TOPIC 2 Multiplication Facts: Use Patterns

Math and Science Project 57
Review What You Know 58
Vocabulary Cards 59

2-1   **2 and 5 as Factors** 61

2-2   **9 as a Factor** 67

2-3   **Apply Properties: Multiply by 0 and 1** 73

2-4   **Multiply by 10** 79

2-5   **Multiplication Facts: 0, 1, 2, 5, 9, and 10** 85

2-6   **PROBLEM SOLVING**
       Model with Math 91

Fluency Practice Activity 97
Vocabulary Review 98
Reteaching 99
Topic Assessment 101
Topic Performance Assessment 103

You can use patterns to help remember multiplication facts.

DATA

9s Facts

$0 \times 9 = 0$

$1 \times 9 = 9$

$2 \times 9 = 18$

$3 \times 9 = 27$

$4 \times 9 = 36$

$5 \times 9 = 45$

$6 \times 9 = 54$

$7 \times 9 =$

$8 \times 9 =$

$9 \times 9 =$

TOPIC 3 Apply Properties: Multiplication Facts for 3, 4, 6, 7, 8

Math and Science Project 105
Review What You Know 106
Vocabulary Cards 107

3-1 The Distributive Property 109

3-2 Apply Properties: 3 as a Factor 115

3-3 Apply Properties: 4 as a Factor 121

3-4 Apply Properties: 5 and 6 as Factors 127

3-5 Apply Properties: 8 as a Factor 133

3-6 Practice Multiplication Facts 139

3-7 The Associative Property: Multiply with 3 Factors 145

3-8 PROBLEM SOLVING
Repeated Reasoning 151

Fluency Practice Activity 157
Vocabulary Review 158
Reteaching 159
Topic Assessment 161
Topic Performance Assessment 163

Properties can help you use known facts to find unknown facts.

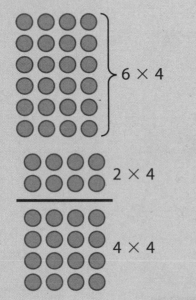

TOPIC 4 Use Multiplication to Divide: Division Facts

Math and Science Project 165
Review What You Know 166
Vocabulary Cards 167

4-1   **Relate Multiplication and Division** 169

4-2   **Use Multiplication to Divide with 2, 3, 4, and 5** 175

4-3   **Use Multiplication to Divide with 6 and 7** 181

4-4   **Use Multiplication to Divide with 8 and 9** 187

4-5   **Multiplication Patterns: Even and Odd Numbers** 193

4-6   **Division Involving 0 and 1** 199

4-7   **Practice Multiplication and Division Facts** 205

4-8   **Solve Multiplication and Division Equations** 211

4-9   **PROBLEM SOLVING**
      Make Sense and Persevere 217

Fluency Practice Activity 223
Vocabulary Review 224
Reteaching 225
Topic Assessment 229
Topic Performance Assessment 233

Multiplication facts can help you learn division facts.

Multiplication
3 rows of 10 drums
$3 \times 10 = 30$
30 drums

Division
30 drums in 3 equal rows
$30 \div 3 = 10$
10 drums in each row

TOPIC 5 Fluently Multiply and Divide within 100

Math and Science Project 235
Review What You Know 236

5-1 Patterns for Multiplication Facts 237

5-2 Use a Multiplication Table 243

5-3 Find Missing Numbers in a Multiplication Table 249

5-4 Use Strategies to Multiply 255

5-5 Solve Word Problems:
Multiplication and Division Facts 261

5-6 Write Math Stories: Multiplication 267

5-7 Write Math Stories: Division 273

5-8 PROBLEM SOLVING
Look For and Use Structure 279

Fluency Practice Activity 285
Vocabulary Review 286
Reteaching 287
Topic Assessment 291
Topic Performance Assessment 295

You can use a multiplication table to find missing factors.

$3 \times 5 = 15$ $15 \div 3 = 5$

×	0	1	2	3	4	5
0	0	0	0	0	0	0
1	0	1	2	3	4	5
2	0	2	4	6	8	10
3	0	3	6	9	12	15

TOPIC 6 Connect Area to Multiplication and Addition

Math and Science Project 297
Review What You Know 298
Vocabulary Cards 299

6-1   **Cover Regions** 301

6-2   **Area: Non-Standard Units** 307

6-3   **Area: Standard Units** 313

6-4   **Area of Squares and Rectangles** 319

6-5   **Apply Properties: Area and the Distributive Property** ... 325

6-6   **Apply Properties: Area of Irregular Shapes** 331

6-7   **PROBLEM SOLVING**
      Look for and Use Structure 337

Fluency Practice Activity 343
Vocabulary Review 344
Reteaching 345
Topic Assessment 349
Topic Performance Assessment 353

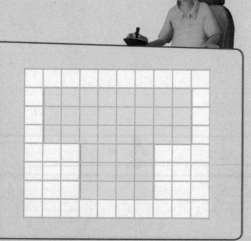

You can find the area of a shape by counting the number of unit squares needed to cover it.

TOPIC 7 Represent and Interpret Data

Math and Science Project 355
Review What You Know 356
Vocabulary Cards 357

7-1   **Read Picture Graphs and Bar Graphs** 359

7-2   **Make Picture Graphs** 365

7-3   **Make Bar Graphs** 371

7-4   **Solve Word Problems Using Information in Graphs** 377

7-5   **PROBLEM SOLVING**
       Precision 383

Fluency Practice Activity 389
Vocabulary Review 390
Reteaching 391
Topic Assessment 395
Topic Performance Assessment 399

Glossary G1

You can use a scaled bar graph to help compare data.

Amount Greg Saved Each Month

TOPIC 8 in volume 2
Use Strategies and Properties to Add and Subtract

Math and Science Project 401
Review What You Know 402
Vocabulary Cards 403

8-1 Addition Properties 405

8-2 Algebra: Addition Patterns 411

8-3 Round Whole Numbers 417

8-4 Mental Math: Addition 423

8-5 Mental Math: Subtraction 429

8-6 Estimate Sums 435

8-7 Estimate Differences 441

8-8 Relate Addition and Subtraction 447

8-9 PROBLEM SOLVING
Model with Math 453

Fluency Practice Activity 459
Vocabulary Review 460
Reteaching 461
Topic Assessment 465
Topic Performance Assessment 469

TOPIC 9 in volume 2
Fluently Add and Subtract within 1,000

Math and Science Project 471
Review What You Know 472
Vocabulary Cards 473

9-1 Use Partial Sums to Add 475

9-2 Add 3-Digit Numbers 481

9-3 Continue to Add 3-Digit Numbers 487

9-4 Add 3 or More Numbers 493

9-5 Use Partial Differences to Subtract 499

9-6 Subtract 3-Digit Numbers 505

9-7 Continue to Subtract 3-Digit Numbers 511

9-8 PROBLEM SOLVING
Construct Arguments 517

Fluency Practice Activity 523
Vocabulary Review 524
Reteaching 525
Topic Assessment 529
Topic Performance Assessment 533

TOPIC 10 in volume 2
Multiply by Multiples of 10

Math and Science Project 535
Review What You Know 536
Vocabulary Cards 537

10-1 Use an Open Number Line to Multiply 539

10-2 Use Properties to Multiply 545

10-3 Multiply by Multiples of 10 551

10-4 PROBLEM SOLVING
Look for and Use Structure 557

Fluency Practice Activity 563
Vocabulary Review 564
Reteaching 565
Topic Assessment 567
Topic Performance Assessment 569

TOPIC 11 in volume 2
Use Operations with Whole Numbers to Solve Problems

Math and Science Project 571
Review What You Know 572

11-1 Solve 2-Step Word Problems:
Addition and Subtraction 573

11-2 Solve 2-Step Word Problems:
Multiplication and Division 579

11-3 Solve 2-Step Word Problems: All Operations 585

11-4 PROBLEM SOLVING
Critique Reasoning 591

Fluency Practice Activity 597
Vocabulary Review 598
Reteaching 599
Topic Assessment 601
Topic Performance Assessment 603

TOPIC 12 in volume 2
Understand Fractions as Numbers

Math and Science Project 605
Review What You Know 606
Vocabulary Cards 607

12-1   **Divide Regions into Equal Parts** 609

12-2   **Fractions and Regions** 615

12-3   **Understand the Whole** 621

12-4   **Number Line: Fractions Less Than 1** 627

12-5   **Number Line: Fractions Greater Than 1** 633

12-6   **Line Plots and Length** 639

12-7   **More Line Plots and Length** 645

12-8   **PROBLEM SOLVING**
Make Sense and Persevere 651

Fluency Practice Activity 657
Vocabulary Review 658
Reteaching 659
Topic Assessment 663
Topic Performance Assessment 667

TOPIC 13 in volume 2
Fraction Equivalence and Comparison

Math and Science Project 669
Review What You Know 670
Vocabulary Cards 671

13-1   **Equivalent Fractions: Use Models** 673

13-2   **Equivalent Fractions: Use the Number Line** 679

13-3   **Use Models to Compare Fractions:**
Same Denominator 685

13-4   **Use Models to Compare Fractions:**
Same Numerator 691

13-5   **Compare Fractions: Use Benchmarks** 697

13-6   **Compare Fractions: Use the Number Line** 703

13-7   **Whole Numbers and Fractions** 709

13-8   **PROBLEM SOLVING**
Construct Arguments 715

Fluency Practice Activity 721
Vocabulary Review 722
Reteaching 723
Topic Assessment 727
Topic Performance Assessment 731

TOPIC 14 in volume 2
Solve Time, Capacity, and Mass Problems

Math and Science Project 733
Review What You Know 734
Vocabulary Cards 735

14-1 Time to the Minute 739

14-2 Units of Time: Measure Elapsed Time 745

14-3 Units of Time: Solve Word Problems 751

14-4 Estimate Liquid Volume 757

14-5 Measure Liquid Volume 763

14-6 Estimate Mass 769

14-7 Measure Mass 775

14-8 Solve Word Problems Involving Mass and Liquid Volume 781

14-9 PROBLEM SOLVING
Reasoning 787

Fluency Practice Activity 793
Vocabulary Review 794
Reteaching 795
Topic Assessment 799
Topic Performance Assessment 803

TOPIC 15 in volume 2
Attributes of Two-Dimensional Shapes

Math and Science Project 805
Review What You Know 806
Vocabulary Cards 807

15-1 Describe Quadrilaterals 811

15-2 Classify Shapes 817

15-3 Analyze and Compare Quadrilaterals 823

15-4 PROBLEM SOLVING
Precision 829

Fluency Practice Activity 835
Vocabulary Review 836
Reteaching 837
Topic Assessment 839
Topic Performance Assessment 841

TOPIC 16 in volume 2
Solve Perimeter Problems

Math and Science Project 843
Review What You Know 844
Vocabulary Cards 845

16-1 Understand Perimeter 847

16-2 Perimeter of Common Shapes 853

16-3 Perimeter and Unknown Side Lengths 859

16-4 Same Perimeter, Different Area 865

16-5 Same Area, Different Perimeter 871

16-6 PROBLEM SOLVING
Reasoning 877

Fluency Practice Activity 883
Vocabulary Review 884
Reteaching 885
Topic Assessment 887
Topic Performance Assessment 889

You can find the perimeter of a shape by adding the lengths of its sides.

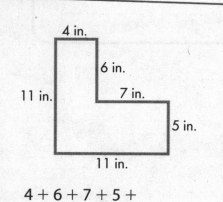

$$4 + 6 + 7 + 5 + 11 + 11 = 44$$

The perimeter of the figure is 44 inches.

STEP UP to Grade 4 in volume 2

STEP UP Lessons Opener 891

1 Place Value Relationships 893

2 Mental Math: Multiply by Multiples of
10, 100, and 1,000 897

3 Mental Math: Multiply Multiples of 10 901

4 Use Models to Multiply 2-Digit Numbers
by Multiples of 10 905

5 Interpret Remainders 909

6 Model Addition of Fractions 913

7 Decompose Fractions 917

8 Lines, Rays, and Angles 921

9 Understand Angles and Unit Angles 925

10 Lines 929

Glossary G1

These lessons help prepare you for Grade 4.

Problem Solving Handbook

Math practices are ways we think about and do math.

Math practices will help you solve problems.

Math Practices

1. **Make sense of problems and persevere in solving them.**

2. **Reason abstractly and quantitatively.**

3. **Construct viable arguments and critique the reasoning of others.**

4. **Model with mathematics.**

5. **Use appropriate tools strategically.**

6. **Attend to precision.**

7. **Look for and make use of structure.**

8. **Look for and express regularity in repeated reasoning.**

There are good Thinking Habits for each of these math practices.

Make sense of problems and persevere in solving them.

Good math thinkers make sense of problems and think of ways to solve them.

If they get stuck, they don't give up.

Mia has $36. Kate has $17 less than Mia. Do Mia and Kate together have enough money to buy a bike for $54?

Here I listed what I know and what I am trying to find.

What I know:
- Mia has $36.
- Kate has $17 less than $36.
- The bike costs $54.

What I need to find:
- Whether Kate and Mia have at least $54 in all.

Thinking Habits

Be a good thinker! These questions can help you.

- What do I need to find?
- What do I know?
- What's my plan for solving the problem?
- What else can I try if I get stuck?
- How can I check that my solution makes sense?

2 Reason abstractly and quantitatively.

Good math thinkers know how to think about words and numbers to solve problems.

I drew a bar diagram that shows how things in the problem are related.

Jake bought a coat for $47. He also bought a shirt. Jake spent $71 in all. How much did he spend on the shirt?

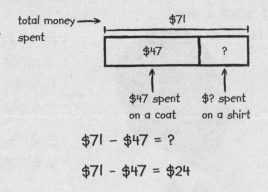

total money spent →

$71
$47	?

$47 spent on a coat $? spent on a shirt

$71 − $47 = ?

$71 − $47 = $24

Thinking Habits

Be a good thinker! These questions can help you.

- What do the numbers and symbols in the problem mean?

- How are the numbers or quantities related?

- How can I represent a word problem using pictures, numbers, or equations?

Construct viable arguments and critique the reasoning of others.

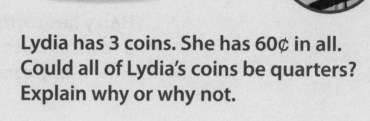

Good math thinkers use math to explain why they are right. They can talk about the math that others do, too.

I wrote a clear argument with words, numbers, and symbols.

Lydia has 3 coins. She has 60¢ in all. Could all of Lydia's coins be quarters? Explain why or why not.

Marta's Work

Lydia's coins cannot all be quarters.

1 quarter is 25¢.

3 quarters is 25¢, 50¢, 75¢.

75¢ > 60¢

So, 3 quarters is more money than Lydia actually has.

Thinking Habits

Be a good thinker! These questions can help you.

- How can I use numbers, objects, drawings, or actions to justify my argument?

- Am I using numbers and symbols correctly?

- Is my explanation clear and complete?

- What questions can I ask to understand other people's thinking?

- Are there mistakes in other people's thinking?

- Can I improve other people's thinking?

4 Model with mathematics.

Good math thinkers choose and apply math they know to show and solve problems from everyday life.

Harry has carrots in his garden. Harry has 5 rows of carrots with 4 carrots in each row. How many carrots are in Harry's garden?

$4 + 4 + 4 + 4 + 4 = 20$

There are 20 carrots in Harry's garden.

I used what I know about arrays and addition. I drew a picture to help.

Thinking Habits

Be a good thinker! These questions can help you.

- How can I use math I know to help solve this problem?

- How can I use pictures, objects, or an equation to represent the problem?

- How can I use numbers, words, and symbols to solve the problem?

Use appropriate tools strategically.

Good math thinkers know how to pick the right tools to solve math problems.

I decided to use place-value blocks to help me compare. I can use them to show the hundreds, the tens, and the ones.

Carla has 234 stickers. Dan has 242 stickers. Who has more stickers?

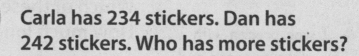

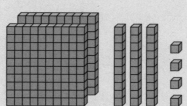
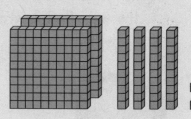

242 is greater than 234.
Dan has more stickers.

Thinking Habits

Be a good thinker! These questions can help you.

- Which tools can I use?

- Why should I use this tool to help me solve the problem?

- Is there a different tool I could use?

- Am I using the tool appropriately?

6 Attend to precision.

Good math thinkers are careful about what they write and say, so their ideas about math are clear.

Which of these two paths is longer? How much longer?

I was precise with my measurements and the way that I wrote my solution.

Blue path: 3 cm + 3 cm = 6 cm
Yellow path: 4 cm + 1 cm = 5 cm
6 cm – 5 cm = 1 cm
The blue path is 1 cm longer than the yellow path.

Thinking Habits

Be a good thinker! These questions can help you.

- Am I using numbers, units, and symbols appropriately?

- Am I using the correct definitions?

- Am I calculating accurately?

- Is my answer clear?

7 Look for and make use of structure.

Good math thinkers look for patterns or relationships in math to help solve problems.

I broke apart 67 to solve 123 - 67.

A store has 123 apples. 67 apples are sold. How many apples does the store have left?

123 - 67 = ?

I know 67 = 60 + 7.
123 - 60 = 63
63 - 7 = 56

So, 123 - 67 = 56.
The store has 56 apples left.

Thinking Habits

Be a good thinker! These questions can help you.

- What patterns can I see and describe?

- How can I use the patterns to solve the problem?

- Can I see expressions and objects in different ways?

Look for and express regularity in repeated reasoning.

Good math thinkers look for things that repeat, and they make generalizations.

I used reasoning to generalize about calculations.

Find the sum for each of these addends.

185 + 100 = ?

? = 292 + 100

100 + 321 = ?

Daniel's Work

185 + 100 = 285

392 = 292 + 100

100 + 321 = 421

100 is added in each problem.

Adding 100 makes the hundreds digit go up by 1.

Thinking Habits

Be a good thinker! These questions can help you.

- Are any calculations repeated?

- Can I generalize from examples?

- What shortcuts do I notice?

Problem Solving Guide

These questions can help you solve problems.

Make Sense of the Problem

Reason Abstractly and Quantitatively

- What do I need to find?
- What given information can I use?
- How are the quantities related?

Think About Similar Problems

- Have I solved problems like this before?

Persevere in Solving the Problem

Model with Math

- How can I use the math I know?
- How can I represent the problem?
- Is there a pattern or structure I can use?

Use Appropriate Tools Strategically

- What math tools could I use?
- How can I use those tools strategically?

Check the Answer

Make Sense of the Answer

- Is my answer reasonable?

Check for Precision

- Did I check my work?
- Is my answer clear?
- Did I construct a viable argument?
- Did I generalize correctly?

Some Ways to Represent Problems

- Draw a Picture
- Make a Bar Diagram
- Make a Table or Graph
- Write an Equation

Some Math Tools

- Objects
- Grid Paper
- Rulers
- Technology
- Paper and Pencil

Problem Solving Recording Sheet

This sheet helps you organize your work.

Name **Carlos**

Teaching Tool **1**

Problem Solving Recording Sheet

Problem:
Cory wants to buy a video game that costs $60. He has $48 saved. On Monday he used part of his savings to buy a shirt for $15. How much more money does Cory need to save to buy the video game?

MAKE SENSE OF THE PROBLEM

Need to Find

Money needed to buy video game

Given

Video game costs $60
Saved $48
Used $15 of savings

PERSEVERE IN SOLVING THE PROBLEM

Some Ways to Represent Problems

☐ Draw a Picture
☑ Make a Bar Diagram
☐ Make a Table or Graph
☐ Write an Equation

Some Math Tools

☐ Objects
☐ Grid Paper
☐ Rulers
☐ Technology
☑ Paper and Pencil

Solution and Answer

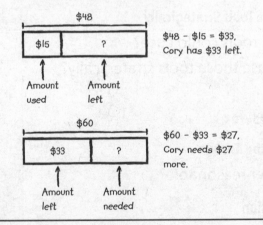

$48 − $15 = $33,
Cory has $33 left.

$60 − $33 = $27,
Cory needs $27 more.

CHECK THE ANSWER

Estimate
50 − 20 = 30   60 − 30 = 30
Check
33 + 15 = 48   27 + 33 = 60

My answer is reasonable and makes sense.
My answer is correct.

T1

Bar Diagrams

You can draw a **bar diagram** to show how the quantities in a problem are related. Then you can write an equation to solve the problem.

Add To

Draw this **bar diagram** for situations that involve *adding* to a quantity.

Result → 82

15   67

↑   ↑
Start   Change

Result Unknown

Greg bought a baseball and a baseball glove. How much did he pay for both?

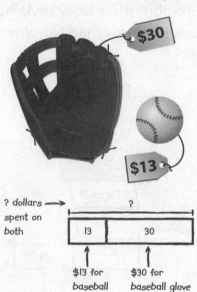

$30

$13

? dollars →
spent on
both   ?

13   30

↑   ↑
$13 for $30 for
baseball baseball glove

13 + 30 = ?

Greg spent $43 on both.

Start Unknown

Robin had some rings. Her sister gave her the rings shown below. After that, Robin had 90 rings. How many rings did Robin start with?

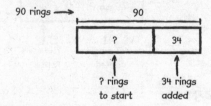

90 rings → 90

?   34

↑   ↑
? rings   34 rings
to start added

? + 34 = 90

Robin started with 56 rings.

Bar Diagrams

You can use bar diagrams to make sense of addition and subtraction problems.

Take From

Draw this **bar diagram** for situations that involve *taking* from a quantity.

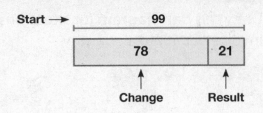

Start → 99

| 78 | 21 |

↑ Change   ↑ Result

Result Unknown

Maurice had 78 e-mails. He deleted 49 of them. How many e-mails did Maurice keep?

78 e-mails → to start   78

| 49 | ? |

↑ 49 e-mails deleted   ↑ ? e-mails kept

$78 - 49 = ?$

Maurice kept **29** e-mails.

Start Unknown

Layla picked some apples at an orchard. She gave the apples below to her grandmother. Now Layla has 29 apples left. How many apples did Layla pick?

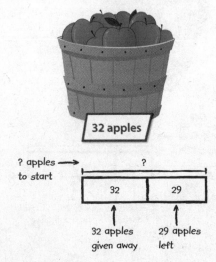

32 apples

? apples → to start   ?

| 32 | 29 |

↑ 32 apples given away   ↑ 29 apples left

$? - 32 = 29$

Layla had 61 apples before she gave some to her grandmother.

The **bar diagrams** on this page can help you make sense of more addition and subtraction situations.

Put Together/Take Apart

Draw this **bar diagram** for situations that involve *putting together* or *taking apart* quantities.

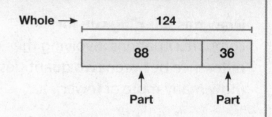

Whole → 124 | 88 | 36 | Part Part

Whole Unknown

The bar graph shows how far Lana drove her car for 3 days. How many total miles did she drive?

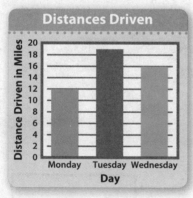

Distances Driven

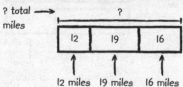

? total miles → [12 | 19 | 16] ?

12 miles 19 miles 16 miles

$12 + 19 + 16 = ?$

Lana drove a total of 47 miles.

Part Unknown

Pier school collected a total of 46 toys during two weeks of a toy drive for charity. How many toys were collected during the second week?

28 toys collected first week

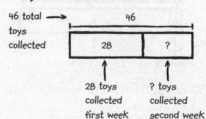

46 total toys collected → [28 | ?] 46

28 toys collected first week   ? toys collected second week

$28 + ? = 46$ or $46 - 28 = ?$

Pier school collected 18 toys during the second week.

Bar Diagrams

Pictures help you understand a problem.

Compare: Addition and Subtraction

Draw this **bar diagram** for *compare* situations involving the difference between two quantities (how many more or fewer).

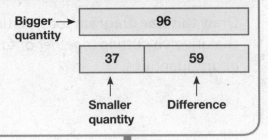

Bigger quantity → 96

37 | 59

Smaller quantity | Difference

Difference Unknown

The larger dog weighs 82 pounds. The smaller dog weighs 6 pounds. How many more pounds does the larger dog weigh?

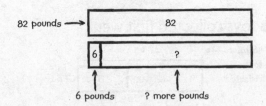

82 pounds → 82

6 | ?

6 pounds | ? more pounds

$6 + ? = 82$ or $82 - 6 = ?$

The larger dog weighs 76 more pounds.

Smaller Unknown

Tim has 12 more postage stamps than Pedro. Tim has 30 postage stamps. How many postage stamps does Pedro have?

30 stamps Tim has → 30

? | 12

? stamps Pedro has | 12 more stamps

$30 - 12 = ?$ or $? + 12 = 30$

Pedro has 18 postage stamps.

The **bar diagrams** on this page can help you solve problems involving multiplication and division.

Equal Groups: Multiplication and Division

Draw this **bar diagram** for situations that involve *equal groups*.

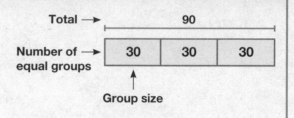

Number of Groups Unknown

Josie spent $40 on tickets to a movie for herself and some friends on Saturday. How many tickets did Josie buy?

$? \times 8 = 40$ or $40 \div 8 = ?$

Josie bought 5 tickets.

Group Size Unknown

Marie placed an equal number of marbles in each bag below. She has 36 total marbles. How many marbles did Marie place in each bag?

$4 \times ? = 36$ or $36 \div 4 = ?$

Marie placed 9 marbles in each bag.

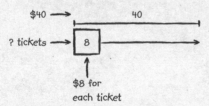

Understand Multiplication and Division of Whole Numbers

Essential Question: What are different meanings of multiplication and division?

Digital Resources

Solve Learn Glossary Practice Buddy

Tools Assessment Help Games

Some animals form groups.

Being in a group can help birds survive.

That's teamwork! Here's a project on animals with multiplication and division.

Math and Science Project: Forming Groups

Do Research Many kinds of animals form groups. Use the Internet or other sources to discover which animals form groups. When do they do this? What are the benefits for these animals of being in a group?

Journal: Write a Report Include what you found. Also include in your report:

- Draw pictures of animals in equal groups. Give a reason why those animals formed groups.

- Use a multiplication equation to show the total number of animals. Use a division equation to show the number in each group.

Name _Adhrit_

Review What You Know

• add ✓	• subtract
• skip count ✓	• ones ✓

1. If you combine different sized groups to find how many in all, you _add_ .

2. _ones_ are groups of single objects.

3. When you say the numbers 5, 10, 15, 20, you _skipcount._

Adding

Find each sum.

4. $5 + 5 + 5$ 15

5. $7 + 7$ 14

6. $3 + 3 + 3$ 9

7. $2 + 2 + 2 + 2$ 8

8. $6 + 6 + 6$ 18

9. $9 + 9 + 9$ 27

Subtracting

Find each difference.

10. $21 - 7$ 14
    $14 - 7$ 7
    $7 - 7$ 0

11. $15 - 5$ 10
    $10 - 5$ 5
    $5 - 5$ 0

12. $27 - 9$ 18
    $18 - 9$ 9
    $9 - 9$ 0

Skip Counting on the Number Line

13. If you continue skip counting, what is the next number on the number line?

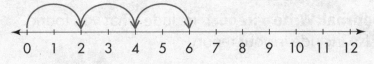

0 1 2 3 4 5 6 7 8 9 10 11 12

Ⓐ 8

Ⓑ 10

Ⓒ 12

Ⓓ 14

My Word Cards

Use the examples for each word on the front of the card to help complete the definitions on the back.

equal groups

multiplication

$4 \times 3 = 12$

factors

$7 \times 3 = 21$

factors

product

$7 \times 3 = 21$

product

equation

addition	subtraction
$2 + 5 = 7$	$7 - 5 = \square$
multiplication	division
$2 \times 5 = 10$	$10 \div \square = 2$

unknown

$\square \div 8 = 2$ $4 \times ? = 32$ $9 \times 8 = g$

unknown

number line

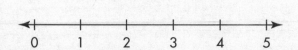

array

3 columns

2 rows

My Word Cards

Complete each definition. Extend learning by writing your own definitions.

✁

multiplication is an operation that gives the total number when you join equal groups.

equal grops have the same number of items in each group.

The answer to a multiplication problem is called the _product_.

The numbers that are multiplied together to give a product are called _factor_.

A symbol or letter that stands for a number in an equation is called an _unknown_.

A number sentence that uses an equal sign (=) to show the value to its left is the same as the value to its right is called an _equation_.

An _array_ is a way of displaying objects in equal rows and columns.

A line divided into equal units and numbered in order is called a _nube line_.

My Word Cards

Use the examples for each word on the front of the card to help complete the definitions on the back.

row

2 rows

column

3 columns

Commutative (Order) Property of Multiplication

$5 \times 7 = 35$

division

$12 \div 3 = 4$

Total   Number of equal groups   Number in each group

My Word Cards

Objects that are arranged in a line up and down are in a _____.

Objects that are arranged in a line across are in a _____.

_____ is an operation that tells how many equal groups there are or how many are in each group.

Numbers can be multiplied in any order and the product will be the same because of the _____ _____ _____.

Name _____Adnr'it_____

Solve & Share

Ms. Witt bought 3 boxes of paint with 5 jars of paint in each box. What is the total number of jars Ms. Witt bought? *Solve this problem any way you choose.*

$$5+5+5 = 15$$
$$5 \times 3 = 15$$

I can ...
use addition or multiplication to join equal groups.

I can also make sense of problems.

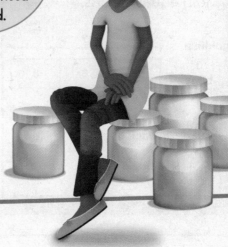

Make sense of this problem. Think about what you know and what you need to find.

Look Back! **Model with Math** How can you use a picture to show the math you did in the problem?

Essential Question ## How Can You Find the Total Number of Objects in Equal Groups?

A

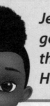

Jessie used 3 bags to bring home the goldfish she won at the Fun Fair. She put the same number of goldfish in each bag. How many goldfish did she win?

I can use counters to show the groups.

8 goldfish in each bag

B The counters show 3 groups of 8 goldfish.

You can use addition to join equal groups.

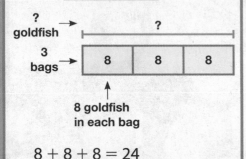

? goldfish
3 bags → | 8 | 8 | 8 |
8 goldfish in each bag

$8 + 8 + 8 = 24$

C Multiplication is an operation that gives the total number when you join equal groups.

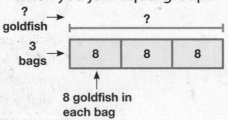

? goldfish
3 bags → | 8 | 8 | 8 |
8 goldfish in each bag

3 times 8 equals 24

$3 \times 8 = 24$

factor factor product

Factors are the numbers that are being multiplied. The product is the answer to a multiplication problem.

D You can write equations.

An unknown is a symbol that stands for a number in an equation.

Addition equation:
$8 + 8 + 8 = ?$
$8 + 8 + 8 = 24$

Multiplication equation:
$3 \times 8 = ?$
$3 \times 8 = 24$

Jessie won 24 goldfish.

Convince Me! **Model with Math** Suppose Jessie won 5 bags of 8 goldfish. Draw a bar diagram and write an addition equation and a multiplication equation to represent the problem.

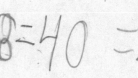

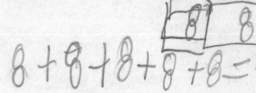
$8 + 8 + 8 + 8 + 8 = 40$ $5 \times 8 = 40$

Practice Buddy Tools Assessment

☆ Guided Practice ☆

Do You Understand?

1. **Reasoning** Can you write
   $5 + 5 + 5 + 5 = 20$ as a multiplication
   equation? Explain. _add 5 4 times_

   _5X4_

2. **Reasoning** Can you write
   $3 + 4 + 7 = 14$ as a multiplication
   equation? Explain. _add 72 times_

   _7X2_

3. Write an addition equation and a
   multiplication equation to solve this
   problem.
   Jessie buys 4 packages of stones. There
   are 6 stones in each package. How
   many stones does Jessie buy?

   _6x4=24   6+6+6+6=24_

Do You Know How?

Complete **4** and **5**. Use the pictures
to help.

4.
2 groups of _4_
$4 + 4 =$ _8_
$2 \times$ _4_ $=$ _8_

5.
_3_ groups of 6
$6 +$ _6_ $+$ _6_ $=$ _18_
$3 \times$ _6_ $=$ _10_

Independent Practice ☆

Leveled Practice Complete **6** and **7**. Use the pictures to help.

6.
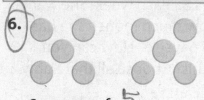
2 groups of _5_
$5 +$ _5_ $=$ _10_
$2 \times$ _5_ $=$ _10_

7.

5 groups of _4_
$4 + 4 + 4 +$ _4_ $+ 4 =$ _20_
$5 \times$ _4_ $= 20$

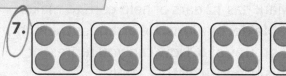
In **8–11**, complete each equation. Use counters or draw a picture to help.

8. $8 + 8 + 8 + 8 = 4 \times$ ___

9. ___ $+$ ___ $+$ ___ $= 3 \times 7$

10. $9 +$ _9_ $+$ _9_ $= 3 \times$ _9_

11. $6 + 6 + 6 + 6 + 6 =$ _5_ $\times$ _6_

Problem Solving

12. **Be Precise** Debra draws this shape on the back of her notebook.

What is the name of the shape Debra draws? How do you know? *it has*
heagoo ＆ vertex

13. **Model with Math** Salvatore gets 50 trading cards for his birthday. He trades some cards with his friend Madison. Salvatore gives 22 cards to Madison, and Madison gives 18 cards to Salvatore. Then Salvatore's sister gives him 14 cards. How many trading cards does Salvatore have now? Use math to represent the problem.

28 - 22 = 28
28

14. **Higher Order Thinking** Luke says you can always add and you can always multiply to join groups. Is he correct? Explain why or why not. *Yes*
becaus it makes
it esaer

15. **Critique Reasoning** Lois says any addition equation where the addends are all the same can be written as a multiplication equation. Is Lois correct? Explain why or why not. *Yes*
it is a little ditter

 Assessment

16. Mark has 12 ears of field corn to make table decorations. He arranges them in 2 groups of 6. How can you represent this? Choose all that apply.

- ☐ 12×2
- ☒ $2 + 2 + 2 + 2 + 2 + 2$
- ☒ $6 + 6$
- ☒ 2×6
- ☐ $12 + 2 + 6$

17. Jenna saves $5 each week. She wants to know how much money she has saved after 6 weeks. How can you represent this? Choose all that apply.

- ☒ $5 + 5 + 5 + 5 + 5 + 5$
- ☐ 5×5
- ☐ $5 + 6$
- ☒ $6 + 6 + 6 + 6 + 6$
- ☒ 5×6

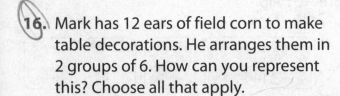

Name _Adhr'it_

☆ Solve & Share

Harvey the Hop Toad jumps 4 times in the same direction. He jumps 5 inches in each jump. How can you show how far he goes on a number line?

I can ...
use a number line to represent and solve multiplication facts.

I can also model with math to solve problems.

Model with math.
A number line can be used to record and count equal groups.

0 1 2 3 4 5 6 7 8 9 10 11 12 13 14 15 16 17 18 19 20 21 22

Look Back! Generalize How are Harvey's jumps on the number line like repeated addition? How are they like skip counting?

How Can You Use a Number Line to Show Multiplication?

Essential Question

Clara is making gift bags for her 5 friends. She wants to put 3 glitter pens in each gift bag. How many glitter pens does Clara need?

You can use a number line and skip counting to show multiplication.

   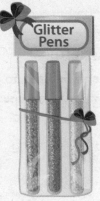 

B

Draw arrows on the number line to show the number of glitter pens for each gift bag.

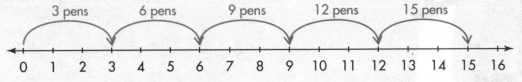

3 pens   6 pens   9 pens   12 pens   15 pens

0 1 2 3 4 5 6 7 8 9 10 11 12 13 14 15 16

Skip counting: 3, 6, 9, 12, 15

Multiplication: $5 \times 3 = 15$

Clara needs 15 glitter pens.

Convince Me! Reasoning What would skip counting by 6 look like on the number line?

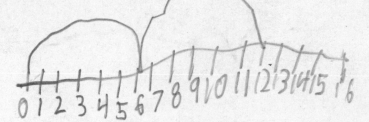

☆ Guided Practice

Do You Understand?

1. On page 14, why do you skip count by 3s on the number line?

2. On page 14, why do you make five jumps on the number line?

3. Reasoning How would the jumps on the number line look different if there were 4 pens in each gift bag?

Do You Know How?

In **4**, complete the arrows on the number line to show the jumps and fill in the blanks.

4. Jim ran 3 miles a day for 4 days in a row. How many miles did he run?

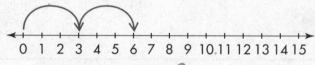

0 1 2 3 4 5 6 7 8 9 10 11 12 13 14 15

Number of jumps: _2_

I skip counted by _3_.

Jim ran _6_ miles.

$\underline{3} \times \underline{2} = \underline{6}$

☆ Independent Practice ☆

In **5**, show how you found the solution using the number line.

5. Judy has 6 fruit baskets. She wants to put 2 apples into each basket. How many apples will she need? Draw the remaining jumps on the number line with arrows to show how many apples Judy will need.

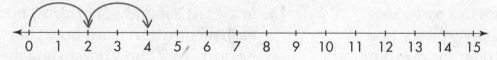

0 1 2 3 4 5 6 7 8 9 10 11 12 13 14 15

Judy will need ____ apples.

In **6** and **7**, show the multiplication fact with arrows on the number line. Write the product.

6. $7 \times 2 = 14$

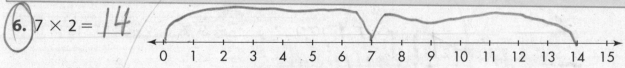

0 1 2 3 4 5 6 7 8 9 10 11 12 13 14 15

7. $3 \times 3 =$ ____

0 1 2 3 4 5 6 7 8 9 10 11 12 13 14 15

Problem Solving

8. Nikki wants to use 3 glass beads in a necklace she is making. She wants to make 6 necklaces. How many glass beads will Nikki need? Write an addition equation and a multiplication equation.

? beads

3	3	3	3	3	3

↑
3 beads on each necklace

9. **Math and Science** Guinea pigs in the wild usually live in groups of between 5 and 10. The group members can warn each other of danger. If there are 2 groups of 7 guinea pigs, how many guinea pigs are there in all? Use the number line to solve.

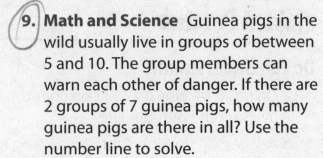

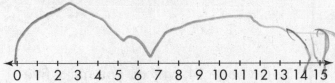

10. **Make Sense and Persevere** Tim drew this number line to show the multiplication fact 4 × 2 = 8.

0 1 2 3 4 5 6 7 8 9 10 11 12 13 14 15

Which parts represent the factors? Which part shows the product?

11. **Higher Order Thinking** Draw a number line to compare skip counting by 3s four times and skip counting by 4s three times. How are they different? How are they alike?

✓ **Assessment**

12. Suki invites 5 friends to a party. She gives each friend 2 party favors. How many party favors does she give out? Show how to find the answer using the number line.

0 1 2 3 4 5 6 7 8 9 10 11 12 13 14 15

10 party favors

13. In the last 5 months Stan read 3 books each month. How many books has he read in all? Show how to find the answer using the number line.

0 1 2 3 4 5 6 7 8 9 10 11 12 13 14 15 16

15 books

Name _____

Homework & Practice 1-2
Multiplication on the Number Line

Another Look!

There are 4 fruit bars in a package. Abby buys 5 packages. How many fruit bars does she buy?

Use a number line. Skip count by 4s, five times.

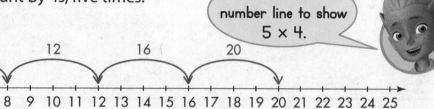

You can use a number line to show 5×4.

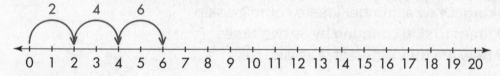

4   8   12   16   20

0 1 2 3 4 5 6 7 8 9 10 11 12 13 14 15 16 17 18 19 20 21 22 23 24 25

Number of jumps: 5   Number in each jump: 4

$5 \times 4 = 20$ Abby buys 20 fruit bars.

In **1–3**, use the number line.

1. Jack puts 2 photos on each of 7 pages of his photo album. How many photos does he use? Complete the jumps on the number line by adding arrows.

2   4   6

0 1 2 3 4 5 6 7 8 9 10 11 12 13 14 15 16 17 18 19 20

Number of jumps: _____   Number in each jump: _____

_____ × _____ = _____

Jack uses _____ photos.

2. Why do you skip count by 2s on the number line?

3. Why do you make 7 jumps on the number line?

---

4. Tony buys 7 packages of mini-muffins. There are 3 mini-muffins in each package. How many mini-muffins does Tony buy? Use the number line to help find the answer.

0 1 2 3 4 5 6 7 8 9 10 11 12 13 14 15 16 17 18 19 20 21 22

5. Mrs. Calvino's classroom has 6 rows of desks. Each row has 4 desks. Explain how to use skip counting to find how many desks there are.

6. Alyssa has saved $77 from mowing lawns. She spends $34 on back-to-school shopping. How much of her savings does Alyssa have left?

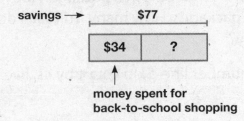

savings → $77
$34 | ?

↑
money spent for
back-to-school shopping

7. Critique Reasoning Tina drew this number line to show $5 \times 3 = 15$.

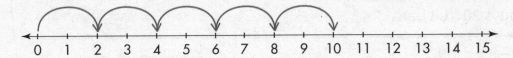

0 1 2 3 4 5 6 7 8 9 10 11 12 13 14 15

Is her number line correct? Why or why not?

8. Higher Order Thinking Draw a number line to compare skip counting by 4s four times to skip counting by 8s two times. How are they alike? How are they different? Explain.

✓ **Assessment**

9. Diane uses 2 feet of ribbon to decorate each gift she is wrapping. She wraps 7 gifts. How much ribbon does she need? Show how to find the answer using the number line.

0   2   4   6   8   10   12   14

☐ feet

10. Jerry has a bookshelf with 4 shelves. He places 4 books on each of the shelves. How many books are on the bookshelf? Show how to find the answer using the number line.

0 1 2 3 4 5 6 7 8 9 10 11 12 13 14 15 16

☐ books

Name _A dhr'it_

☆ Solve & Share ☆

Mark put sports cards in an album. He put 4 rows of cards on each page. He put 3 cards in each row. How many cards are on each page? **Solve this problem any way you choose.**

I can ...
use arrays to show and solve multiplication problems.

I can also choose and use a math tool to solve problems.

You can use tools. Sometimes using objects can help you solve a problem. Show your work in the space below!

Look Back! **Make Sense and Persevere** Will your answer be the same if Mark puts 3 rows of 4 cards on each page? Explain.

Essential Question **How Does an Array Show Multiplication?**

A

Dana keeps her swimming medal collection in a display on the wall.

> *The display has 4 rows. Each row has 5 medals. How many medals are in Dana's collection?*

The medals are in an array. An array shows objects in equal rows and columns.

B The counters show 4 rows and 5 columns.

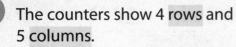
5 columns

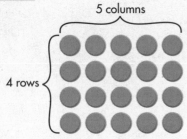
4 rows

Each row is a group. You can use addition or skip counting to find the total.

Addition: $5 + 5 + 5 + 5 = 20$
Skip counting: 5, 10, 15, 20

C Multiplication can also be used to find the total in an array.

You say, "4 times 5 equals 20."

$$4 \times 5 = 20$$

number of rows   number in each row

There are 20 medals in Dana's collection.

Convince Me! **Construct Arguments** Jason also has a swimming medal collection. His display has 5 rows with 5 medals in each row. Who has more medals, Jason or Dana? Draw an array then write an addition equation and a multiplication equation to show your work.

$5 + 5 + 5 + 5 + 5 = 25$
$5 \times 5 = 25$

Name _Adnrit_

☆ Guided Practice *

Do You Understand?

1. Look at page 20. What does the first factor tell you about the array?

2. Mia puts muffins in 4 rows with 7 muffins in each row. Draw an array to find the total number of muffins.

Do You Know How?

In **3** and **4**, write a multiplication equation for each array.

3.

$3 \times 4 = 12$

4.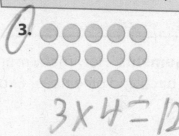

Independent Practice ☆

In **5–7**, fill in the blanks to show addition, skip counting, and multiplication for each array.

5.
$6 + \underline{6} + \underline{6} = 18$
$6, \underline{12, 18}$
$3 \times \underline{6} = 18$

6.
$4 + \underline{} + \underline{} + \underline{} = 16$
$4, \underline{}, \underline{}, \underline{}$
$4 \times \underline{} = 16$

7.
$\underline{} + \underline{} + \underline{} + \underline{} + \underline{} = 25$
$\underline{}, \underline{}, \underline{}, \underline{}, \underline{}$
$\underline{} \times \underline{} = 25$

In **8** and **9**, draw an array to show each equation. Write the product.

8. $5 \times 6 = 30$

9. $2 \times 9 = \underline{}$

*For another example, see Set C on page 51.

Topic 1 | Lesson 1-3

21

Problem Solving

10. Look for Relationships Liza draws these two arrays. How are the arrays alike? How are they different?

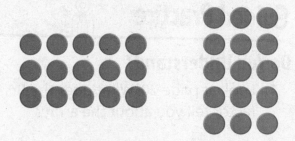

11. Construct Arguments How many more oak trees are there than birch and pine trees? Explain how you know.

DATA	Trees in the Park	
	Birch	~~HHL HHL~~ ///
	Oak	~~HHL HHL HHL~~ //
	Maple	~~HHL HHL~~
	Pine	//

12. Higher Order Thinking Margo has 23 pictures. Can she use all the pictures to make an array with exactly two equal rows? Why or why not?

no it 'is not a even huber.

13. Delbert puts 5 nickels in each of his 3 empty piggy banks. How many nickels did Delbert put in the banks? Write a multiplication equation to show how you solved the problem.

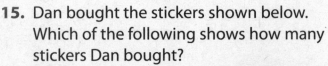

5 nickels in each bank

✓ Assessment

14. Mr. Lopez planted 8 rows of apple trees on his farm. The apple trees are in 5 columns. How many trees are there in all?

Ⓐ 5 trees

Ⓑ 8 trees

Ⓒ 13 trees

Ⓓ 40 trees

15. Dan bought the stickers shown below. Which of the following shows how many stickers Dan bought?

Ⓐ 5 + 5

Ⓑ 5 × 4

Ⓒ 5 + 4

Ⓓ 5 − 4

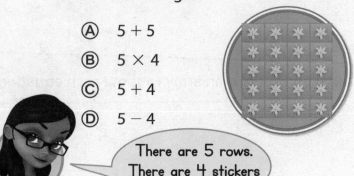

There are 5 rows. There are 4 stickers in each row.

Name _____

Another Look!

Scott arranges some apples in an array. He makes 4 rows with 3 apples in each row. How many apples does Scott have?

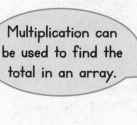
Multiplication can be used to find the total in an array.

The array shows 4 rows of 3 apples.

$3 + 3 + 3 + 3 = 12$

3, 6, 9, 12

Say, "4 times 3 equals 12."

Write: $4 \times 3 = 12$.

In **1–3**, fill in the blanks to show addition, skip counting, and multiplication for each array.

1.

$3 + $ ____ $ + $ ____ $ = 9$

3, __, __

$3 \times $ ____ $ = 9$

2.

$4 + $ ____ $ = $ ____

__, __

$2 \times $ ____ $ = $ ____

3.

____ $ + $ ____ $ + $ ____ $ = 15$

__, __, 15

____ $ \times $ ____ $ = 15$

In **4–7**, draw an array. Write an addition equation and a multiplication equation for your array.

4. 3×4

5. 2×3

6. 2×5

7. 3×6

8. **Vocabulary** Paula says that she can draw an array with a total of 17 counters placed in 3 rows. Is she correct? If she is, draw the array. If she is not, explain why not.

9. **Make Sense and Persevere** Shelly wants to plant 6 rows of flowers, with 7 flowers in each row. What addition equation and what multiplication equation can she write to find how many flowers she needs to plant? Which equation do you find easier to use? Why?

10. **Reasoning** Marie has one of the solid figures shown below.

Cylinder   Sphere   Cone

Marie's solid figure has 2 flat surfaces, 0 edges, and 0 vertices. Which solid figure does Marie have?

11. **Higher Order Thinking** Vince has 16 beads. How many different arrays can Vince draw to represent the total number of beads he has? List the sizes of the arrays.

 Assessment

12. Jana makes the array below to show how she wants to arrange some pictures. Which multiplication equation describes Jana's array?

    Ⓐ $3 \times 12 = 36$

    Ⓑ $2 \times 18 = 36$

    Ⓒ $6 \times 6 = 36$

    Ⓓ $4 \times 9 = 36$

13. Carole makes an array of magnets on her refrigerator. She makes 7 rows with 8 magnets in each row. Which of the following shows how to find the total number of magnets in Carole's array?

    Ⓐ   7, 14, 21, 28, 35, 42, 49

    Ⓑ 7×8

    Ⓒ $7 + 7 + 7 + 7 + 7 + 7 + 7$

    Ⓓ $8 + 7$

Name _Adhrict B_

Solve & Share

Cathy arranged seashells in two different arrays. One array has 2 rows with 6 shells in each row. The other array has 6 rows with 2 shells in each row. Do both arrays have the same number of shells? Draw the arrays, then write a multiplication equation for each.

I can ...
multiply factors in any order to solve multiplication problems.

I can also look for patterns to solve problems.

You can use structure. What do you notice is the same in each array?

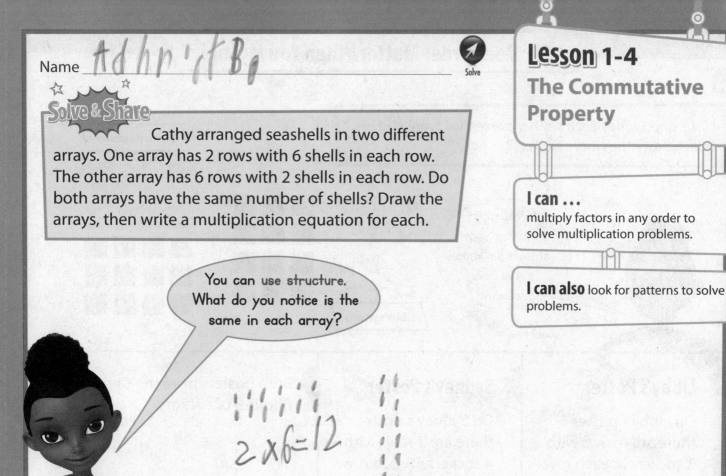

$2 \times 6 = 12$

$6 \times 2 = 12$

Look Back! **Look for Relationships** Explain what happened to the product when you changed the order of the factors.

Essential Question Does Order Matter When You Multiply?

A

Libby and Sydney each say her poster has more stickers. Which poster has more stickers?

Sydney's poster

Remember, an array shows objects in equal rows and columns.

Libby's poster

B ## Libby's Poster

On Libby's poster, there are 4 rows with 3 stickers in each row. Here are two ways to write this:

$3 + 3 + 3 + 3 = 12$

and

$4 \times 3 = 12$

C ## Sydney's Poster

On Sydney's poster, there are 3 rows with 4 stickers in each row. Here are two ways to write this:

$4 + 4 + 4 = 12$

and

$3 \times 4 = 12$

D Both posters have the same number of stickers.

The Commutative (Order) Property of Multiplication says you can multiply numbers in any order and the product is the same. So, $4 \times 3 = 3 \times 4$.

Convince Me! Look for Relationships Circle the pair of equations that shows the Commutative Property of Multiplication. Explain your answer.

$2 \times 4 = 8$

$2 \times 8 = 16$

$2 \times 4 = 8$

$4 \times 2 = 8$

$2 + 2 + 2 + 2 = 8$

$4 \times 2 = 8$

$4 \times 2 = 2 \times 4 = 8$

Name _Adhrit B_

☆ Guided Practice*

Do You Understand?

1. Complete the following statement.

   $6 \times 4 = 24$, so $4 \times 6 =$ _24_.

2. **Use Structure** What multiplication fact can be paired with $2 \times 8 = 16$ to make a pair of facts showing the Commutative Property of Multiplication?

3. Why is the Commutative Property of Multiplication sometimes called the *order* property?

Do You Know How?

In **4**, draw an array and give the product for each fact.

4. $5 \times 2 =$ _9_ $2 \times 5 =$ ____

In **5** and **6**, complete the equation.

5. $5 \times 2 =$ _2_ $\times 5$

6. $6 \times 1 = 1 \times$ ____

☆ Independent Practice ☆

In **7** and **8**, write a multiplication equation for each array in the pair.

7.
   $6 \times 2 = 12$

   $2 \times 6 = 12$

8.

In **9**, draw an array to show each equation. Write the products.

9. $5 \times 6 =$ _30_ $6 \times 5 =$ _30_

In **10–12**, fill in the missing number.

10. $5 \times 3 =$ ____ $\times 5$ 11. $8 \times$ _4_ $= 4 \times 8$ 12. ____ $\times 6 = 6 \times 7$

Problem Solving

13. Effie earns $26 from babysitting and $45 from mowing lawns. She spends $12 on lunch. How much money does Effie have now?

Bar diagrams can show addition or subtraction.

59

14. Use Structure Chen arranged 32 berries in the array shown below.

What other array can he use to show the same number of berries?

15. Higher Order Thinking Ramón says he can use the Commutative Property of Multiplication to show the product of 4 × 6 is the same as the product of 3 × 8. Is he correct? Why or why not?

$4 \times 6 = 24$
$3 \times 8 = 24$

16. **Vocabulary** Fill in the blanks. You can show the Commutative Property of Multiplication using 2 arrays. The number of _____ in the first array is equal to the number of _____ in the second array. The number of _____ in the first array is equal to the number of _____ in the second array.

✓ **Assessment**

17. How do the arrays at the right show the Commutative Property of Multiplication?

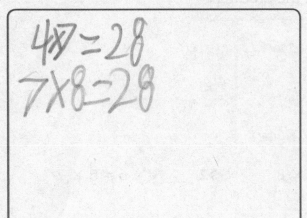

$4 \times 7 = 28$
$7 \times 8 = 28$

Name _____

Another Look!

This array shows 2 rows of 3 pennies.

This array shows 3 rows of 2 pennies.

$2 \times 3 = 6$

$3 \times 2 = 6$

An array shows objects in equal rows.

You can use the **Commutative Property of Multiplication** to multiply the numbers in any order.

$2 \times 3 = 6$ so $3 \times 2 = 6$

In **1** and **2**, draw an array to show each equation. Write the products.

1. $2 \times 8 =$ ____ $8 \times 2 =$ ____

2. $4 \times 4 =$ ____

In **3–10**, complete each multiplication equation. You may use counters or draw pictures to help.

3. $3 \times 4 = 12$, so ____ $\times 3 = 12$.

4. $5 \times 6 = 30$, so ____ $\times 5 = 30$.

5. $5 \times 2 = 10$, so $2 \times$ ____ $= 10$.

6. $4 \times 8 = 32$, so ____ $\times 4 = 32$.

7. $7 \times 9 = 63$, so ____ $\times$ ____ $= 63$.

8. $7 \times 8 = 56$, so ____ $\times$ ____ $= 56$.

9. $3 \times 8 = 24$, so ____ $\times$ ____ $= 24$.

10. $5 \times 3 = 15$, so ____ $\times$ ____ $= 15$.

11. Use Structure Use the Commutative Property of Multiplication to draw the second array. Complete the multiplication equations.

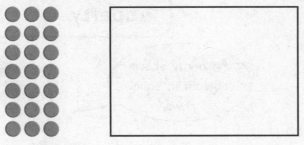

$7 \times 3 =$ _____ $3 \times$ _____ $=$ _____

12. Construct Arguments Scott puts some sports stickers in rows. He makes 6 rows with 5 stickers in each row. If he puts the same number of stickers in 5 equal rows, how many stickers would be in each row? How do you know?

A good math explanation can include words, numbers, and symbols.

13. Karen arranges 24 star stickers in the array shown below.

What other array could the same number of stickers be arranged in?

14. Higher Order Thinking Ed arranged some tiles in different arrays. One array has 3 rows with 6 tiles in each row. The other array has 2 rows with 9 tiles in each row. Ed says that he can use the Commutative Property to show that the arrays both have 18 tiles. Is he correct? Explain.

 Assessment

15. Taylor made these arrays to show the Commutative Property of Multiplication. Is that what the arrays show? Why or why not?

Name _Adhrit B._

Solve & Share

Four friends picked 20 apples. They want to share them equally. How many apples should each person get? **Solve this problem any way you choose.**

I can ...
use objects or pictures to show how objects can be divided into equal groups:

I can also model with math to solve problems.

$$20 \div 4 = 5$$
each will get 5 apples

Model with math. Drawing a picture that represents the problem can help you solve it. Show your work!

Look Back! **Use Appropriate Tools** Can you use counters to help you solve this problem? Explain.

Essential Question: How Many Are in Each Group?

A

Three friends have 12 toys to share equally. How many toys will each friend get?

Think of arranging 12 toys into 3 equal groups.

Division is an operation that is used to find how many equal groups there are or how many are in each group.

B

What You Think

Put one toy at a time in each group.

12 toys

4 toys for each friend

When all the toys are grouped, there will be 4 in each group.

C

What You Write

You can write a division equation to find the number in each group.

$$12 \div 3 = 4$$

Total — Number of equal groups — Number in each group

Each friend will get 4 toys.

Convince Me! **Be Precise** What would happen if 3 friends wanted to share 13 toys equally?

No. The 3 friend couldnot share the toys because 13÷3 is not posible

---

Practice Buddy Tools Assessment

☆ Guided Practice ☆

Do You Understand?

1. 18 eggs are divided into 3 rows. How many eggs are in each row? Use the bar diagram to solve.

18

?	?	?

$18 \div 3 = \underline{6}$ eggs

2. Be Precise Can 12 grapes be shared equally among 5 children with no grapes remaining? Explain.

Do You Know How?

In **3** and **4**, draw a picture to solve.

3. 15 bananas are shared equally by 3 monkeys. How many bananas does each monkey get?

$15 \div 3 = 5$

4. 16 plants are divided equally into 4 pots. How many plants are in each pot?

Independent Practice ☆

In **5** and **6**, draw a picture to solve.

5. 18 marbles are divided equally into 6 sacks. How many marbles are in each sack?

$18 \div 6 = 3$

6. 16 crayons are shared equally by 2 people. How many crayons does each person have?

In **7–10**, complete each equation.

7. $12 \div 2 = \boxed{6}$

12

?	?

8. $16 \div 8 = \boxed{2}$

16

?	?	?	?	?	?	?	?

9. $9 \div 3 = \underline{3}$

10. $14 \div 7 = \underline{2}$

Problem Solving

11. Critique Reasoning Jim is putting 18 pens into equal groups. He says if he puts them into 2 equal groups he will have more pens in each group than if he puts them in 3 equal groups. Is Jim correct? Explain.

12. Make Sense and Persevere Ms. Terry's class is hosting a fundraising challenge. The students in her class are divided into 4 teams. Each team has an equal number of students. Do you have enough information to find how many students are on each team? Explain.

13. Erika draws a hexagon. Maria draws a pentagon. Who draws the shape with more sides? How many more sides does that shape have?

14. Model with Math The flag bearers in a parade march in 9 rows with 5 flags in each row. Write an equation to show how many flags there are.

45

15. Number Sense Jenn equally shares 40 jellybeans with some friends. Is the number that each friend gets greater than 40 or less than 40? Explain.

16. Higher Order Thinking Joy has 12 shells. She gives 2 shells to her mom. Then she and her sister share the other shells equally. How many shells does Joy get? How many shells does her sister get? How do you know?

$12 - 2 = 10$

$10 \div 2 = 5$

✔ **Assessment**

17. Max has the 14 stickers shown at the right. He wants to put an equal number of stickers on each of 2 posters. Draw circles in each box to represent the stickers Max puts on each poster.

Poster 1

Poster 2

Help Practice Tools Games
       Buddy

Another Look!

A.J. has 15 T-shirts. He sorted them equally into 5 laundry bins. How many T-shirts did A.J. put in each bin? You can use a bar diagram to solve.

15 T-shirts →   15
5 bins → | 3 | 3 | 3 | 3 | 3 |
              ↑
        3 T-shirts in each bin

There are 15 T-shirts. There are 5 groups.
There are 3 T-shirts in each group.
So, 15 ÷ 5 = 3.

A.J. put 3 T-shirts in each laundry bin.

Division can show how many items are in each equal group.

In **1**, use the bar diagram to help divide.

1. There are 12 tennis balls that need to be packaged equally into 4 cans.

   How many tennis balls will be in each can?

   12 tennis balls →   12
   4 cans → | ? | ? | ? | ? |
                 ↑
           ? tennis balls in each can

   There are ____ tennis balls.

   There are ____ groups.

   There are ____ tennis balls in each group.

   12 ÷ ____ = ____

In **2–7**, put an equal number of objects in each group. Use counters or draw a picture to solve. Write the unit for each answer.

2. Sort 16 apples equally into 2 baskets. How many apples are in each basket?

3. Arrange 20 chairs equally at 4 tables. How many chairs are at each table?

4. 7 rabbits share 21 carrots equally. How many carrots does each rabbit get?

5. 5 children share 25 dimes equally. How many dimes does each child get?

6. Divide 14 books equally on 2 shelves. How many books are on each shelf?

7. 24 people divide among 3 elevators equally. How many people are in each elevator?

8. **Construct Arguments** Can you divide 14 shirts into 2 equal piles? Why or why not?

9. In February 2015, there were 28 days, all in complete weeks. There are 7 days in a complete week. How many weeks were there in February 2015?

10. **Be Precise** Ron and Pam each have 20 pennies. Ron puts his pennies into 4 equal groups. Pam puts her pennies into 5 equal groups. Who has more pennies in each group? Explain.

11. Write the division equation that matches the bar diagram.

16			
?	?	?	?

12. **Algebra** There are 92 students in the third and fourth grades at Johnsonville Elementary. Of these, 47 are in fourth grade. Write an equation to find how many third graders there are. Use a question mark to represent the unknown number and solve.

13. **Higher Order Thinking** Kyra has a rock collection. When she puts her rocks into 2 equal piles, there are no rocks left over. When she puts her rocks into 3 equal piles, there are still no rocks left over. When she puts her rocks into 4 equal piles, there are still no rocks left over. How many rocks could Kyra have?

 Assessment

14. Sam, Clara, and Dylan are each making a necklace. They divide 26 beads equally. Draw pictures in the boxes to show how many beads each person will get. Draw any remaining beads in the Leftover box.

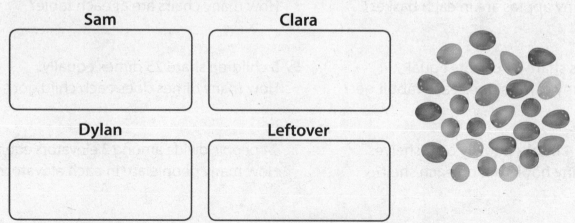

Sam

Clara

Dylan

Leftover

Name _Adhrit B._

Solve

Solve & Share

Li made 12 tacos. He wants to give some of his friends 2 tacos each. If Li does not get any of the tacos, how many of his friends will get tacos? *Solve this problem any way you choose.*

I can ...
use repeated subtraction to understand and solve division problems.

I can also reason about math.

You can use reasoning. How can what you know about sharing help you solve the problem? Show your work in the space below!

$$12 \div 2 = 6$$

Look Back! **Use Appropriate Tools** How can counters or other objects help you show your work?

How Can You Divide Using Repeated Subtraction?

A

June has 10 strawberries to serve to her guests. If each guest eats 2 strawberries, how many guests can June serve?

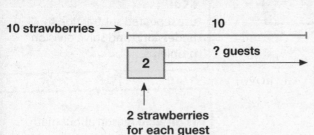

10 strawberries → 10

2 ? guests

↑
2 strawberries
for each guest

B

You can use repeated subtraction to find how many groups of 2 are in 10.

$10 - 2 = 8$
$8 - 2 = 6$
$6 - 2 = 4$
$4 - 2 = 2$
$2 - 2 = 0$

You can subtract 2 five times. There are five groups of 2 in 10.

There are no strawberries left.

June can serve 5 guests.

C

You can write a division equation to find the number of groups.

Write: $10 \div 2 = ?$

Read: Ten divided by 2 equals what number?

Solve: $10 \div 2 = 5$

June can serve 5 guests.

Convince Me! **Model with Math** In the example above, what if each guest ate 5 strawberries? Use the math you know to represent the problem and find how many guests June could serve.

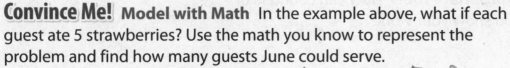

$10 - 5 = 5 \cdot 1$ $10 \div 5 = 2$
$5 - 5 = 0 \cdot 2$

Name _Adhrit_

☆ Guided Practice ☆

Do You Understand?

1. Show how you can use repeated subtraction to find how many groups of 4 there are in 20. Then write a division equation to solve the problem.

$20 \div 4 = 5$ $20 - 4 = 16$
$16 - 4 = 12$
$12 - 4 = 8$
$8 - 4 = 4$
$4 - 4 = 0$

Do You Know How?

In **2** and **3**, use counters or draw a picture to solve.

2. The bell choir has 16 gloves. There are 2 gloves in each pair. How many pairs of gloves are there?

$16 \div 8$

3. Ruth has 15 dog treats. She gives each of her dogs 3 treats. How many dogs does Ruth have?

$15 \div 3 = 5$

☆ Independent Practice ☆

Leveled Practice In **4** and **5**, complete the equations.

4. Ruth picks 14 apples. She places 7 apples in each bag. How many bags does Ruth have?

$14 - 7 = 7$
$7 - 7 = 0$
$14 \div 7 = 2$

Ruth has 2 bags.

5. The wagons on the farm have 4 wheels each. There are 12 wheels. How many wagons are on the farm?

$12 - 4 = 8$
$8 - 4 = 4$
$4 - 4 = 0$
$12 \div 4 = 3$

There are __ wagons.

In **6** and **7**, use counters or draw a picture to solve.

6. Shirley bought 30 markers that came in packages of 5 markers each. How many packages did Shirley buy?

7. Marcus has 18 pencils. He places 2 pencils on each desk. How many desks are there?

Problem Solving

8. **Generalize** The chart shows the number of pennies each of three friends has in her pocket. Each friend divides her money into piles of 3 coins. Write division equations to show how many equal piles each friend can make. Explain what repeats in the equations and how it helps you solve.

Money in Pockets		
Claudia	:	18 cents
Zoe	:	12 cents
Jenna	:	15 cents

9. If Zoe makes columns of 6 pennies each, how many rows does she make?

$12 \div 6 = 2$

10. **Model with Math** Bella has $52. She spends $21, then finds $12. How much money does she have now? Use math to represent the problem.

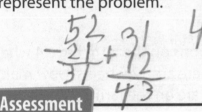

$$\begin{array}{r} 52 \\ -21 \\ \hline 31 \end{array} \quad \begin{array}{r} 31 \\ +12 \\ \hline 43 \end{array} \quad 43$$

11. **Higher Order Thinking** An ice cream store plans to make 8 new flavors each year. How many years will it take for the store to make 80 flavors? Write and solve an equation.

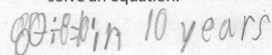

$80 \div 8 = 10$ in 10 years

✓ Assessment

12. Eric writes the following:

$20 - 5 = 15$
$15 - 5 = 10$
$10 - 5 = 5$
$5 - 5 = 0$

What equation could Eric use to represent the same problem?

Ⓐ $5 \times 5 = 25$

Ⓑ $5 \div 5 = 1$

Ⓒ $15 \div 5 = 3$

Ⓓ $20 \div 5 = 4$

13. Jacqui writes the following:

$24 - 8 = 16$
$16 - 8 = 8$
$8 - 8 = 0$

Which problem is Jacqui trying to solve?

Ⓐ $24 \div 8$

Ⓑ $24 \div 6$

Ⓒ $24 - 16$

Ⓓ 24×3

Name _____

Another Look!

Layla has 20 raffle tickets.
There are 5 tickets in each book.
How many books of raffle tickets
does Layla have? Find $20 \div 5 = \boxed{}$.

$$
\left.\begin{array}{l}
20 - 5 = 15 \\
15 - 5 = 10 \\
10 - 5 = 5 \\
5 - 5 = 0
\end{array}\right\} \text{There are four groups of 5 in 20.}
$$

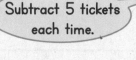

Subtract 5 tickets
each time.

You subtracted 5 four times. So, $20 \div 5 = 4$.

Layla has 4 books of raffle tickets.

In **1**, use repeated subtraction to help you solve.

1. Ryan has 10 markers.
   There are 5 markers in each box.
   How many boxes of markers are there?
   Find $10 \div 5 = \boxed{}$.

   $10 - 5 = $ _____

   $5 - $ _____ $= $ _____

   I subtracted 5 two times.

   So, _____ $\div$ _____ $=$ _____.

   Ryan has _____ boxes of markers.

In **2** and **3**, use bar diagrams or counters or draw a picture to solve.

2. There are 16 books. The librarian arranged
   4 books on each shelf. How many shelves
   are there?

   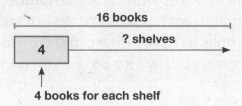
   16 books
   ? shelves
   4
   4 books for each shelf

3. Joseph had 28 paintbrushes to give to
   4 members of the Art Club. He wanted to
   give an equal number of brushes to each
   member. How many brushes did each
   member get?

Daniel has to carry 32 boxes to his room. He can carry 4 boxes on each trip. How many trips will Daniel take? Show your work.

You can use repeated subtraction or draw a picture to solve.

5. **Model with Math** The United States Mint released five state quarters every year. There are 50 states. How many years did it take for all 50 state quarters to be released? Write and solve an equation.

6. Write an equation that represents the bar diagram below.

40

| 8 | 8 | 8 | 8 | 8 |

7. **Number Sense** Compare 249 and 271. Write the greater number in word form.

8. **Higher Order Thinking** A newspaper has more than 30 pages and fewer than 40 pages. The newspaper is divided into sections, and each section has exactly 8 pages. How many sections does the newspaper have?

✓ Assessment

9. The store clerk has 21 mugs to display on shelves. She wants to display an equal number of mugs on each shelf with no mugs left over. Which problem below shows a way she can do this?

Ⓐ 21 ÷ 2

Ⓑ 21 ÷ 5

Ⓒ 21 ÷ 7

Ⓓ 21 ÷ 10

10. Tamara has 20 dolls. She wants to store them in boxes with an equal number of dolls in each box. She does not want any dolls left over. How can she divide the dolls equally into boxes with none left over?

Ⓐ Put 3 dolls in each box.

Ⓑ Put 4 dolls in each box.

Ⓒ Put 6 dolls in each box.

Ⓓ Put 8 dolls in each box.

Name _____

Solve & Share

Carolyn earned $8 a week for 2 weeks. She wants to buy some books that cost $4 each. How many books can she buy?

Choose a tool to represent and solve the problem. Explain why you chose that tool.

I can ...
think strategically to determine which tool will be most useful.

I can also multiply and divide to solve problems.

Thinking Habits

Be a good thinker! These questions can help you.

- Which tools can I use?
- Why should I use this tool to help me solve the problem?
- Is there a different tool I could use?
- Am I using the tool appropriately?

Look Back! Use Appropriate Tools Explain how you used the tool you chose.

Essential Question

How Can You Use Appropriate Tools to Represent and Solve Problems?

A

A hardware store has boxes of 18 light bulbs. 3 light bulbs cost $4. How much does it cost to buy a whole box of light bulbs? Choose a tool to represent and solve the problem.

Sometimes you can use more than one tool to help you solve problems.

What do I need to do?

I need to choose an appropriate tool to help me find how much it costs to buy a box of 18 light bulbs.

B

Which tools can I use to help me solve this problem?

I can

- decide which tools are appropriate.

- use cubes and counters to solve this problem.

- use the tools correctly.

C

Here's my thinking...

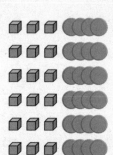

I will use two tools. Both counters and ones cubes are easy to count and move around.

Each cube is 1 light bulb.
I will separate 18 cubes into groups of 3.

Each counter is $1.
I will put 4 counters with each group of 3 light bulbs.

There are 24 counters.
A box of light bulbs costs $24.

Convince Me! **Use Appropriate Tools** What other tools could you use to solve this problem?

☆ Guided Practice ☆

Use Appropriate Tools

3 friends each have 8 books. They put their books into 4 equal piles. How many books are in each pile?

You can also use a digital tool. Technology can help you solve a problem.

1. Choose a tool to represent the problem. Explain why you chose that tool.

2. Solve the problem. Explain how you used the tool you chose.

☆ Independent Practice ☆

Use Appropriate Tools

15 students are working in equal groups to make posters. There are 5 students in each group. For each group of students, there needs to be 2 adults helping. How many adults are needed?

3. Choose a tool to represent the problem. Explain why you chose that tool.

4. Solve the problem. Explain how you used the tool you chose.

5. The posters need to be 20 inches long. What tool could the students use to check the posters are the correct size? Explain how they could use this tool.

Problem Solving

Bottle Cap Display

The soda bottle caps at the right are shared equally between Kerry and Nita. There are 4 orange bottle caps. Kerry wants to arrange her bottle caps into an array.

6. **Make Sense and Persevere** What do you need to find out before you make an array? Show a way to find this. You can use a tool to help.

7. **Use Appropriate Tools** Choose a tool to represent the array of soda bottle caps. Explain why you chose that tool.

8. **Model with Math** Draw a picture to show one way the array might look. Then write a multiplication equation for the array.

9. **Use Structure** Write a different multiplication equation with the same two factors you used in **8**. Has the product changed? Explain.

> Think about what you need to do in the problem. Then choose a tool that can help you solve it.

10. **Critique Reasoning** Kerry says she can use a tens rod to represent the array. Do you agree? Explain.

Another Look!

Mal downloads 4 songs each week for 5 weeks. Then he sorts the songs into equal groups. There are 10 songs in each group. How many groups are there?

Tell how you can use tools to help solve the problem.

- I can decide which tool is appropriate.

- I can use a tool to represent the situation.

- I can use the tool correctly.

Solve the problem. Explain how you used the tool you chose.

I can use grid paper. Each shaded square represents 1 song.

I shade 4 squares for each week. There are 20 songs. Then I separate them into groups of 10. There are 2 groups.

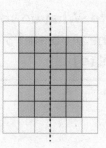

Grid paper, counters, cubes, or other objects can all be used as tools to help solve problems.

Use Appropriate Tools

Niko bought 4 stamps each week for 3 weeks. He wants to put 6 stamps on each page of his album. How many pages will Niko use?

1. Tell how you can use tools to help solve the problem.

2. Choose a tool to represent the problem.
   Explain why you chose that tool.

3. Solve the problem. Explain how you used the tool you chose.

Summer Jobs
The table at the right shows how much Tony earns per hour for his summer jobs. One day Tony spends 3 hours running errands. He wants to use the money from this job to buy two banners.

Tony's Summer Jobs	
Job	**Hourly Pay**
Walking Dogs	$8
Mowing Lawns	$10
Running Errands	$6

DATA

4. **Use Appropriate Tools** Choose a tool to represent the problem. Explain why you chose that tool.

5. **Make Sense and Persevere** What do you need to find out before you can solve the problem? Show a way to find this. You can use a tool to help.

6. **Reasoning** Does Tony have enough money? Use what you know to solve the problem.

You can use tools to represent different parts of a problem.

7. **Make Sense and Persevere** Did you need all the information in the table to solve the problem? Explain.

8. **Construct Arguments** Tony decides not to buy the banners. Does he have enough money to buy one cap instead? Explain why or why not.

Find a Match

Work with a partner. Point to a clue. Read the clue.

Look below the clues to find a match. Write the clue letter in the box next to the match.

Find a match for every clue.

I can ...
add and subtract within 20.

Clues

A Is equal to 9 + 11	**E** Is equal to 19 − 9	**I** Is equal to 2 − 2
B Is equal to 13 − 6	**F** Is equal to 9 + 6	**J** Is equal to 9 + 10
C Is equal to 8 + 8	**G** Is equal to 10 − 7	**K** Is equal to 16 − 8
D Is equal to 12 − 8	**H** Is equal to 8 + 9	**L** Is equal to 6 + 7

☐ 3 + 0	☐ 10 + 6	☐ 9 − 9
☐ 15 − 8	☐ 13	☐ 4 + 4
☐ 17	☐ 13 − 9	☐ 12 + 8
☐ 5 + 5	☐ 8 + 7	☐ 19

TOPIC 1 Vocabulary Review

Glossary

Word List

- array
- column
- Commutative Property of Multiplication
- division
- equal groups
- equation
- factors
- multiplication
- number line
- product
- row
- unknown

Understand Vocabulary

Choose the best term from the Word List. Write it on the blank.

1. Addition and _____ are operations you can use to join _____.

2. You solve an equation by finding the value that is _____.

3. You can use a(n) _____ to display objects in equal rows and columns.

4. A line marked in equal units and numbered in order is called a(n) _____.

For each of these terms, give an example and a non-example.

	Example	Non-example
5. division	_____	_____
6. equation	_____	_____
7. Commutative Property of Multiplication	_____	_____

Use Vocabulary in Writing

8. Explain how you can multiply 3 × 4. Use at least 2 terms from the Word List in your explanation.

Reteaching

Set A pages 7–12

How many is 3 groups of 4?

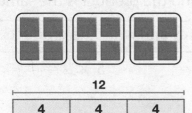

| 12 |
| 4 | 4 | 4 |

$4 + 4 + 4 = 12$

$3 \times 4 = 12$

$4 + 4 + 4 = 3 \times 4$

Remember that you can use addition or multiplication to join equal groups.

Complete each equation. Use counters or draw a picture to help.

1. $2 + 2 + 2 = 3 \times$ ____

2. ____ $+$ ____ $+$ ____ $= 3 \times 6$

3. $8 +$ ____ $+$ ____ $=$ ____ $\times 8$

Set B pages 13–18

Skip count by 4s three times.

You can use a number line to find 3×4.

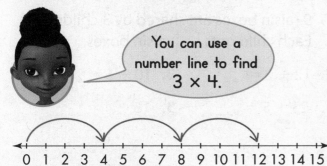

Number of jumps: 3
Number in each jump: 4

$3 \times 4 = 12$

Remember that you can show skip counting on a number line.

Use the number line to complete each multiplication equation.

1. $2 \times 3 =$ ____

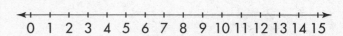
0 1 2 3 4 5 6 7 8 9 10 11 12 13 14 15

2. $4 \times 3 =$ ____

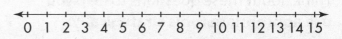
0 1 2 3 4 5 6 7 8 9 10 11 12 13 14 15

Set C pages 19–24

Find 4×6.
The array shows 4 rows of 6 counters.

Each row is an equal group. You can use addition, skip counting, or multiplication to find the total.

$6 + 6 + 6 + 6 = 24$

6, 12, 18, 24

$4 \times 6 = 24$

Remember that an array shows objects in equal rows.

Show how to use addition, skip counting, and multiplication for each array.

1.

2.

This array shows 3 rows of 4.

$3 \times 4 = 12$

This array shows 4 rows of 3.

$4 \times 3 = 12$

So, $3 \times 4 = 4 \times 3$.

Remember that the Commutative Property of Multiplication says you can multiply factors in any order and the product is the same.

Draw an array and write the products.

1. $2 \times 5 =$ _____ $5 \times 2 =$ _____

Set E pages 31–36, 37–42

2 friends share 6 fruit snacks equally. How many fruit snacks does each friend get?

$6 \div 2 = 3$ fruit snacks

You can use repeated subtraction.

$6 - 2 = 4$ You subtract 2 from 6 three
$4 - 2 = 2$ times to reach zero.
$2 - 2 = 0$

$6 \div 2 = 3$

Remember that division is an operation to find the number of equal groups or the number in each equal group.

1. 9 raisin boxes are shared by 3 children. Each child gets ☐ raisin boxes.

2. $12 \div 2 =$ _____   **3.** $10 \div 5 =$ _____

4. $25 \div 5 =$ _____   **5.** $16 \div 4 =$ _____

Set F pages 43–48

Think about these questions to help you **use appropriate tools strategically**.

Thinking Habits

Which tools can I use?

Why should I use this tool to help me solve the problem?

Is there a different tool I could use?

Am I using the tool appropriately?

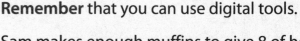

Remember that you can use digital tools.

Sam makes enough muffins to give 8 of her friends 3 muffins each. Each tray holds 6 muffins. How many trays does she need?

1. Choose a tool to represent the problem. Explain why you chose that tool.

2. Solve. Explain how the tool helped.

Name _____

1. Jace drew a picture. Choose all of the equations that go with Jace's picture.

- ☐ 1 + 2 + 1 + 3 = 8
- ☐ 2 + 2 + 8 = 12
- ☐ 2 + 2 + 2 + 2 = 8
- ☐ 4 + 2 + 2 = 8
- ☐ 4 × 2 = 8

2. Aidan puts 2 turtles in each of 4 aquariums. What is the total number of turtles? Show the multiplication problem on a number line. Then write the answer.

☐ turtles

3. Minh paints 12 rooms. To paint 3 rooms, he needs 2 cans of paint. He wants to know how many cans he needs in all. Which tools would be appropriate for Minh to use to solve the problem? Choose all that apply.

- ☐ Counters
- ☐ Ruler
- ☐ Pencil and paper
- ☐ Tiles
- ☐ Money

4. Megan organized her photos in this array. Draw a different array that has the same factors. Then write multiplication equations for each array.

5. Josiah makes six 3-point baskets in his basketball game. For questions 5a–5d, choose *Yes* or *No* to tell if the equation shows a way to find the number of points that Josiah scores.

5a. 6 × 3 = 18   ○ Yes ○ No

5b. 2 × 6 = 12   ○ Yes ○ No

5c. 3 + 3 + 3 +
       3 + 3 + 3 = 18   ○ Yes ○ No

5d. 6 + 6 = 12   ○ Yes ○ No

6. Teresa is growing 2 rows of tomato plants, with 4 plants in each row. Draw an array to show the plants. Find the total number of plants.

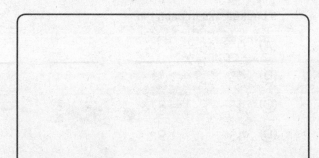

7. Ann has 25 tennis balls. She wants to put them into cans that hold 3 balls each. Can there be equal shares of balls with no balls remaining? Why or why not?

10. Zak uses repeated subtraction to find 48 ÷ 8. How many groups of 8 does Zak subtract?

11. Saima makes 14 muffins to give to her friends. She wants to give 2 muffins to each friend at her party.

Part A

Explain how Saima can figure out how many friends to invite.

8. Crystal draws jumps on a number line to solve a multiplication problem. Which multiplication equation does her number line show?

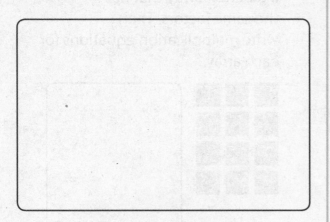

Part B

Explain a different way that Saima can figure out how many friends to invite.

9. Al needs to put 9 basketballs in each bin. He has 45 basketballs. Which equation can help you find how many bins Al can fill?

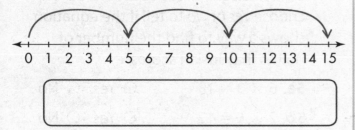

Ⓐ 9 ÷ 45 = ☐

Ⓑ 45 × 5 = ☐

Ⓒ 45 ÷ ☐ = 8

Ⓓ 45 ÷ ☐ = 9

Name _____

Sticker Collection
Jamie saved money to buy a sticker album.
The money he has saved each week is shown in the table.

Sticker Prices
• Green sticker albums cost $6.
• Blue sticker albums cost $9.
• Yellow sticker albums cost $12.
• Stickers cost $1 for 3 stickers.

Use the **Money Saved Each Week** table to answer
Question 1.

Money Saved Each Week	
Week	Dollars Saved per Week
1	$3
2	$3
3	$3
4	$3

1. How much money has Jamie saved after 4 weeks?
   Write an addition equation to solve.

Use the **Sticker Prices** list to answer Questions 2–4.

2. Jamie divides his money into two equal parts. Jamie spends 1 part on a
   sticker album. Which of the albums can Jamie buy?

3. Jamie spends the other part of his money on stickers.
   How many stickers can Jamie buy?

4. After spending his money, Jamie decides that he wants a second album.
   He plans to save $3 per week until he can also buy a blue sticker album.
   How many weeks does Jamie need to save money?

Use the **Sticker Arrays** table to answer Question 5.

5. Jamie wants to organize his stickers into arrays on a page of the album. Jamie started to make a table to show three ways he could do this.

Sticker Arrays		
Array	**Number of Rows**	**Stickers in Each Row**
Way 1	6	3
Way 2	2	9
Way 3	_____	_____

Part A

Draw arrays to show the two ways Jamie planned to organize his stickers.

Way 1

Way 2

Part B

Draw an array to show another way Jamie could organize his stickers. Complete the Sticker Arrays table for Way 3.

Way 3

6. Write multiplication equations for each array to check that Jamie uses all of his stickers in each plan. Do two ways show the same factors? Explain.

Multiplication Facts : Use Patterns

Essential Question: How can unknown multiplication facts be found using patterns and properties?

Digital Resources

Solve Learn Glossary Practice Buddy

Tools Assessment Help Games

Force makes objects move.

You can use patterns to predict how objects will move!

Let's move some numbers! Here's a project on motion and patterns.

Math and Science Project: Motion Patterns

Do Research Swings, see-saws, and some other playground objects move with force. Use the Internet or other sources to see what happens when these objects move. Record the number of times that someone pushes or pulls to make the object move. Record the number of times that the object moves.

Journal: Write a Report Include what you found. Also in your report:

- Explain any patterns you found. Tell how you can use your patterns to predict how the objects will move in the future.

- Write an equation for one of the patterns.

- Explain what the numbers in your equation represent.

Review What You Know

A-Z Vocabulary

Choose the best term from the box.
Write it on the blank.

| • multiplication | • factors |
| • array | • product |

1. The _____ is the answer to a multiplication problem.

2. Numbers that are being multiplied are _____.

3. An operation that gives the total when you join equal groups is _____.

Multiplication as Repeated Addition

Complete each equation.

4. $2 + 2 + 2 + 2 = 4 \times$ ____

5. $9 +$ ____ $+$ ____ $=$ ____ $\times 9$

6. ____ $+$ ____ $+$ ____ $+ 5 =$ ____ $\times 5$

7. $2 \times 6 =$ ____ $+$ ____

Multiplication on the Number Line

8. Marty drew this number line.

   Which multiplication fact does the number line show?

   Ⓐ $3 \times 5 = 15$ Ⓑ $3 \times 4 = 12$ Ⓒ $3 \times 3 = 9$ Ⓓ $3 \times 6 = 18$

9. Show the multiplication fact on the number line. Write the product.

   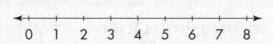

   $3 \times 2 =$ ____

The Commutative Property

10. How do the arrays represent the Commutative Property of Multiplication?

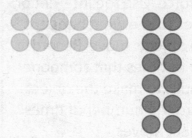

My Word Cards

Use the examples for each word on the front of the card to help complete the definitions on the back.

A-Z
Glossary

multiple

0, 5, 10, 15, and 20 are
multiples of 5.

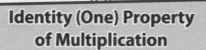
Identity (One) Property of Multiplication

$$4 \times 1 = 4$$
$$5 \times 1 = 5$$

Zero Property of Multiplication

$$4 \times 0 = 0$$
$$5 \times 0 = 0$$

My Word Cards

Complete each definition. Extend learning by writing your own definitions.

The _____

_____

_____

states that the product of any number and 1 is that number.

The product of a given number and any other whole number is called a

_____.

The _____

_____ states that the product of any number and zero is zero.

Name **Adhrit B.**

Solve & Share

Each chicken has 2 legs. How many legs are there in a group of 9 chickens? Show how you decided.

I can ...
use patterns to multiply by 2 and 5.

I can also make sense of problems.

You can make sense of the problem by using a number line or a table to record and analyze information.

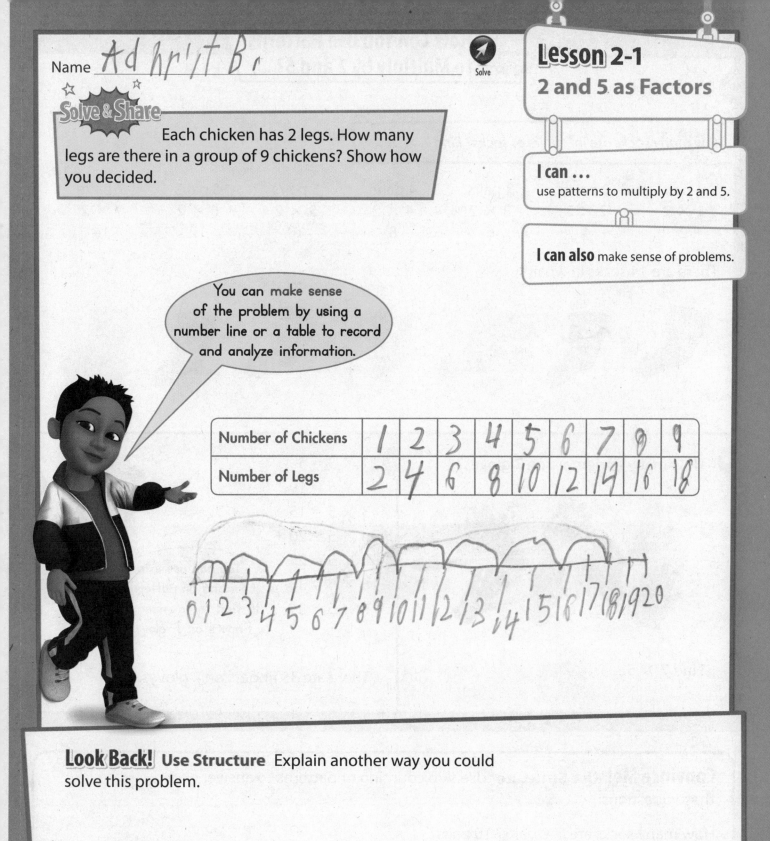

Number of Chickens	1	2	3	4	5	6	7	8	9
Number of Legs	2	4	6	8	10	12	14	16	18

0 1 2 3 4 5 6 7 8 9 10 11 12 13 14 15 16 17 18 19 20

Look Back! **Use Structure** Explain another way you could solve this problem.

A

How many socks are in 7 pairs of socks? Find 7 × 2.

1 pair	2 pairs	3 pairs	4 pairs	5 pairs	6 pairs	7 pairs
1 × 2	2 × 2	3 × 2	4 × 2	5 × 2	6 × 2	7 × 2
2	4	6	8	10	12	14

There are 14 socks in 7 pairs.

B

How many fingers are on 7 gloves?

Find 7 × 5.

C

1 × 5 = 5
2 × 5 = 10
3 × 5 = 15
4 × 5 = 20
5 × 5 = 25
6 × 5 = 30
7 × 5 = 35

You can use skip counting or patterns to find the number of fingers on 7 gloves.

There are 35 fingers on 7 gloves.

Convince Me! **Use Structure** Use skip counting or patterns to answer these questions:

How many socks are in 9 pairs? 10 pairs?

9 × 2 = 18 = 10 × 2 = 20

How many fingers are on 9 gloves? 10 gloves?

9 + 9 + 9 + 9 + 9 = 45   50   10 + 10 + 10 + 10 + 10 = 50

Another Example!

Multiples are the products of a number and other whole numbers.

DATA	**2s Facts**	
	$0 \times 2 = 0$	$5 \times 2 = 10$
	$1 \times 2 = 2$	$6 \times 2 = 12$
	$2 \times 2 = 4$	$7 \times 2 = 14$
	$3 \times 2 = 6$	$8 \times 2 = 16$
	$4 \times 2 = 8$	$9 \times 2 = 18$

DATA	**5s Facts**	
	$0 \times 5 = 0$	$5 \times 5 = 25$
	$1 \times 5 = 5$	$6 \times 5 = 30$
	$2 \times 5 = 10$	$7 \times 5 = 35$
	$3 \times 5 = 15$	$8 \times 5 = 40$
	$4 \times 5 = 20$	$9 \times 5 = 45$

The products for the 2s facts are multiples of 2. Multiples of 2 end in 0, 2, 4, 6, or 8.

The products for the 5s facts are multiples of 5. Multiples of 5 end in 0 or 5.

☆ Guided Practice ☆

Do You Understand?

1. Is 25 a multiple of 2 or 5? How do you know? No

$25 \div 2 = 24 \, R \, 1$
$25 \div 5 = 5$

2. **Use Structure** Bert says 2×9 is 19. How can you use patterns to show Bert's answer is wrong?

Do You Know How?

In **3–5**, find each product.

3. $2 \times 4 =$ __8__    $2 \times 1 = 2$
                          $2 \times 2 = 4$
                          $2 \times 3 =$ ____
                          $2 \times 4 =$ ____

4.   8
    $\times 2$

5.   5
    $\times 8$
    40

☆ Independent Practice ☆

In **6–12**, find the missing product or factor.

6. $2 \times 2 =$ ____

7. $3 \times$ ____ $= 15$

8. __7__ $\times 2 = 14$

9.   6
    $\times 5$

10.   4
    $\times 2$

11.   9
    $\times 2$

12.   5
    $\times 7$

Problem Solving ☆

13. Make Sense and Persevere
Eric has some nickels. He says they are worth exactly 34 cents. Can you tell if Eric is correct or not? Why or why not?

14. Critique Reasoning Brian said $78 + 92 + 85$ is greater than 300. Explain why Brian's answer is not reasonable.

---

15. Shannon traded 6 nickels in for dimes. How many dimes did Shannon receive?

$6 \times 10 = 60$

16. Math and Science Mike watches how the pendulum swings in his clock. He notices that it swings 1 time every 2 seconds. How long will it take to swing 5 times?

10

---

17. April has the coins shown below.

April counted the value of her coins in cents. List the numbers April would have named.

18. Higher Order Thinking Jake went bowling. On his first turn, he knocked down 2 pins. On his second turn, he knocked down twice as many pins. So far, how many pins has Jake knocked down? How do you know?

✓ **Assessment**

19. Write each number in the correct column to show if it is a multiple of 2 or 5.

Multiple of 2	Multiple of 5

5   6   10   14   18   25

Name _____

Another Look!

When you multiply by 2, you can use a doubles fact. For example, 2 × 6 is the same as adding 6 + 6. Both equal 12.

When you multiply by 5, you can use a pattern to find the product.

2s Facts	
2 × 0 = 0	2 × 5 = 10
2 × 1 = 2	2 × 6 = 12
2 × 2 = 4	2 × 7 = 14
2 × 3 = 6	2 × 8 = 16
2 × 4 = 8	2 × 9 = 18

5s Facts	
5 × 0 = 0	5 × 5 = 25
5 × 1 = 5	5 × 6 = 30
5 × 2 = 10	5 × 7 = 35
5 × 3 = 15	5 × 8 = 40
5 × 4 = 20	5 × 9 = 45

Each multiple of 2 ends in 0, 2, 4, 6, or 8.　　Each multiple of 5 ends in 0 or 5.

In **1–17**, solve each equation.

1. 2 × 5 = ?

5 + 5 = ____

2 × 5 = ____

2. 2 × 4 = ?

4 + 4 = ____

2 × 4 = ____

3. 1 × 2 = ?

1 + 1 = ____

2 × 1 = ____

4. 5 × ____ = 25

5. 3 × 5 = ____

6. 35 = 7 × ____

7. ____ × 8 = 16

8. 5 × 9 = ____

9. 2 × 7 = ____

10.　　5
　　× 4

11.　　1
　　× 5

12.　　2
　　× 0

13.　　8
　　× 2

14. What is 9 times 2? ____

15. What is 5 times 8? ____

16. What is 6 times 2? ____

17. What is 5 times 0? ____

18. Georgia is making sock puppets. Each pair of socks costs $2. Georgia bought 6 pairs of socks. How much did she spend? Draw a number line to solve.

19. (A-Z) **Vocabulary** Write an equation where 45 is the product.

20. Reasoning There are 5 school days in each week. How many school days are in 9 weeks? Explain.

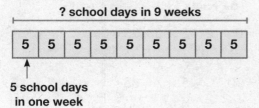

? school days in 9 weeks

| 5 | 5 | 5 | 5 | 5 | 5 | 5 | 5 | 5 |

↑
5 school days
in one week

21. Make Sense and Persevere
Tara walks 2 miles each day. How many miles does Tara walk in a week? How did you find the answer?

22. Mika drew this shape. What is the name of the shape Mika drew? Mika then drew a shape that has 2 fewer sides. What is the name of that shape?

23. Higher Order Thinking How can adding doubles help you multiply by 2? Give an example.

✓ **Assessment**

24. Write the expressions in the correct column.

Product is 10	Product is 12	Product is 35

2×5 7×5 6×2 2×6 5×2 5×7

Name _____

Solve & Share

Maria bought 4 packages of bottled water. There are 9 bottles in each package. How many bottles did Maria buy? Explain how you solved this problem.

I can ...
use patterns to multiply by 9.

I can also make math arguments.

An array or a data table can help you construct arguments.

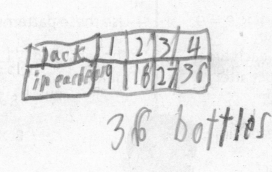

pack	1	2	3	4
in each	9	18	27	36

36 bottles

Look Back! **Make Sense and Persevere** If Maria bought 9 packages of bottled water and there were 4 bottles in each package, would the number of bottles she bought be the same or different? Explain.

Essential Question: **How Can Patterns Be Used to Find 9s Facts?**

A

The owner of a flower shop puts 9 roses in each package. How many roses are in 8 packages?

You can use patterns to find 8 × 9.

9s Facts

DATA

0 × 9 =	0
1 × 9 =	9
2 × 9 =	18
3 × 9 =	27
4 × 9 =	36
5 × 9 =	45
6 × 9 =	54
7 × 9 =	63
8 × 9 =	■
9 × 9 =	

B **One Way**

Use these patterns. Start with 1 × 9 = 9.

The ones digit decreases by 1 each time. So, the ones digit in the product after 63 in the facts table above is 2.

The tens digit increases by 1 each time.

So, the tens digit in the product after 63 in the facts table above is 7.

8 × 9 = 72

There are 72 roses in 8 packages.

C **Another Way**

Use these patterns to find the product.

The tens digit is 1 less than the factor being multiplied by 9.

$$8 - 1 = 7$$
$$8 \times 9 = 72$$
$$7 + 2 = 9$$

The digits of the product have a sum of 9 or a multiple of 9.

Convince Me! **Use Structure** Use the patterns above to find 9 × 9. Explain how you found the product. yoo need to "if 8x9=72 then add 9 to get the product of 9x9.

68 **Topic 2** | Lesson 2-2

Copyright © Savvas Learning Company LLC. All Rights Reserved.

Name _____

☆ Guided Practice *

Do You Understand?

1. **Critique Reasoning** Paul thinks 3×9 is 24. Use a 9s pattern to show Paul is wrong.

2. **Look for Relationships** Look at the table of 9s facts on page 68. Describe a number pattern in the multiples of 9.

Do You Know How?

In **3–10**, find each product.

3. $9 \times 2 =$ _18_

4. $5 \times 9 =$ _45_

5. $7 \times 9 =$ _63_

6. $4 \times 9 =$ _36_

7. $2 \times 9 =$ _18_

8. $6 \times 9 =$ _54_

> You can use patterns to solve multiplication facts with 9s.

9.   3
$\underline{\times\ 9}$
  _27_

10.   8
$\underline{\times\ 9}$
  _72_

☆ Independent Practice ☆

In **11–22**, find the missing product or factor.

11. $9 \times 0 =$ _____

12. $2 \times$ _____ $= 18$

13. _____ $\times 9 = 72$

14. $9 \times 9 =$ _____

15.   4
$\underline{\times\ 9}$
  _36_

16.   9
$\underline{\times\ 5}$

17.   9
$\underline{\times\ 7}$

18.   9
$\underline{\times\ 1}$

19. What is 9×3? _____

20. What is 9×6? _____

21. What is 0×9? _____

22. What is 9×8? _____

Problem Solving

In **23–25**, use the table to the right.

23. Reasoning The library is having a used book sale. How much do 4 hardcover books cost? Draw a number line to show the answer.

Library Book Sale	
Paperback Books	$5
Hardcover Books	$9
Magazines	$2

DATA

24. Higher Order Thinking How much more would Chico spend if he bought 3 hardcover books rather than 3 paperback books? Show how you found the answer.

25. Make Sense and Persevere Maggie bought only magazines. The clerk told her she owed $15. How does Maggie know the clerk made a mistake?

26. The owner of a flower shop put 9 sunflowers in each of 6 vases. Then he counted the flowers by 9s. List the numbers he named.

27. Number Sense Chris and Jerome played a video game. Chris scored 437 points. Jerome scored 398 points. Who scored more points? Explain your answer using >, <, or =.

✓ Assessment

28. Which numbers are **NOT** multiples of 9? Choose all that apply.

- [ ] 9
- [x] 16
- [ ] 18
- [x] 21
- [x] 23

29. Which numbers are multiples of 9? Choose all that apply.

- [ ] 18
- [ ] 36
- [ ] 42
- [ ] 54
- [ ] 69

Help Practice Tools Games
      Buddy

Homework & Practice 2-2

9 as a Factor

Another Look!

9s Facts
$0 \times 9 = 0$
$1 \times 9 = 9$
$2 \times 9 = 18$
$3 \times 9 = 27$
$4 \times 9 = 36$
$5 \times 9 = 45$
$6 \times 9 = 54$
$7 \times 9 =$
$8 \times 9 = \blacksquare$
$9 \times 9 =$

DATA

The table shows patterns in the 9s facts.

- The tens digit in a product will be 1 less than the factor being multiplied by 9.
- The sum of the digits of the product will always be 9 or a multiple of 9, unless the other factor is 0.

Find 9×7.

The tens digit must be 1 less than 7.
The tens digit is 6.

The sum of the digits is 9.
$6 + 3 = 9$, so the ones digit is 3.

The product is 63.

You can use patterns to help remember 9s facts.

In **1–13**, solve each equation.

1. $3 \times 9 = ?$

Tens digit: $3 - 1 =$ _____

Sum of digits:

_____ + _____ = 9

$3 \times 9 =$ _____

2. $2 \times 9 = ?$

Tens digit: $2 - 1 =$ _____

Sum of digits:

_____ + _____ = 9

$2 \times 9 =$ _____

3. $1 \times 9 = ?$

Tens digit: $1 - 1 =$ _____

Sum of digits:

_____ + _____ = 9

$1 \times 9 =$ _____

4. $9 \times 0 =$ _____

5. $9 \times$ _____ $= 54$

6. $81 = 9 \times$ _____

7. $\begin{array}{r} 9 \\ \times\ 8 \\ \hline \end{array}$

8. $\begin{array}{r} 7 \\ \times\ 9 \\ \hline \end{array}$

9. $\begin{array}{r} 4 \\ \times\ 9 \\ \hline \end{array}$

10. $\begin{array}{r} 2 \\ \times\ 9 \\ \hline \end{array}$

11. Find 6 times 9.

12. Find 5 times 9.

13. Find 0 times 9.

14. Reasoning Paula's hair was put into 9 braids. Each braid used 4 beads. How many beads were used? Explain how you found the product.

15. Algebra Tony has 9 sets of baseball cards. Each set contains 6 cards. Write 2 equations that Tony could use to find how many cards he has.

16. Critique Reasoning Sasha says if she knows the product of 9 × 8, she also knows the product of 8 × 9. Is Sasha correct? Why or why not?

17. Make Sense and Persevere Dustin had $52. He got $49 more and then he spent some money. Dustin has $35 left. How much money did Dustin spend?

18. Higher Order Thinking Jordan received 9 text messages last week. She received 3 times more text messages this week than last week. How many text messages did Jordan receive this week?

19. Construct Arguments Rita bought 5 pairs of socks. Each pair cost $4. How much did Rita spend on socks? Explain how you know.

$4.00

✓ **Assessment**

20. Which numbers are factors of 45? Choose all that apply.

_____ × _____ = 45

☐ 4
☐ 5
☐ 6
☐ 8
☐ 9

21. Which numbers are factors of 18? Choose all that apply.

_____ × _____ = 18

☐ 2
☐ 3
☐ 6
☐ 8
☐ 9

Name _____

Solve & Share

Carlos said that 6 times 0 equals 6. Do you agree? Explain your thinking.

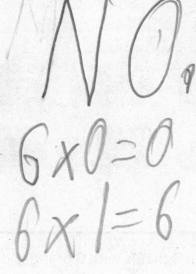

NO,

$6 \times 0 = 0$

$6 \times 1 = 6$

I can ...
use patterns and properties to multiply by 0 and 1.

I can also be precise in my work.

> Be precise. What does it mean to multiply something by zero?

Look Back! **Make Sense and Persevere** Draw a picture to show $5 \times 0 = 0$.

A

What Are the Patterns in Multiples of 1 and 0?

Kira has 8 plates with 1 orange on each plate. How many oranges does Kira have?

You can use patterns to find 8 × 1.

B 8 groups with 1 in each group equals 8 in all.

$$8 \times 1 = 8$$

Kira has 8 oranges.

1 plate with 8 oranges also equals 8 oranges.

$$1 \times 8 = 8$$

The Identity (One) Property of Multiplication: When you multiply a number by 1, the product is that number.

C If Kira has 4 plates with 0 oranges on each plate, she has 0 oranges.

$$4 \times 0 = 0$$

If $4 \times 0 = 0$, then $0 \times 4 = 0$.

The Zero Property of Multiplication: When you multiply a number by 0, the product is 0.

Convince Me! **Use Appropriate Tools** How would you use counters to show 7 × 1? How many counters would you have in all?

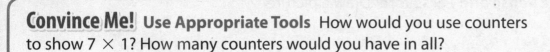

7 because 7 × 1 = 7

0 0 0 0 0 0 0 7 counters

Guided Practice

Do You Understand?

1. **Make Sense and Persevere** Draw a number line to show $8 \times 1 = 8$.

2. Chad has 6 plates. There is 1 apple and 0 grapes on each plate. How many apples are there? How many grapes are there?

Do You Know How?

In **3–8**, find each product.

3.

$3 \times 1 =$ _____

4.

$3 \times 0 =$ _____

5. $1 \times 7 =$ _____

6. $5 \times 0 =$ _____

7.
$$\begin{array}{r} 4 \\ \times\, 0 \\ \hline \end{array}$$

8.
$$\begin{array}{r} 2 \\ \times\, 1 \\ \hline \end{array}$$

You can use the Identity and Zero Properties of Multiplication to find these products.

Independent Practice

In **9–15**, find each product.

9. $0 \times 4 =$ 0

10. $1 \times 6 =$ 6

11. $4 \times 1 =$ 4

12.
$$\begin{array}{r} 9 \\ \times\, 1 \\ \hline 9 \end{array}$$

13.
$$\begin{array}{r} 0 \\ \times\, 2 \\ \hline 0 \end{array}$$

14.
$$\begin{array}{r} 1 \\ \times\, 1 \\ \hline 1 \end{array}$$

15.
$$\begin{array}{r} 6 \\ \times\, 0 \\ \hline 0 \end{array}$$

In **16–21**, write $<$, $>$, or $=$ in each ◯ to compare.

16. 1×6 ⊘ 8×0

17. 0×6 ⊜ 6×0

18. 0×7 ⊘ 5×1

19. 0×0 ⊜ 0×9

20. 1×7 ⊘ 5×1

21. 1×4 ⊜ 4×1

Problem Solving

22. Critique Reasoning Brent drew this model to show 5 groups of 1 is the same as 1 group of 5. Is Brent correct? Explain how you know.

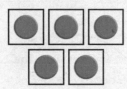 =

23. Make Sense and Persevere A unicycle relay team has 4 riders. Each rider has one unicycle. If each unicycle has 1 wheel, how many wheels does the team have? What property of multiplication can you use to find the answer?

24. Tickets for a school concert are free to students. The cost is $1 for each adult. What is the total cost of tickets for 5 students?

25. Higher Order Thinking The product of two factors is 0. One of the factors is 0. Can you tell what the other factor is? Explain your answer.

$0 \times 0 = 0$

26. Reasoning The children in the third-grade classes are having a bike parade. Barb's class has 18 bikes. Tim's class has some rows of bikes with 5 bikes in each row. Tim's class has more bikes than Barb's class. How many rows of bikes could Tim's class have? Explain.

✓ **Assessment**

27. Is the equation correct? Choose *Yes* or *No*.

27a. $1 \times 4 = 1$ ○ Yes   ⊘ No

27b. $4 \times 4 = 0$ ○ Yes   ◉ No

27c. $7 \times 1 = 7$ ◉ Yes   ○ No

27d. $0 \times 9 = 9$ ○ Yes   ◉ No

Help Practice Tools Games
Buddy

Another Look!

Zero and one have special multiplication properties.

The Identity (One) Property of Multiplication	The Zero Property of Multiplication
When you multiply a number by 1, the product is that number.	When you multiply a number by 0, the product is 0.
Examples:	Examples:
$4 \times 1 = 4$ $16 \times 1 = 16$	$5 \times 0 = 0$ $123 \times 0 = 0$
$1 \times 9 = 9$ $13 \times 1 = 13$	$17 \times 0 = 0$ $0 \times 58 = 0$
$51 \times 1 = 51$ $1 \times 48 = 48$	$0 \times 51 = 0$ $74 \times 0 = 0$

In **1–6**, draw a picture to represent the multiplication fact and then solve.

1. $1 \times 3 =$ _____

2. $0 \times 6 =$ _____

3. $9 \times 0 =$ _____

4. $5 \times 0 =$ _____

5. $1 \times 7 =$ _____

6. $0 \times 4 =$ _____

In **7–10**, find each product.

7.   7
      $\times\ 1$

8.   8
      $\times\ 0$

9.   8
      $\times\ 1$

10.   10
       $\times\ 0$

In **11–13**, write $<$, $>$, or $=$ in each $\bigcirc$ to compare.

11. $0 \times 4 \bigcirc 0 \times 4$

12. $1 \times 8 \bigcirc 6 \times 1$

13. $1 \times 5 \bigcirc 5 \times 1$

14. **Number Sense** Chen says the product of 4×0 is the same as the sum of $4 + 0$. Is Chen correct? Explain.

15. **Model with Math** Sara put 7 boxes in her closet. Each box is for holding a different type of seashell. So far, there are 0 shells in each box. How many shells does Sara have? Tell what math you used to find the answer.

16. Bob made a picture graph of the marbles he and his friends have. How many more marbles does Bob have than Kayla? Explain how you found the answer.

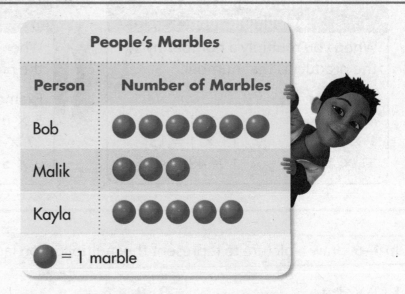

People's Marbles

Person	Number of Marbles
Bob	●●●●●●
Malik	●●●
Kayla	●●●●●

● = 1 marble

17. **Reasoning** Kirsten has 6 coins. She puts the same number of coins in each of 3 envelopes. How many coins did Kirsten put in each envelope?

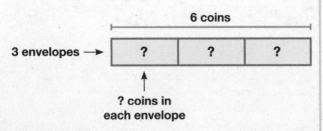

6 coins

3 envelopes → | ? | ? | ? |

? coins in each envelope

18. **Higher Order Thinking** Chef Morgan's restaurant has 24 tables. Fifteen of the tables each have one flower in a vase. The remaining tables have 5 flowers in each vase. How many flowers are there? Show how you found the answer.

19. Can you multiply the numbers on the left side of the equal sign to get the number on the right side of the equal sign? Choose *Yes* or *No*.

19a. $0 \times 2 = 0$ ○ Yes ○ No **19b.** $1 \times 1 = 1$ ○ Yes ○ No

19c. $1 \times 4 = 5$ ○ Yes ○ No **19d.** $5 \times 0 = 5$ ○ Yes ○ No

Name _____

Solve & Share

Duke runs 10 miles each week. How many miles will he run in 6 weeks? 7 weeks? 8 weeks? Describe patterns you find. **Solve these problems any way you choose.**

I can ...
use patterns to multiply by 10.

I can also generalize from examples.

You can generalize. What repeats in this problem?

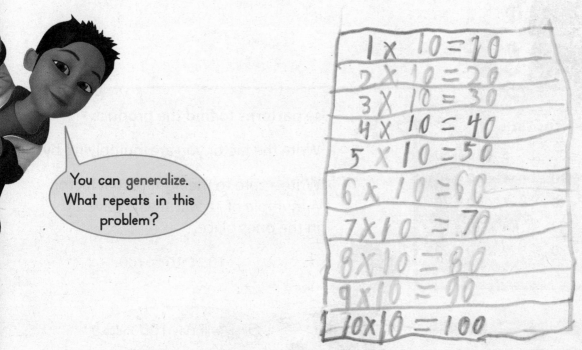

$1 \times 10 = 10$
$2 \times 10 = 20$
$3 \times 10 = 30$
$4 \times 10 = 40$
$5 \times 10 = 50$
$6 \times 10 = 60$
$7 \times 10 = 70$
$8 \times 10 = 80$
$9 \times 10 = 90$
$10 \times 10 = 100$

Look Back! **Look for Relationships** How are the patterns when multiplying by 10 related to the patterns when multiplying by 5?

What Are the Patterns in Multiples of 10?

A

Greg wants to train for a race that is 10 weeks away. The chart shows his training schedule. How many miles will Greg run to train for the race?

You can use patterns to find 10 × 10.

Weekly Training Schedule	
Activity	**Miles**
Swimming	4 miles
Running	10 miles
Biking	9 miles

B

10s Facts	
0 × 10 = 0	5 × 10 = 50
1 × 10 = 10	6 × 10 = 60
2 × 10 = 20	7 × 10 = 70
3 × 10 = 30	8 × 10 = 80
4 × 10 = 40	9 × 10 = 90
	10 × 10 = ?

Use patterns to find the product.

- Write the factor you are multiplying by 10.

- Write a zero to the right of that factor. A multiple of 10 will always have a 0 in the ones place.

$$10 \times 10 = 100$$

Greg will run 100 miles.

Convince Me! **Use Structure** How many miles will Greg swim in 10 weeks? Write an equation, and explain how to use a pattern to find the product.

(student handwriting) he will swim 40 miles

0 × 10 = 0   3 × 10 = 30
1 × 10 = 10   4 × 10 = 40
2 × 10 = 20

Another Example!

You can use a number line to find 3×10.

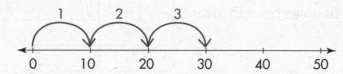

$3 \times 10 = 30$

☆ Guided Practice

Do You Understand?

1. **Reasoning** Is 91 a multiple of 10? Explain.

2. **Generalize** If you multiply any one-digit number by 10, what do you write in the tens digit of the product?

Do You Know How?

In **3–6**, find each product.

3. $2 \times 10 = \underline{2}\,0$

4. $6 \times 10 = \underline{6}\,0$

5. $8 \times 10 = \underline{80}$

6. $9 \times 10 = \underline{90}$

Independent Practice ☆

In **7** and **8**, use the number lines to help find the product.

7. $1 \times 10 = \underline{\qquad}$

8. $5 \times 10 = \underline{50}$

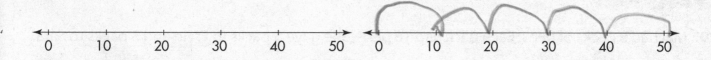

In **9–14**, find the missing product or factor.

9. $10 \times 2 = \underline{\qquad}\,0$

10. $9 \times 10 = \underline{\qquad}\,0$

11. $7 \times 10 = \underline{\qquad}\,0$

12. $3 \times 10 = \underline{30}$

13. $5 \times \underline{\qquad} = 50$

14. $80 = 10 \times \underline{\qquad}$

Problem Solving

15. Reasoning Eddie borrowed $65 from his dad. Every month, he pays back $12. Complete the table to find how much money Eddie still owes his dad after 4 months.

Month	Amount Eddie Owes
April	$65 − $12 = _____
May	_____ − $12 = _____
June	_____ − _____ = _____
July	_____ − _____ = _____

16. Model with Math Kimmy bought 7 tickets to a concert. Each ticket costs $10. She also paid $5 to have the tickets delivered. Write equations to show how much money Kimmy spent in all.

17. Use Structure Write an addition equation and a multiplication equation for the array below.

18. Use the table to find the total number of juice boxes bought for a school picnic.

Food Item	Number of Packages	Number in Each Package
Hot dogs	8	10
Rolls	10	9
Juice boxes	7	10

DATA

Juice boxes: _70_

19. Higher Order Thinking Look at the table at the top of page 80. Greg multiplied 5 × 10 to find how many more miles he biked than swam in the 10 weeks. Does that make sense? Why or why not?

✓ Assessment

20. Mai had 8 packs of pens. Each pack had 10 pens. She gave 5 packs to Ervin and 3 packs to Sara.

Part A

How many pens did Mai start with?

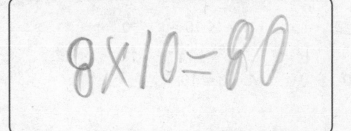

$8 \times 10 = 80$

Part B

Did Mai give more pens to Ervin or to Sara? Explain how you know.

Name _____

Another Look!

The table shows multiplication facts for 10.

10s Facts	
$10 \times 0 = 0$	$10 \times 5 = 50$
$10 \times 1 = 10$	$10 \times 6 = 60$
$10 \times 2 = 20$	$10 \times 7 = 70$
$10 \times 3 = 30$	$10 \times 8 = 80$
$10 \times 4 = 40$	$10 \times 9 = 90$
	$10 \times 10 = 100$

All multiples of 10 end with zero.

Find 5×10.

To find the answer, you can use a number line, or you can write a zero after the 5.

or $5 \times 10 = 50$

In **1** and **2**, use the number lines to help find the product.

1. $2 \times 10 =$ _____

2. $4 \times 10 =$ _____

In **3–12**, find the product.

3. $10 \times 6 =$ _____

4. $10 \times 10 =$ _____

5. $0 \times 10 =$ _____

6. $1 \times 10 =$ _____

7. $10 \times 3 =$ _____

8. $9 \times 10 =$ _____

9. $\begin{array}{r} 10 \\ \times\ 1 \\ \hline \end{array}$

10. $\begin{array}{r} 10 \\ \times\ 3 \\ \hline \end{array}$

11. $\begin{array}{r} 10 \\ \times\ 8 \\ \hline \end{array}$

12. $\begin{array}{r} 10 \\ \times\ 7 \\ \hline \end{array}$

13. **Reasoning** Joey made this graph to show how many incorrect answers students got on a test. How many students got 3 answers incorrect? How do you know?

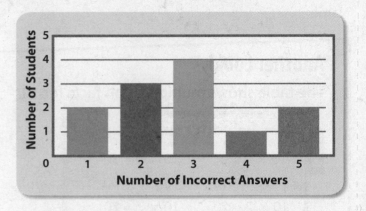

14. **Math and Science** Julie sees a ride that spins 10 turns each minute. She says it will spin 40 turns in 4 minutes. Is Julie correct? Explain.

15. **A-Z Vocabulary** Define *multiple of 10*. Give an example of a multiple of 10.

16. **Critique Reasoning** Greg has 3 rows of stamps with 10 stamps in each row. Greg says there are a total of 35 stamps. Use what you've learned about multiples of 10 to explain why Greg is incorrect.

17. **Higher Order Thinking** Junior says the product of 25 × 10 is 250. How can you use patterns to check Junior's answer?

✓ **Assessment**

18. Benjamin has 5 baskets. Each basket has 10 berries in it.

Part A

Explain how you could find how many berries Benjamin has.

Part B

If Benjamin instead had 10 baskets with 5 berries in each basket, explain how you could find how many berries he has.

Name _Adrit_

☆ ☆
Solve & Share

A company sells boxes of colored pencils. Each box contains 5 pencils. How many pencils are in 5 boxes? 9 boxes? 10 boxes? Explain how you found your answers.

I can ...
use basic multiplication facts to solve problems.

I can also choose and use a math tool to solve problems.

Number of Boxes	1	5	9	10
Number of Colored Pencils	5	25	45	50

You can use appropriate tools to make an array to show the multiplication.

I found that by skip counting by 5

Look Back! **Model with Math** A different company sells boxes that have 9 colored pencils in each box. If the boxes had 9 pencils each, how would the way you solve the problem change? How would your answer change?

Essential Question

How Do You Use Multiplication Facts to Solve Problems?

A

Brendan has archery practice. The target shows the points he gets for hitting a section. How many points did Brendan get from his arrows that hit the black ring? How many points did he get from the red ring?

Section of Target	Number of Arrows
10	3
9	4
5	9
2	8
1	7

The table shows the number of arrows that landed in each section.

B | **8 arrows hit the black ring.**

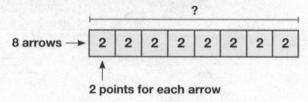

8 arrows →

2 points for each arrow

The bar diagram shows 8 equal groups of 2.
$8 \times 2 = 16$

Brendan got 16 points from the 8 arrows.

C | **4 arrows hit the red ring.**

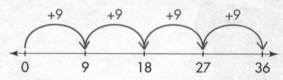

Skip count and record your counts.
9, 18, 27, 36
$4 \times 9 = 36$

Brendan got 36 points from the 4 arrows.

Convince Me! **Be Precise** How many points did Brendan get from the arrows that hit the yellow ring? Explain how you know.

he got 30 point, I know
Brendan hit 10 3 time
and 10x3=30.

Name __Adhrit__

⭐Guided Practice⭐

Do You Understand?

1. To find 6×5, how does knowing $5 \times 6 = 30$ help you?

2. How can you find $8 + 8 + 8 + 8 + 8$ without adding?

Do You Know How?

In 3–9, find each product.

3. $5 \times 9 = $ __45__

4. $2 \times 1 = $ __2__

5. $0 \times 10 = $ __0__

6. $5 \times 4 = $ __20__

7.
$$\begin{array}{r} 1 \\ \times\ 2 \\ \hline 2 \end{array}$$

8.
$$\begin{array}{r} 2 \\ \times\ 7 \\ \hline 14 \end{array}$$

9. What is 4×9?

__36__

Independent Practice⭐

In 10–26, find each product.

10. $2 \times 5 = $ ____

11. $9 \times 0 = $ ____

12. $1 \times 4 = $ ____

13. ____ $= 6 \times 2$

14. $10 \times 6 = $ __60__

15. ____ $= 7 \times 1$

16.
$$\begin{array}{r} 2 \\ \times\ 10 \\ \hline \end{array}$$

17.
$$\begin{array}{r} 2 \\ \times\ 1 \\ \hline \end{array}$$

18.
$$\begin{array}{r} 9 \\ \times\ 9 \\ \hline \end{array}$$

19.
$$\begin{array}{r} 7 \\ \times\ 2 \\ \hline \end{array}$$

20.
$$\begin{array}{r} 9 \\ \times\ 3 \\ \hline \end{array}$$

21.
$$\begin{array}{r} 0 \\ \times\ 7 \\ \hline \end{array}$$

22.
$$\begin{array}{r} 4 \\ \times\ 5 \\ \hline \end{array}$$

23.
$$\begin{array}{r} 5 \\ \times\ 7 \\ \hline \end{array}$$

24. What is 1×1?

__1__

25. What is 10×10?

__100__

26. What is 3×9?

__27__

Problem Solving

27. Critique Reasoning Abdi says that 9×6 is less than 10×4 because 9 is less than 10. Do you agree with Abdi's reasoning? Explain why or why not.

28. Model with Math Victoria has 5 pairs of shoes. What equation could Victoria write to find out how many shoes she has?

29. Show 7:50 on the clock.

30. Robb has 35 red counters and 39 yellow counters. He gives his sister 18 red counters. How many counters does Robb have left?

56

31. Use Structure Kim makes an array with 4 rows and 9 columns. Rashida makes an array with 9 rows and 4 columns. Whose array has more items? Explain.

32. Higher Order Thinking Look at the table on page 86. Think about what you know about Brendan's points. What is the total number of points Brendan scored for all his arrows?

 **Assessment**

33. Draw lines to match each pair of factors on the left with its product on the right.

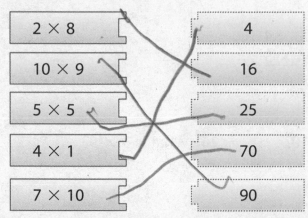

2×8		4
10×9		16
5×5		25
4×1		70
7×10		90

Think about the different ways you know to find multiplication facts.

Name _____

☆ ☆
Solve & Share

At the pet store, Sam bought a hamster that cost $10. He also bought 5 mice at $4 each. How much did Sam spend in all? *Write to explain the math you used to solve this problem.*

I can ...
use math I know to solve problems.

I can also multiply to solve problems.

Thinking Habits

Be a good thinker!
These questions can help

• How can I use math I know to help solve this problem?

• How can I use pictures, objects, or an equation to represent the problem?

• How can I use numbers, words, and symbols to solve the problem?

Look Back! **Model with M**   How would your answer above change if Sam only bought 4 m

Essential Question **How Can You Model with Math?**

A

Keisha bought 2 yards of felt to make some puppets. Tanya bought 6 yards of felt. Each yard of felt costs the same amount. How much did the girls spend on felt in all?

$2 per yard

What math do I need to use to solve this problem?

I need to show what I know and then choose the needed operations.

B How can I model with math?

I can

- use the math I know to solve the problem.

- find and answer any hidden questions.

- use diagrams and equations to represent and solve this problem.

C

Here's my thinking...

I will use bar diagrams and equations.

The hidden question is: How many yards of felt did the girls buy?

? yards

| 2 yards | 6 yards |

$2 + 6 = ?$

$2 + 6 = 8$. The girls bought 8 yards of felt.

So, I need to find the cost of 8 yards at $2 per yard.

? total cost

| $2 | $2 | $2 | $2 | $2 | $2 | $2 | $2 |

$8 \times \$2 = ?$

$8 \times \$2 = \$16$. The girls spent $16.

Convince Me! Model with Math Use these number lines to show another way to represent the problem above.

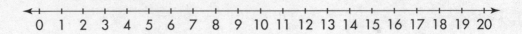

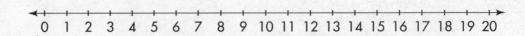

Practice Buddy   Tools   Assessment

Guided Practice*

Model with Math

A pack of gum contains 5 pieces. Phil had 7 packs of gum before he lost 2 pieces. How many pieces of gum does Phil have now?

Model with math. You can represent and solve each step in a two-step problem.

1. What is the hidden question you need to answer before you can solve the problem?

2. Solve the problem. Complete the bar diagrams. Show the equations you used.

One Pack ☐

Phil's Packs ☐☐☐☐☐☐☐

? pieces of gum

_____ pieces of gum

?

Independent Practice*

Model with Math

Jen bought 4 tickets. Amber bought 5 tickets. The tickets cost $2 each. How much did the girls spend on tickets in all?

3. What is the hidden question you need to answer before you can solve the problem?

4. Solve the problem. Complete the bar diagrams. Show the equations you used.

5. How would your equations change if Amber bought only 3 tickets? Explain.

Coffee Shop
David and Jon are placing coffee orders for their friends.
David orders 10 large cups of coffee.
Jon orders 4 fewer large cups than David.
Jon pays for his orders with a $50 bill.
Jon wants to know how much he spent on coffee.

Coffee Shop Prices	
Cup	**Cost**
Small	$2
Regular	$4
Large	$5

DATA

6. **Make Sense and Persevere** What is a good plan to find the amount Jon spent on coffee?

7. **Model with Math** Find how much Jon spent on coffee. Complete the bar diagrams. Show the equations you used.

8. **Critique Reasoning** Jamie says the equation $0 \times \$2 = \$0$ shows the amount Jon spent on small cups of coffee. Is he correct? Explain.

9. **Reasoning** Would David have enough money if he paid for his order with a $20 bill? Explain.

Model with math. Think about the math you know to solve the problem.

Name _____

Another Look!

Ron has 6 bags. He puts 2 red, 3 yellow, and 4 blue marbles in each bag. How many marbles does Ron have in all?

Explain how you can use the math you know to solve the problem.

- I can find and answer any hidden questions.

- I can use bar diagrams and equations to represent and solve the problem.

You can model with math by using bar diagrams to show the whole and the parts.

Solve the problem.

Find the hidden question:
How many marbles are in each bag?

? marbles in each bag

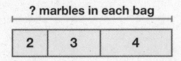

2	3	4

$2 + 3 + 4 = 9$ marbles in each bag

Use the answer to solve the problem.

? marbles

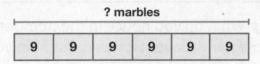

9	9	9	9	9	9

$6 \times 9 = 54$ marbles in all

Model with Math

Paul has 7 piles of sports cards. There are 3 basketball, 3 football, and 4 baseball cards in each pile. How many total sports cards does Paul have?

1. Explain how you can use the math you know to solve the problem.

2. What is the hidden question you need to answer before you can solve the problem?

3. Solve the problem. Complete the bar diagrams. Show the equations you used.

? sports cards in each pile

? sports cards

Jase's Farm
Jase's farm has 9 chickens, each of which laid 3 eggs. Jase's farm has 4 horses. Edna's farm has chickens which laid a total of 23 eggs. Jase wonders whose chickens laid more eggs.

? total chicken eggs

Jase's farm | 3 | 3 | 3 | 3 | 3 | 3 | 3 | 3 | 3 |

4. **Make Sense and Persevere** What is a good plan to find whose chickens laid more eggs?

5. **Reasoning** What do you notice in the numbers shown in the bar diagram above? How can this help you solve the problem?

Model with math.
When you write equations, think about which operations you can use.

6. **Model with Math** Use equations to show if Jase's or Edna's chickens laid more eggs. How many more eggs did those chickens lay?

7. **Use Appropriate Tools** Lucio says he can use counters to represent the number of eggs laid. Explain how he could do this to find out whose chickens laid more eggs.

Name _____

Find a partner. Get paper and a pencil. Each partner chooses a different color: light blue or dark blue.

Partner 1 and Partner 2 each point to a black number at the same time. Both partners add those numbers.

If the answer is on your color, you get a tally mark. Work until one partner has seven tally marks.

I can ...
add within 100.

Partner 1

| 55 |
| 23 |
| 37 |
| 12 |
| 41 |

80	54	94	36
62	25	41	57
76	30	100	82
86	50	73	68
49	67	38	63
59	81	55	51

Partner 2

| 13 |
| 45 |
| 39 |
| 26 |
| 18 |

Tally Marks for Partner 1

Tally Marks for Partner 2

A-Z Glossary

Word List

- bar diagram
- factor
- Identity (One) Property of Multiplication
- multiplication
- multiples
- product
- Zero Property of Multiplication

Understand Vocabulary

Circle all correct responses.

1. Circle each number that is a *product*.

$4 \times 6 = 24$ $7 \times 3 = 21$ $8 \div 4 = 2$

2. Circle each example of the *Identity Property*.

$2 \times 2 = 4$ $5 \times 0 = 0$ $1 \times 6 = 6$

3. Circle each example of the *Zero Property*.

$1 \times 0 = 0$ $0 \times 9 = 0$ $2 \times 5 = 10$

4. Circle each equation that shows *multiplication*.

$5 + 6 = 11$ $4 \times 4 = 16$ $17 - 12 = 5$ $16 \div 2 = 8$

5. Circle each number that is a *multiple* of 9.

16   9   28   27   19   36   18   39

Write T for *true* or F for *false*.

_____ **6.** The number 14 is a *multiple* of 4.

_____ **7.** The *Identity Property* says that any number times 1 equals the number itself.

_____ **8.** A *bar diagram* can be used to show 3×6.

Use Vocabulary in Writing

9. Explain how you can find the product 4×2 and the product 8×2. Use at least 3 terms from the Word List in your explanation.

Set A pages 61–66

Find 6 × 2.

Use skip counting. Draw 6 curved arrows on a number line. Each arrow should be 2 units wide.

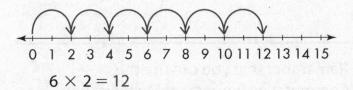

0 1 2 3 4 5 6 7 8 9 10 11 12 13 14 15

6 × 2 = 12

Find 6 × 5.

Use a pattern. Count by 5s. The 6th number in the pattern is the product.

5, 10, 15, 20, 25, 30

6 × 5 = 30

Remember that mutiples of 2 end in 0, 2, 4, 6, or 8. Multiples of 5 end in 0 or 5.

1. 2 × 3 = ____   **2.** 5 × 3 = ____

3. 5 × 5 = ____   **4.** 2 × 6 = ____

5. 8 × 2 = ____   **6.** 7 × 5 = ____

7. 2   **8.** 7
     × 2   × 2

9. 8   **10.** 9
     × 5   × 5

Set B pages 67–72

Find 9 × 4.

List 9s facts.

9 × 1 = 9
9 × 2 = 18
9 × 3 = 27
9 × 4 = 36

Remember that the digits in the multiples of 9 form a pattern.

1. 9 × 5 = ____   **2.** 9 × 7 = ____

3. 6 × 9 = ____   **4.** 8 × 9 = ____

5. 9 × 9 = ____   **6.** 9 × 0 = ____

Set C pages 73–78

Find 0 × 7.

Zero Property of Multiplication: When you multiply a number by 0, the product is 0.

0 × 7 = 0

Find 1 × 7.

Identity (One) Property of Multiplication: When you multiply a number by 1, the product is that number.

1 × 7 = 7

Remember that the product of 0 and any other number is 0. When you multiply a number by 1, the product is that same number.

1. 0 × 4 = ____   **2.** 1 × 9 = ____

3. 0 × 9 = ____   **4.** 1 × 6 = ____

5. 10 × 0 = ____   **6.** 9 × 0 = ____

7. 3 × 1 = ____   **8.** 8 × 1 = ____

9. 0 × 2 = ____   **10.** 1 × 0 = ____

Find 10 × 6.

When multiplying a number by 10, write a zero to the right of the number.

10 × 6 = 60

Remember that when a number is multiplied by 10, the product has a zero in the ones place.

1. 10 × 7 = _____   **2.** 10 × 10 = _____

3. 3 × 10 = _____   **4.** 9 × 10 = _____

5. 10 × 0 = _____   **6.** 1 × 10 = _____

Find 5 × 10.

There are many patterns and properties you can use to multiply.

Use skip counting with 5 facts:
5, 10, 15, 20, 25, 30, 35, 40, 45, 50

Use a pattern for 10 facts:
Write a 0 after the 5: 50

The product is the same.
5 × 10 = 50

Remember that you can use the Commutative Property of Multiplication to multiply 2 factors in any order.

1. 5 × 9 = _____   **2.** 0 × 6 = _____

3. 10 × 3 = _____   **4.** 8 × 1 = _____

5. 7 × 2 = _____   **6.** 9 × 6 = _____

Think about these questions to help you **model with math.**

Thinking Habits

- How can I use math I know to help solve the problem?

- How can I use pictures, objects, or an equation to represent the problem?

- How can I use numbers, words, and symbols to solve the problem?

Remember that representations can help you apply math that you know.

Umar has 5 dimes in his left pocket. He has 3 dimes in his right pocket. A dime is worth 10 cents. How much money does Umar have?

1. Draw a bar diagram to help answer the hidden question.

2. Draw a bar diagram to help answer the main question.

Name _____

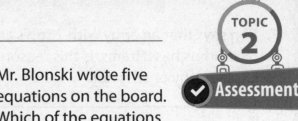

1. A building has 9 rows of mailboxes. There are 6 mailboxes in each row. How many mailboxes are there?

2. Tickets to a juggling show cost $5 for each adult and $2 for each child. 4 adults and 3 children go to see the show. What is the total cost of their tickets?

Part A

Identify any hidden questions.

Part B

Draw bar diagrams for this problem. Show the equations that you used.

3. Mr. Blonski wrote five equations on the board. Which of the equations did he write correctly? Choose all that apply.

☐ $24 \times 0 = 0$

☐ $45 \times 1 = 45$

☐ $67 \times 1 = 1 \times 67$

☐ $38 \times 0 = 38$

☐ $77 + 1 = 77$

4. Mark is thinking of a number that is a multiple of 9. Which of the following could be Mark's number? Choose all that apply.

☐ 27

☐ 45

☐ 48

☐ 67

☐ 81

5. Alex has 5 dimes in his pocket. How much money does Alex have?

6. Choose the greatest product.

(A) 9×1

(B) 10×0

(C) 2×3

(D) 5×2

7. Ben says that an array with 2 rows and 5 columns has 8 items. Is this reasonable? Explain why or why not.

8. Gabe has 4 birdcages. He keeps 5 birds in each cage. Then Gabe buys another birdcage. The new birdcage has the same number of birds. How many birds does Gabe have now? Use a bar diagram to represent the problem.

9. A set of blocks has 4 different types of blocks. There are 10 of each type of block. How many blocks are in the set?

Ⓐ 14 blocks

Ⓑ 30 blocks

Ⓒ 40 blocks

Ⓓ 44 blocks

10. Draw lines to connect equal expressions.

2 × 0		2
2 × 1		3 × 0
2 × 3		3 × 2

11. Ed is thinking of a number that is a multiple of both 2 and 5. For questions 11a–11d, choose Yes or No to tell if it could be Ed's number.

11a. 15   ○ Yes ○ No

11b. 20   ○ Yes ○ No

11c. 25   ○ Yes ○ No

11d. 30   ○ Yes ○ No

12. Dawn has 2 bananas. She cuts each banana into 8 slices. How many slices of banana does Dawn have?

13. Isabella has $45 to spend on shirts. All shirts in the store are on sale for $10 each. How many shirts can Isabella buy? Explain the math that you used.

Name _____

Selling Cards

A soccer team is selling boxes of cards to raise money.
There are boxes of small, medium, and large cards.
The team earns a different amount for each card type.

Boxes Sold

• On Monday, Will sold 4 boxes of large cards.
• On Wednesday, Mia sold 6 boxes of small cards
  and 3 boxes of large cards.

Use the **Selling Boxes of Cards** table and **Boxes Sold** list to answer Questions 1 and 2.

1. How much money did Will earn? Write a
   multiplication equation to solve.

Selling Boxes of Cards	
Card Type	Amount Earned per Box
Box of small cards	$1
Box of medium cards	$2
Box of large cards	$5

2. Complete the chart to find the amount that Mia earned
   for each card type.

Card Type	Number Sold	Amount Earned per Box	Total Earned
small			
medium			
large			

Use the **Selling Boxes of Cards** table to answer Question 3.

3. For 7 days, Logan sold a box of medium cards every day.
   How much did Logan earn? Create a representation for
   the problem.

Boxes Bought
- Mrs. Carlson buys 1 box of medium cards.
- Mr. Choi buys 6 boxes of small cards.
- Mrs. Willis buys 7 boxes of medium cards and 9 boxes of large cards.

Use the **Cards in Each Box** table and **Boxes Bought** list to answer
Questions 4–6.

4. **Part A**

   How many cards does Mr. Choi buy?

   Part B

   What is another way that Mr. Choi can
   buy the same number of cards?

Cards in Each Box

Card Type	Number of Cards
Box of small cards	5
Box of medium cards	9
Box of large cards	10

5. Is there another way that Mrs. Carlson can buy
   the same amount of cards? Explain.

6. Complete the chart to find the number of cards Mrs. Willis buys of each
   card type.

Card Type	Number of Boxes Bought	Number of Cards in a Box	Total Cards
small			
medium			
large			

Apply Properties: Multiplication Facts for 3, 4, 6, 7, 8

Essential Question: How can unknown multiplication facts be found using known facts?

Digital Resources

Solve   Learn   Glossary   Practice Buddy

Tools   Assessment   Help   Games

Some roses are red and some violets are blue, but do you know why?

Flowers inherit their color. They get their color from parent plants.

My mom's roses are yellow! Here's a project on traits of organisms, multiplication, and equations.

Math and Science Project: Inherited Traits

Do Research Some characteristics of organisms are inherited. The traits are passed from generation to generation. In flowers, one of the inherited traits is color. Use the Internet or other sources to make a list of other traits that flowers inherit from their parent plants.

Journal: Write a Report Include what you found. Also in your report:

- Compare your list of traits with lists of traits other students have made. If there is a trait you don't have, add it to your list.

- Draw flowers or animals with similar traits in an array. Show how to break apart the array and use multiplication facts to find the total number.

Name _____

Review What You Know

A-Z Vocabulary

Choose the best term from the box. Write it on the blank.

- skip counting
- The Commutative (Order) Property of Multiplication
- The Identity (One) Property of Multiplication
- The Zero Property of Multiplication

1. _____ says that the product of any number and zero is zero.

2. _____ says that 1 times any number is that number.

3. _____ says that you can multiply factors in any order, and the product stays the same.

Multiplying

Use multiplication to solve.

4. $10 \times 1 =$ _____

5. $2 \times 10 =$ _____

6. $0 \times 5 =$ _____

7. $9 \times 5 =$ _____

8. $2 \times 7 =$ _____

9. $1 \times 8 =$ _____

10. $5 \times 7 = ?$

(A) $7 + 5$ (B) $5 + 7$ (C) 7×5 (D) $7 \div 5$

Adding 2-Digit Numbers

Find the sum.

11. $16 + 12 =$ _____

12. $21 + 14 =$ _____

13. $24 + 12 =$ _____

Arrays

14. How can you represent 6×3 using an array? Draw an array, and explain how to use it to find the product.

My Word Cards

Use the examples for each word on the front of the card to help complete the definitions on the back.

Distributive Property

$7 \times 4 = (5 \times 4) + (2 \times 4)$

5×4

2×4

Associative (Grouping) Property of Multiplication

$(3 \times 2) \times 4 = 24$

$3 \times (2 \times 4) = 24$

$(3 \times 2) \times 4 = 3 \times (2 \times 4)$

My Word Cards

Complete each definition. Extend learning by writing your own definitions.

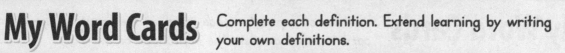

The _____

_____

_____ says that you can change the grouping of the factors and the product will be the same.

The _____ says that a multiplication fact can be broken apart into the sum of two other multiplication facts.

Name _____

Solve

Solve & Share

Find two ways to break the array below into two smaller arrays. What multiplication equation can you write for each array? What is the total? Tell how you decided.

You can be precise. You can explain what your equations mean.

$$5 \times 2 = 10$$
$$5 \times 2 = 10 \; +$$
$$\boxed{20}$$

Look Back! Reasoning Find the total number of items in both of the smaller arrays. Compare their combined total to the total number of items in the one large array. Why are the totals the same even though the arrays are different?

Essential Question **How Can You Break Up a Multiplication Fact?**

A

Maria wants to set up 7 rows of 4 chairs for a meeting. She wants to know how many chairs she needs but does not know the product of 7 × 4.

You can use known facts to help find the product of unknown facts.

B ## What You Think

Maria thinks of **7** rows of 4 chairs as **5** rows of 4 chairs and another **2** rows of 4 chairs.

4

7 {
5 — 5 × 4
2 — 2 × 4

C ## What You Write

The Distributive Property says that a multiplication fact can be broken apart into the sum of two other multiplication facts.

Maria knows the two new facts.

$7 \times 4 = (5 \times 4) + (2 \times 4)$
$7 \times 4 = 20 + 8$
$7 \times 4 = 28$

So, $7 \times 4 = 28$.

Maria needs 28 chairs.

Convince Me! **Use Structure** What are two ways that Maria could break up the array for 7 × 4? Draw a picture of the two new arrays and write the new facts.

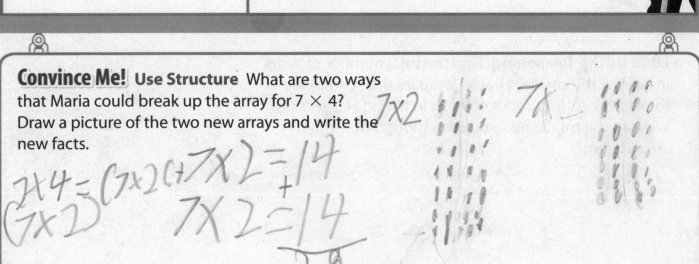

$7 + 4 = (7 \times 2)(+ 7 \times 2 = 14$
(7×2)
$7 \times 2 = 14$

7x2   7x2

28

Name _____

☆ Guided Practice

Do You Understand?

1. Rafael broke up an array for 6 × 3 into two new arrays. Both of his new arrays are the same. What were the two arrays?

2. **Use Structure** Ann broke up a large array into two smaller arrays. The two smaller arrays show 1 × 8 and 4 × 8. What was the large array that Ann started with?

Do You Know How?

In **3** and **4**, use the smaller arrays and the Distributive Property to find each missing factor. You may use counters to help.

3.

4 × 8

$4 \times 8 = (2 \times 8) + (2 \times 8)$

4.

3 × 5

___ × ___ = (___ × 5) + (1 × ___)

Independent Practice ☆

In **5** and **6**, separate the rows in the large array into two smaller arrays. Write the new facts.

5.

$4 \times 5 = (1 \times 5) + (4 \times 5)$

6.

$5 \times 6 = ($___$ \times$___$) + ($___$ \times$___$)$

In **7–10**, use the Distributive Property to find each missing factor. Use counters and arrays to help.

7. $6 \times 8 = (4 \times 6) + (2 \times 8)$

8. $10 \times 3 = ($___$ \times 3) + (2 \times 3)$

9. $(5 \times 7) = (3 \times 7) + (2 \times 7)$

10. $(8 \times$___$) = ($___$ \times 8) + (4 \times 8)$

*For another example, see Set A on page 159.   **Topic 3** | Lesson 3-1   **111**

Problem Solving

11. Model with Math Paige bakes 5 cupcakes. She puts 7 jellybeans on each cupcake. How many jellybeans does Paige need? Use the bar diagram to help write an equation.

? jellybeans

7	7	7	7	7

35 jellybeans

12. Critique Reasoning Fred wants to separate the rows of the array below into a 2 × 4 array and a 3 × 4 array. Can Fred do this? Explain.

13. Lane uses counters to make a 4 × 7 array and a 1 × 7 array. What size array can he make using all of these counters?

5 × 7 = 35

14. Gavin had $75 on Monday. On Tuesday he spent $23. Then he spent $14 on Wednesday. How much money does he have left?

15. A-Z Vocabulary Explain how you can use the *Distributive Property* to solve 9 × 6.

9 × 3 = 27
+
9 × 3 = 27
54

16. Higher Order Thinking How can you use 3 × 5 = 15 to help you find 6 × 5?

✔ **Assessment**

17. Choose all of the ways you can separate the rows of the array at the right.

- ☐ (2 × 7) + (5 × 7)
- ☐ (4 × 7) + (1 × 7)
- ☐ (2 × 7) + (3 × 7)
- ☐ (2 × 5) + (5 × 7)
- ☐ (3 × 7) + (2 × 7)

Help Practice Tools Games
Buddy

Another Look!

The array below shows
6 × 4 or 6 rows of 4 circles.

You can draw a line to break
6 rows of **4** circles into **2** rows
of **4** circles and **4** rows of
4 circles.

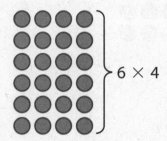

} 6 × 4

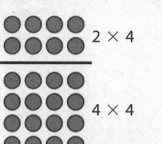

2 × 4

4 × 4

With the Distributive Property,
you can break apart a multiplication fact
into the sum of two other facts.

In **1** and **2**, draw a line to separate each array into two smaller arrays.
Write the new facts.

1.

4 × 3 = (___ × ___) + (___ × ___)

2.

5 × 6 = (___ × ___) + (___ × ___)

In **3–10**, use the Distributive Property to find each missing factor.

3. 4 × 6 = (1 × 6) + (___ × 6)

4. 5 × 8 = (___ × 8) + (2 × 8)

5. 4 × 5 = (___ × 5) + (2 × ___)

6. 7 × 6 = (3 × ___) + (___ × ___)

7. 3 × 8 = (___ × 8) + (2 × ___)

8. 5 × 7 = (2 × ___) + (3 × ___)

9. 4 × 7 = (___ × ___) + (2 × ___)

10. 5 × 5 = (___ × 5) + (4 × ___)

11. Use Structure Tony broke a larger array into a 2 × 3 array and a 4 × 3 array. What did the larger array look like? Draw a picture. Write an equation to show the relationship between the larger array and the two smaller arrays.

12. Higher Order Thinking Rosa says she can break this array into 3 different sets of two smaller arrays. Is Rosa correct? Explain.

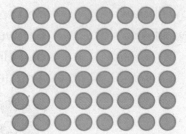

13. Algebra Marcus passed for 16 yards in the first half of a football game. He passed for a total of 49 yards in the entire game. What was Marcus's total passing yardage in the second half?

Write equations to represent and solve the problem. Use ? for the unknown number.

49	
16	?

14. Lulu buys a dress for $67, a hat for $35, and shoes for $49. How much did Lulu spend?

?		
$67	$35	$49

15. Akela drew these smaller arrays to find the product of a larger array. Which of the following equations show the relationship between the larger array and these two smaller arrays? Choose all that apply.

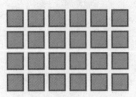

☐ 6 × 6 = (3 × 6) + (3 × 6)

☐ 7 × 6 = (3 × 6) + (4 × 6)

☐ 8 × 7 = (4 × 7) + (4 × 7)

☐ 7 × 6 = (4 × 6) + (3 × 6)

☐ 7 × 7 = (3 × 7) + (4 × 7)

Name _____

★ ☆ ★
Solve & Share

There are 3 rows of pictures on a wall. Each row has 6 pictures. How many pictures are on the wall? *Solve this problem any way you choose.*

I can ...
use tools and properties strategically to solve problems when I multiply by 3.

I can also choose and use a math tool to solve problems.

$$\beta 1 0 0 0 0 \Big| - 2 \times 6$$
$$\overline{1 0 6 1 0 0} \Big| - 1 \times 6$$
$$\overline{0 0 0 0 0}$$

$$3 \times 6 = (2 \times 6) + (1 \times 6) =$$
$$12 + 6 = 18$$

You can use tools. You can draw arrays or make arrays with counters to help you solve the problem. *Show your work!*

Look Back! **Generalize** How can you use what you know about multiplication facts for the 1s and 2s to solve multiplication facts for the 3s?

How Can You Break Apart Arrays to Multiply with 3?

A

The Park District has canoes stored in 3 rows. There are 6 canoes in each row. What is the total number of canoes stored?

You can multiply to find the total for an array.

B

What You Show

Find 3 × 6.

Use 1s facts and 2s facts to help you multiply with 3.

Make an array for each multiplication sentence.

$$2 \times 6 = 12$$

$$12 + 6 = 18$$

$$1 \times 6 = 6$$

C

What You Think

3 × 6 is 3 rows of 6. That is 2 sixes plus 1 more six.

2 sixes are 12.
1 six is 6.

$$12 + 6 = 18$$

$$3 \times 6 = 18$$

There are 18 canoes.

Convince Me! **Use Structure** Suppose there were 7 canoes in each of 3 rows. How can 2 × 7 = 14 help you find the total number of canoes?

$$3 \times 7 = (2 \times 7) + (1 \times 7) =$$
$$14 + 7 = 21$$

add $1 \times 7 = 7$

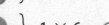

$$2 \times 7 = 14 + 7 = 21$$

Name _____

☆ Guided Practice *

Do You Understand?

1. Selena arranged plants in 3 rows in her garden. She put 6 plants in each row. How many plants did Selena arrange?

18

2. Use Structure Alicia has 3 vases. She wants 9 flowers in each vase. She buys enough flowers for 2 vases. For the third vase, she cuts 9 flowers from her garden. How can Alicia use $2 \times 9 = 18$ to find how many flowers she needs?

Do You Know How?

In **3–8**, multiply. You may use counters or pictures to help.

3. $3 \times 10 =$ *30*   **4.** $3 \times 6 =$ ____

5. $\begin{array}{r} 3 \\ \times 8 \\ \hline 24 \end{array}$ **6.** $\begin{array}{r} 3 \\ \times 2 \\ \hline \end{array}$

7. $\begin{array}{r} 3 \\ \times 7 \\ \hline 21 \end{array}$ **8.** $\begin{array}{r} 3 \\ \times 3 \\ \hline \end{array}$

☆ Independent Practice ☆

Leveled Practice In **9–20**, multiply. You may use counters or pictures to help.

9. 3×4

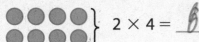

$2 \times 4 =$ *6*

$1 \times 4 =$ *4*

$8 + 4 =$ *12*

10. 3×5

$2 \times 5 =$ ____

$1 \times 5 =$ ____

$10 + 5 =$ ____

11. $2 \times 3 =$ *6*   **12.** $9 \times 3 =$ ____   **13.** $10 \times 3 =$ *30*

14. $8 \times 3 =$ ____   **15.** $5 \times 3 =$ *15*   **16.** $0 \times 3 =$ ____

17. $\begin{array}{r} 7 \\ \times 3 \\ \hline 21 \end{array}$ **18.** $\begin{array}{r} 3 \\ \times 1 \\ \hline \end{array}$ **19.** $\begin{array}{r} 3 \\ \times 3 \\ \hline 9 \end{array}$ **20.** $\begin{array}{r} 4 \\ \times 3 \\ \hline \end{array}$

Problem Solving

21. What is the total number of stamps in a package of car stamps and a package of outer space stamps? Show how you found the answer.

Number of Stamps in Different Packages		
Kind of Stamp	Number of Rows	Number in Each Row
Dinosaur	3	7
Car	3	9
Outer Space	3	8
Reptile	5	6

22. Use Appropriate Tools Cara bought 1 package of reptile stamps. What tool could you use to find the total number of stamps that Cara bought?

23. Critique Reasoning Allison bought 10 packages of energy bars. Each package contains 6 bars. Allison says she has a total of 65 energy bars. Is her answer reasonable? Why or why not?

60 is the answer. she is wrong because 10×6=60.

24. Higher Order Thinking What two multiplication facts can help you find 3×9? How could you use 3×9 to find 9×3?

✓ **Assessment**

25. Mr. Torres has some tomatoes. He arranges them in 3 rows and 8 columns.

Part A

Complete the equation and find the total number of tomatoes.

$(3 \times \underline{4}) + (3 \times \underline{4}) = \underline{24}$ tomatoes

Part B

Draw a picture to represent this problem.

Name _____

Another Look!

You can use arrays to show 3s facts.

Find 2 × 3.

2 × 3 = 6

You can also use a 2s and a 1s fact to find a 3s fact.

Find 7 × 3.
7 × 3 = (7 × 2) + (7 × 1)
7 × 3 = 14 + 7
7 × 3 = 21

In **1–4**, use arrays or the Distributive Property to find each product.

1.

3 × 4 = ____

2. Find 3 × 5.

3 × 5 = (____ × 5) + (1 × ____)

3 × 5 = ____ + ____

3 × 5 = ____

3. Find 4 × 3.

4 × 3 = (4 × ____) + (____ × 1)

4 × 3 = ____ + ____

4 × 3 = ____

4. Find 3 × 6.

3 × 6 = (2 × 6) + (____ × ____)

3 × 6 = ____ + ____

3 × 6 = ____

In **5–14**, find each product.

5. 6 × 3 = ____

6. 3 × 7 = ____

7. 3 × 3 = ____

8. 1 × 3 = ____

9. 3 × 9 = ____

10. 5 × 3 = ____

11. 3
    × 8

12. 3
    × 0

13. 3
    × 2

14. 9
    × 3

15. Generalize How can you use a 2s fact and a 1s fact to find 3 × 8?

16. Construct Arguments Maria said 7 × 3 = 21. Connie said 3 × 7 = 21. Who is correct? Explain.

17. Five people bought tickets to a football game. They bought 3 tickets each. How many tickets were bought? Draw an array.

18. Higher Order Thinking Sid says 26 is a multiple of 3. Is Sid correct? Why or why not?

19. Barney divides a rectangle into fourths. Show two ways he could do this.

Assessment

20. Kenichi's jump rope team is competing in a tournament. There are 10 teams in the tournament.

Jump Rope
Tournament
Teams of 3 Only

Part A

Use the numbers to complete the equation and find the total number of players in the tournament.

$$3 \times 10 = (3 \times \underline{\quad}) + (3 \times \underline{\quad}) = \underline{\quad} \text{ players}$$

Part B

Draw a picture to represent the problem.

Name _Adnrit B0_

Solve & Share

Ed made 8 key chains each week for 4 weeks. How many key chains did Ed make? *Solve this problem any way you choose.*

I can ...
use what I know about multiplying by 2s and properties to multiply by 4.

I can also look for patterns to solve problems.

You can use structure. What number relationships do you see when when you multiply by 4? *Show your work in the space below!*

OOO O OOO
OO O OO
OO O OO
OO OO OO

$4 \times 8 = (4 \times 4) + (4 \times 4) = \boxed{32}$

Look Back! **Look for Relationships** How can you use multiplication facts for 2s to solve multiplication facts for 4s?

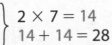 **How Can You Use Doubles to Multiply with 4?**

A

Anna painted piggy banks to sell at the student art show. She painted one bank on each of the 7 days of the week for 4 weeks. How many piggy banks did Anna paint?

Four is a double of 2. So, 4 × 7 is double 2 × 7.

B

What You Show

Find 4 × 7.

You can make arrays.

To multiply with 4, think of a 2s fact and then double it.

2 × 7 = 14

2 × 7 = 14
14 + 14 = 28

C

What You Think

4 × 7 is 4 rows of 7. That is 2 sevens plus 2 sevens.

2 sevens are 14.

14 + 14 = 28
So, 4 × 7 = 28.

Anna painted 28 piggy banks.

Convince Me! **Construct Arguments** Zach knows 2 × 8 = 16. Explain how he can find 4 × 8.

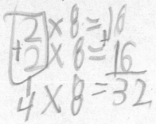

$2 × 8 = 16$
$+ 2 × 8 = 16$
$4 × 8 = 32$

⭐Guided Practice⭐

Do You Understand?

1. Besides using a 2s fact and doubling it, what is another way to break apart 4×7 using facts you already know?

2. Nolan made lamps to sell at the school art show. He made 9 lamps each week for 4 weeks. How many lamps did Nolan make?

36

Do You Know How?

In **3–8**, multiply. You may use counters or pictures to help.

3. $3 \times 4 =$ _____

4. $5 \times 4 =$ 20

5. $4 \times 9 =$ _____

6. $1 \times 4 =$ 4

7.   2
    $\times 4$

8.   10
    $\times 4$
    40

⭐Independent Practice⭐

Leveled Practice In **9–17**, multiply. You may use counters or pictures to help.

9. Find 4×6.

$2 \times 6 =$ _____

$2 \times 6 =$ _____

$12 + 12 =$ _____

So, $4 \times 6 =$ _____.

10. Find 4×9.

$2 \times 9 =$ 18

$2 \times 9 =$ 18

$18 + 18 =$ 36

So, $4 \times 9 =$ 36.

11. $4 \times 8 =$ _____

12. $4 \times 3 =$ 12

13. $6 \times 4 =$ _____

14.   7
    $\times 4$
    28

15.   9
    $\times 4$

16.   4
    $\times 5$
    20

17.   4
    $\times 2$

Problem Solving

18. Make Sense and Persevere James needs to buy supplies for his trail walk. What is the total number of cereal bars James needs to buy? Explain how you used the table to find the answer.

14

19. Reasoning How many more apples than juice drinks does James need? Show how you found the answer.

Trail Walk Supplies

Item	Number of Packages Needed	Number of Items in Each Package
Apples	2	8
Cereal Bars	4	6
Juice Drinks	4	3

20. Math and Science Martin studied slugs in science class. He learned each slug has 4 feelers. That evening, he saw 7 slugs. How many feelers did all the slugs have? What are two strategies you can use to find the answer?

28

21. Higher Order Thinking Lila makes a chart that has 9 rows and 4 columns. How many spaces are in her chart? Explain why Lila can use 9s facts or 4s facts to solve.

✔ **Assessment**

---

22. Bess has boxes of candles on the table. Each box has 4 candles. If Bess skip counts the candles in groups of 4, which list shows numbers she names?

Ⓐ 8, 12, 16, 20   Ⓒ 4, 6, 12, 14

Ⓑ 8, 12, 14, 18   Ⓓ 4, 8, 10, 14

23. Ramona has 9 candy boxes with 4 chocolate-covered cherries in each. Which of the following shows a way she can find how many candies there are in all?

Ⓐ $(4 \times 2) + (4 \times 2)$

Ⓑ $(9 \times 2) + (9 \times 2)$

Ⓒ $(9 \times 2) + (4 \times 2)$

Ⓓ $(9 + 2) \times (4 + 2)$

Help · Practice Buddy · Tools · Games

Homework & Practice 3-3

Apply Properties: 4 as a Factor

Another Look!

If you know a 2s multiplication fact, you can find a 4s multiplication fact.

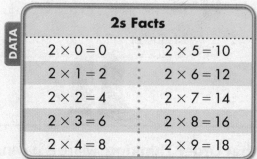

2s Facts	
$2 \times 0 = 0$	$2 \times 5 = 10$
$2 \times 1 = 2$	$2 \times 6 = 12$
$2 \times 2 = 4$	$2 \times 7 = 14$
$2 \times 3 = 6$	$2 \times 8 = 16$
$2 \times 4 = 8$	$2 \times 9 = 18$

DATA

Find 4×3. Draw an array.

$2 \times 3 = 6$

$2 \times 3 = 6$

$6 + 6 = 12$

So, $4 \times 3 = 12$.

In **1** and **2**, use a 2s fact to find the product of the 4s fact.

1. Find 4×9.

___ $\times 9 =$ ___

$2 \times$ ___ $=$ ___

___ $+ 18 =$ ___

So, $4 \times 9 =$ ___.

2. Find 4×2.

___ $\times 2 =$ ___

$2 \times$ ___ $=$ ___

___ $+ 4 =$ ___

So, $4 \times 2 =$ ___.

In **3–14**, find the product.

3. $4 \times 6 =$ ___

4. $8 \times 4 =$ ___

5. $4 \times 9 =$ ___

6. $2 \times 4 =$ ___

7. $4 \times 1 =$ ___

8. $4 \times 7 =$ ___

9. $0 \times 4 =$ ___

10. $4 \times 4 =$ ___

11. $4 \times 10 =$ ___

12. $3 \times 4 =$ ___

13. $5 \times 4 =$ ___

14. $4 \times 0 =$ ___

15. **Make Sense and Persevere** Jero and Max rented a canoe for 4 hours. They each rented a life jacket. How much money did they spend? How did you find the answer?

Canoeing	
Cost per hour	$4
Life jacket rental	$6

16. Tina paid for 6 hours of canoeing and 1 life jacket rental with two twenty-dollar bills. How much change did Tina get back? Show your work.

17. **Critique Reasoning** Rob says he can use 2 × 5 to find 4 × 5. Is he correct? Explain.

18. **Higher Order Thinking** Mark is having a party. He invited 35 people. Mark set up 8 tables with 4 chairs at each table. Does Mark have enough tables and chairs for all his guests? Explain.

✓ Assessment

19. Emmitt is grilling hot dogs for a cookout. He has 7 plates and put 4 hot dogs on each plate. Which of the following is **NOT** a way to find how many hot dogs Emmitt grilled?

    Ⓐ Make two 4 × 3 arrays

    Ⓑ Multiply 7 × 4

    Ⓒ Add 2 × 7 and 2 × 7

    Ⓓ Multiply 4 × 7

20. Jillian bought 3 boxes of crayons. Each box had the same number of crayons. How many crayons did Jillian buy?

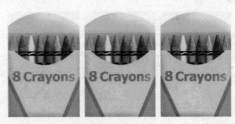

    Ⓐ 16 crayons

    Ⓑ 24 crayons

    Ⓒ 32 crayons

    Ⓓ 36 crayons

Name _____

Solve & Share

Students set up 6 rows of seats for a music concert. They put 6 seats in each row. What is the total number of seats? *Solve this problem any way you choose.*

You can model with math. Pictures, numbers, symbols, and words can be used to represent and solve multiplication problems. *Show your work in the space below!*

I can ...
make and use models to solve multiplication problems that have 6 and 7 as factors.

I can also look for patterns to solve problems.

Look Back! **Look for Relationships** How can 3s facts help you solve 6s facts?

Essential Question **How Can You Break Apart Arrays to Multiply?**

A

The members of the band march in 6 equal rows. There are 8 band members in each row. How many are in the band?

You can multiply to find the total for an array.

B **What You Show**

Find 6 × 8.

Use 5s facts and 1s facts.

Make an array for each multiplication sentence.

5 × 8 = 40

1 × 8 = 8

C **What You Think**

6 × 8 is 6 rows of 8. That is 5 eights plus 1 more eight.

5 eights are 40.
8 more is 48.
40 + 8 = 48

So, 6 × 8 = 48.

The band has 48 members.

Convince Me! **Use Structure** Use a 5s fact and a 1s fact to find 6 × 9. Draw two arrays. Explain your drawings.

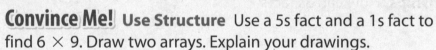

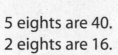
Another Example !

Find 7×8. Use 5s facts and 2s facts to help you multiply by 7.

$5 \times 8 = 40$

$2 \times 8 = 16$

7×8 equals 7 rows of 8.
That is 5 eights plus 2 eights.

5 eights are 40.
2 eights are 16.

$40 + 16 = 56$

So, $7 \times 8 = 56$.

Guided Practice *

Do You Understand?

1. **Model with Math** The students who are graduating are standing in 7 equal rows. There are 9 students in each row. How many students are graduating? Use a 5s fact and a 2s fact.

2. Chrissy bakes 3 cherry pies. She cuts each pie into 6 slices. How many slices does Chrissy have?

Do You Know How?

In **3–8**, multiply. You may draw pictures or use counters to help.

3. $6 \times 10 =$ _____   4. $7 \times 6 =$ _____

5. $\begin{array}{r} 7 \\ \times\,7 \\ \hline \end{array}$ 6. $\begin{array}{r} 9 \\ \times\,7 \\ \hline \end{array}$

7. Find 4 times 7. _____

8. Multiply 6 times 5. _____

 Independent Practice *

In **9–16**, find the product. You may draw pictures to help.

9. $\begin{array}{r} 5 \\ \times\,7 \\ \hline \end{array}$ 10. $\begin{array}{r} 3 \\ \times\,6 \\ \hline \end{array}$ 11. $\begin{array}{r} 7 \\ \times\,8 \\ \hline \end{array}$ 12. $\begin{array}{r} 1 \\ \times\,7 \\ \hline \end{array}$

13. $\begin{array}{r} 10 \\ \times\,6 \\ \hline \end{array}$ 14. $\begin{array}{r} 4 \\ \times\,7 \\ \hline \end{array}$ 15. $\begin{array}{r} 7 \\ \times\,3 \\ \hline \end{array}$ 16. $\begin{array}{r} 8 \\ \times\,6 \\ \hline \end{array}$

Problem Solving

17. Model with Math The National Toy Train Museum has 5 exhibits for trains. In one of the exhibits, the trains are on 5 tracks. How many trains are on display at that exhibit? Write an equation to solve the problem.

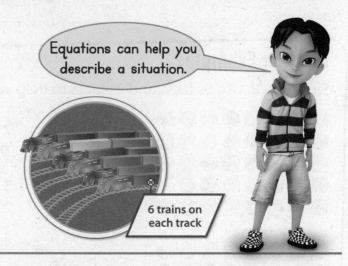

Equations can help you describe a situation.

6 trains on each track

---

18. Tracy used the flat surface of a cube to draw a plane shape. What plane shape did Tracy draw? How do you know?

19. The dance team lines up in 4 rows of 6 dancers each. How many dancers are on the dance team?

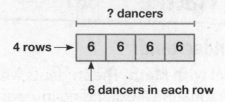

? dancers

4 rows → | 6 | 6 | 6 | 6 |

6 dancers in each row

---

20. Higher Order Thinking Marge says 7×0 is equal to $7 + 0$. Is Marge correct? Why or why not?

21. One train has 77 seats. Another train has 32 fewer seats. How many seats are on both trains?

✓ **Assessment**

22. Miguel has the baskets of oranges shown at the right. Each basket holds 6 oranges. How many oranges does Miguel have? Explain how to use 2 other known facts to solve this problem.

Name _____

Another Look!

You can use multiplication facts you already know to find other multiplication facts.

Find 6 × 9. Use a 3s fact.

$3 \times 9 = 27$

$3 \times 9 = 27$

$27 + 27 = 54$

So, 6 × 9 = 54.

Find 7 × 5. Use a 2s fact.

$2 \times 5 = 10$

$5 \times 5 = 25$

$10 + 25 = 35$

So, 7 × 5 = 35.

In **1** and **2**, use known facts to find each product.

1. 6 × 4 = ?

$3 \times 4 =$ ____

$3 \times 4 =$ ____

$12 +$ ____ = ____

So, 6 × 4 = ____.

2. 7 × 4 = ?

$2 \times 4 =$ ____

$5 \times 4 =$ ____

____ + ____ = ____

So, 7 × 4 = ____.

In **3–11**, find each product.

3. 2 × 7 = ____

4. 6 × 7 = ____

5. 7 × 9 = ____

6. 6 × 4 = ____

7. 6 × 8 = ____

8. 7 × 7 = ____

9. 6 × 2 = ____

10. 8 × 7 = ____

11. 3 × 7 = ____

12. Emmet buys 7 egg salad sandwiches at Sam's Café. How much money does Emmet spend?

13. Make Sense and Persevere Al buys 4 chicken salad sandwiches and 3 tuna salad sandwiches. How much money does Al spend? How did you find the answer?

Sandwiches	
Tuna Salad	$6
Egg Salad	$4
Chicken Salad	$7

14. Math and Science Raul's science class is studying chicken eggs. The eggs take 3 weeks to hatch. There are 7 days in each week. How many days does it take for the eggs to hatch?

15. Number Sense What multiplication fact can be found by using the arrays for 2×9 and 5×9?

16. Use Appropriate Tools Nan made an array to find $5 \times 3 = 15$. How can she use a tool to show 6×3?

17. Higher Order Thinking Harold says, "To find 6×8, I can use the facts for 5×4 and 1×4." Do you agree? Explain.

✔ **Assessment**

18. Emily has 7 apples. She cuts each apple into 6 slices. How many slices does Emily have? Write an equation to show how you solved the problem.

Name _____

☆ ☆
Solve & Share

There are 8 rows of prizes. There are 6 prizes in each row. How many prizes are there? *Solve this problem any way you choose.*

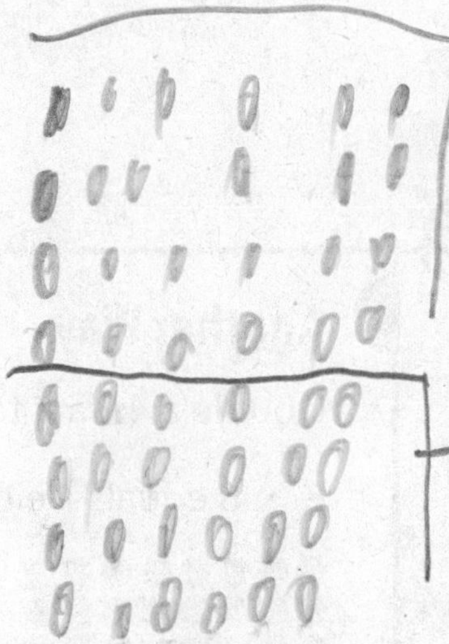

I can ...
use known facts and properties to multiply by 8.

I can also make sense of problems.

$$4 \times 6 = 24$$
$$+$$
$$4 \times 6 = 24$$
$$48$$

You can make sense of problems by using known facts to solve unknown facts. *Show your work!*

Look Back! **Generalize** Tell how you can use 2s, 3s, or 4s facts to solve the problem.

Essential Question **How Can You Use Doubles to Multiply with 8?**

A

At a school fun fair, students try to toss a table tennis ball into a bowl. There are 8 rows of bowls. There are 8 bowls in each row. How many bowls are there?

What 2s and 4s facts can you find in the bowl array?

B ## One Way

Use 2s facts to find 8×8.

8×8 equals 4 groups of 2 eights.

$\left.\begin{array}{l}\bullet\bullet\bullet\bullet\bullet\bullet\bullet\bullet\\\bullet\bullet\bullet\bullet\bullet\bullet\bullet\bullet\end{array}\right\}$ $2 \times 8 = 16$

$\left.\begin{array}{l}\bullet\bullet\bullet\bullet\bullet\bullet\bullet\bullet\\\bullet\bullet\bullet\bullet\bullet\bullet\bullet\bullet\end{array}\right\}$ $2 \times 8 = 16$

$\left.\begin{array}{l}\bullet\bullet\bullet\bullet\bullet\bullet\bullet\bullet\\\bullet\bullet\bullet\bullet\bullet\bullet\bullet\bullet\end{array}\right\}$ $2 \times 8 = 16$

$\left.\begin{array}{l}\bullet\bullet\bullet\bullet\bullet\bullet\bullet\bullet\\\bullet\bullet\bullet\bullet\bullet\bullet\bullet\bullet\end{array}\right\}$ $2 \times 8 = 16$

$16 + 16 + 16 + 16 = 64$

So, $8 \times 8 = 64$.

C ## Another Way

Double a 4s fact to find 8×8.

8×8 equals 4 eights plus 4 eights.

$\left.\begin{array}{l}\bullet\bullet\bullet\bullet\bullet\bullet\bullet\bullet\\\bullet\bullet\bullet\bullet\bullet\bullet\bullet\bullet\\\bullet\bullet\bullet\bullet\bullet\bullet\bullet\bullet\\\bullet\bullet\bullet\bullet\bullet\bullet\bullet\bullet\end{array}\right\}$ $4 \times 8 = 32$

$\left.\begin{array}{l}\bullet\bullet\bullet\bullet\bullet\bullet\bullet\bullet\\\bullet\bullet\bullet\bullet\bullet\bullet\bullet\bullet\\\bullet\bullet\bullet\bullet\bullet\bullet\bullet\bullet\\\bullet\bullet\bullet\bullet\bullet\bullet\bullet\bullet\end{array}\right\}$ $4 \times 8 = 32$

$32 + 32 = 64$

So, $8 \times 8 = 64$.

Convince Me! **Use Structure** How does knowing $5 \times 8 = 40$ help you find 8×8?

I now 3+5=8 so I can split 8 into 3+5. I now 5×8=40 and I now 3×8=24 so I sould add 40+24=64

Practice Buddy   Tools   Assessment

☆ Guided Practice*

Do You Understand?

1. Multiply 8 times 3. Write and solve a multiplication equation.

2. Multiply 5 times 8. Write and solve a multiplication equation.

3. Multiply 8 times 1. Write and solve a multiplication equation.

Do You Know How?

In **4–9**, multiply. You may draw pictures or use counters to help.

4. $8 \times 7 =$ ____

5. $8 \times 4 =$ _32_

6. $6 \times 8 =$ ____

7. $10 \times 8 =$ ____

8.   9
   $\times\,8$

9.   8
   $\times\,3$

☆ Independent Practice ☆

In **10–23**, find the product. You may draw pictures to help.

10. $8 \times 4 =$ _32_

11. $1 \times 8 =$ ____

12. $2 \times 8 =$ ____

13. $5 \times 8 =$ ____

14. $8 \times 2 =$ ____

15. $8 \times 6 =$ _48_

16.   8
    $\times\,8$

17.   8
    $\times\,5$

18.   0
    $\times\,8$

19.   4
    $\times\,8$

20.   10
    $\times\,8$
    _80_

21.   8
    $\times\,1$

22.   3
    $\times\,8$

23.   7
    $\times\,8$

Problem Solving

24. Use Structure Ming bought 8 belts for gifts. How much money did Ming spend? Show how you can use a 4s fact to find the answer.

$4 \times 9 = 36$ $4 \times 9 = 36 + 36 = 72$

25. Make Sense and Persevere Willa bought a shirt and a sweater. She had $14 left. How much money did Willa start with? How do you know?

DATA	Clothing Sale	
	Shirt	$23
	Belt	$9
	Sweater	$38
	Pair of jeans	$42

26. Model with Math Mr. Garner spends $52 on groceries and $24 on gas. How much did Mr. Garner spend? Write an equation and solve.

?	
$52	$24

27. Algebra Mischa bought 7 boxes of orange tiles. There are 8 tiles in each box. How many tiles did Mischa buy? Write an equation and solve. Use ? to represent the unknown quantity of tiles.

28. Aaron bought 6 packs of sports cards. There are 7 cards in each pack. How many sports cards did Aaron buy in all? Use properties to solve the problem.

29. Higher Order Thinking Sophi says, "To find 8 × 8, I can find 8 × (4 + 4)." Do you agree? Explain.

✔ **Assessment**

30. Ms. Vero has boxes of crayons in her classroom closet. Each box has 8 crayons in it. Draw lines to show how many total crayons are found in each group of crayon boxes.

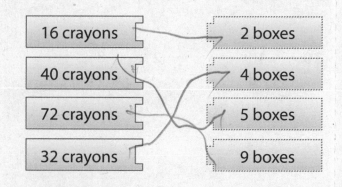

16 crayons	2 boxes
40 crayons	4 boxes
72 crayons	5 boxes
32 crayons	9 boxes

Help Practice Buddy Tools Games

Another Look!

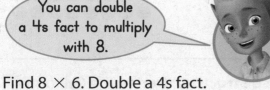

You can double a 4s fact to multiply with 8.

Find 8 × 6. Double a 4s fact.

4 × 6 = 24

4 × 6 = 24
24 + 24 = 48

So, 8 × 6 = 48.

4s Facts	
4 × 0 = 0	4 × 5 = 20
4 × 1 = 4	4 × 6 = 24
4 × 2 = 8	4 × 7 = 28
4 × 3 = 12	4 × 8 = 32
4 × 4 = 16	4 × 9 = 36

DATA

In **1** and **2**, double a 4s fact to find the product.

1. 8 × 5 = ?

4 × 5 = _____

4 × 5 = _____

20 + _____ = _____

So, 8 × 5 = _____.

2. 8 × 3 = ?

4 × 3 = _____

4 × 3 = _____

_____ + _____ = _____

So, 8 × 3 = _____.

In **3–9**, find the products.

3. 2 × 8 = _____

4. 4 × 8 = _____

5. 8 × 5 = _____

6. 7
     × 8

7. 8
     × 9

8. 1
     × 8

9. 8
     × 6

10. Luis made the arrays shown at the right to find 5 × 8. Explain how he could change the arrays to find 7 × 8. Add to Luis's drawing to show your solution.

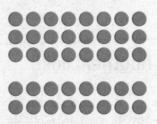

---

11. Math and Science An octopus has 8 arms. At the aquarium there are 3 octopuses in one tank. How many arms do the octopuses have all together? What are two strategies you can use to find the answer?

12. Use Structure During the California Gold Rush, miners sometimes paid $10 for a glass of water. What was the total cost if 8 miners each bought one glass of water? How can you use a 4s fact to find the answer?

---

13. How many pints are in 5 gallons?

1 gallon = 8 pints

14. Higher Order Thinking Lani said all of the multiples of 8 are also multiples of 2. Jamila said all of the multiples of 8 are also multiples of 4. Who is correct? Explain.

---

15. Ted works in a store where rolls are sold in packages of 8. Customers came in asking Ted for 16, 48, 8, and 40 rolls. Draw lines to connect each quantity of rolls to the number of packages Ted should tell the customers to buy.

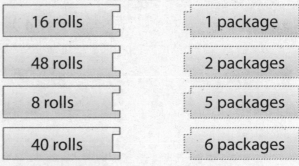

16 rolls		1 package
48 rolls		2 packages
8 rolls		5 packages
40 rolls		6 packages

Name _____

Solve

Solve & Share

Jermaine has 7 coolers. Each cooler contains 8 bottles of sports drink. How many bottles of sports drink does Jermaine have in all? *Solve this problem any way you choose.*

I can ...
use strategies and tools to represent and solve multiplication facts.

I can also model with math to solve problems.

You can model with math. Pictures, objects, words, numbers, and symbols can be used to represent and solve the problem. *Show your work in the space below!*

$$7 \times 8 = (3 \times 8) + (4 \times 8) =$$

Look Back! **Construct Arguments** Jermaine instead has 8 coolers with 7 bottles of sports drink in each cooler. Does that change the total number of bottles of sports drinks that he has? Explain why or why not.

Essential Question: How Do You Use Strategies to Multiply?

A

Justin and Dolores made a dragon float for a parade. They connected 9 equal sections to make the dragon's body. What is the total length of the dragon's body in feet?

The dragon's body is made of equal sections, so you can multiply to find its length.

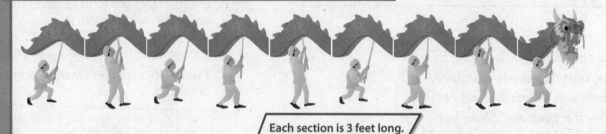

Each section is 3 feet long.

B **One Way**

Draw a picture to find 9 × 3.

9 × 3 means 9 groups of 3. Combine the groups to find the product.

Dragon's body length
?

| 3 | 3 | 3 | 3 | 3 | 3 | 3 | 3 | 3 |

↑
3 feet each section

9 × 3 = 27.

The dragon's body is 27 feet long.

C **Another Way**

Use known facts to find 9 × 3.

Use 4s facts and 5s facts to help.

4 × 3 = 12

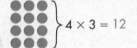
5 × 3 = 15

12 + 15 = 27

The dragon's body is 27 feet long.

Convince Me! **Make Sense and Persevere** What two other facts can you use to find 9 × 3? Explain.

9 × 3 = (1 × 3) + (8 × 3) = 9 + 18 = 27

Name _____

★ Guided Practice ★

Do You Understand?

1. What known facts can you use to find 7 × 5?

2. To find 8 × 6, how does knowing 6 × 6 = 36 help you?

Do You Know How?

In **3–8**, multiply.

3. 3 × 7 = *21*   4. 6 × 5 = _____

5. 9 × 4 = _____   6. 3 × 0 = _____

7. 1
   × 7
   ____

8. 10
   × 8
   ____

Independent Practice ★

In **9–25**, use known facts and strategies to find the product.

9. 7 × 7 = *49*

10. 8 × 2 = _____

11. 3 × 10 = _____

12. *72* = 8 × 9

13. _____ = 4 × 6

14. _____ = 4 × 4

15. 10   16. 2   17. 1   18. 2
    × 7   × 6   × 3   × 7
    ____   ____   ____   ____
    70   *14*

19. 8   20. 10   21. 4   22. 8
    × 0   × 6   × 7   × 9
    ____   ____   ____   ____
                                      28

23. What is 6 × 9? _____   24. What is 7 × 2? *14*   25. What is 8 × 1? _____

Problem Solving

26. Reasoning Mr. Ling walks 5 miles each day. How many total miles does he walk in one week? Explain.

Remember, there are 7 days in a week.

27. David wants to buy new shoes and a jersey. The shoes cost $56. The jersey costs $42. How much money does David need to buy both items?

?	
$56	$42

98

28. Model with Math Ms. Wilson drank three 8-ounce glasses of tea before lunch. Then she drank three 8-ounce glasses of water before dinner. How many ounces of liquid did she drink in all? Write an equation to help solve.

29. Higher Order Thinking Show how you can use known facts to find 4×11. Explain how you chose the known facts.

30. Critique Reasoning Mr. Evans needs to assign 32 students into 8 equal groups. He says, "I can use repeated subtraction. Since I subtract 3 times, each group has 3 students." Do you agree with Mr. Evans? Explain why or why not.

$32 - 16 = 16$
$16 - 8 = 8$
$8 - 8 = 0.$

4

Assessment

31. Rory played 9 holes of golf. On each hole it took him 4 strokes to get his ball in the hole. Choose *Yes* or *No* to tell if each equation can be used to find the total number of strokes it took Rory to complete 9 holes.

$(8 \times 4) + (1 \times 4) = ?$ ○ Yes ○ No
$9 \times 4 = ?$ ○ Yes ○ No
$(3 \times 3) + (1 \times 4) = ?$ ○ Yes ○ No
$9 \times (2 \times 2) = ?$ ○ Yes ○ No

32. Rachel has a collection of 24 ceramic figures. She displays them in equal groups in her room. Choose *Yes* or *No* to tell if each example is a possible way to display all of Rachel's figures.

8 groups of 4 ○ Yes ○ No
3 groups of 6 ○ Yes ○ No
6 groups of 4 ○ Yes ○ No
3 groups of 8 ○ Yes ○ No

Name _____

Another Look!

Find 8 × 4.

You can use a picture or known facts to find 8 × 4.

Picture

8 × 4 means 8 groups of 4.

?
| 4 | 4 | 4 | 4 | 4 | 4 | 4 | 4 |

Combine equal groups to find the product.

So, 8 × 4 = 32.

Known Facts

Use 4s facts to help.

4 × 4 = 16

4 × 4 = 16

16 + 16 = 32

So, 8 × 4 = 32.

In **1** and **2**, use a picture and known facts to find the product.

1. 3 × 6 = ?

?
| 6 | 6 | |

6   12   _____

3 × 6 = _____

2 × 6 = _____

1 × 6 = _____

12 + _____ = _____

2. 3 × 3 = ?

?
| 3 | 3 | |

3   6   _____

3 × 3 = _____

2 × 3 = _____

1 × 3 = _____

6 + _____ = _____

In **3–8**, multiply.

3. 3 × 2 = _____

4. 8 × 3 = _____

5. 6 × 7 = _____

6. 10 × 7 = _____

7. 4 × 0 = _____

8. 7 × 2 = _____

9. **Make Sense and Persevere** The home team had 4 three-pointers, 10 two-pointers, and 6 free throws. The visiting team scored 5 three-pointers, 8 two-pointers, and 5 free throws. Which team scored more points? Explain.

Think about what you know, and what you need to find.

Basketball Points	
Type	**Points**
Three-Pointer	3 points
Two-Pointer	2 points
Free Throw	1 point

10. **Higher Order Thinking** Martina has 3 bags of tennis balls. There are 6 pink, 5 yellow, and 2 white balls in each bag. How many tennis balls does Martina have in all? Show how you found the answer.

11. **Number Sense** Without multiplying, how can you tell which product will be greater, 4×3 or 4×5? Explain.

✓ **Assessment**

12. A park ranger is counting visitors who drive into a national park. In 30 minutes, she counts 7 cars with 4 passengers in each. Choose *Yes* or *No* to tell if each equation shows a way to find how many visitors the park ranger counted.

$4 \times 7 = ?$ ◯ Yes ◯ No

$4 \times 7 + 30 = ?$ ◯ Yes ◯ No

$(2 \times 7) + (2 \times 7) = ?$ ◯ Yes ◯ No

$(4 \times 3) + (4 \times 4) = ?$ ◯ Yes ◯ No

13. Harris buys one cap for every city he has visited in the United States. The number of caps he has is shown below. Choose *Yes* or *No* to tell if each equation shows a way to find how many cities Harris has visited.

$3 \times 6 = ?$ ◯ Yes ◯ No

$(2 \times 5) + (1 \times 5) = ?$ ◯ Yes ◯ No

$(3 + 5) \times 3 = ?$ ◯ Yes ◯ No

$3 \times 5 = ?$ ◯ Yes ◯ No

Name _____

☆ ☆
Solve & Share

Gina has 2 quilts. Each quilt has 5 rows with 3 squares in each row. How many squares are in both quilts? *Solve this problem any way you choose.* Then find another way to solve the problem.

Lesson 3-7
The Associative Property: Multiply with 3 Factors

I can ...
multiply 3 factors in any order to find a product.

I can also make sense of problems.

$$2 \times (5 \times 3) = 30$$
$$2 \times 15 = 30$$ answer

You can make sense of problems and persevere in solving them. You can solve this problem in more than one way. *Show your work!*

Look Back! **Construct Arguments** Did you get a different answer when you solved the problem a different way? Explain why or why not.

How Can You Multiply 3 Numbers?

A

Drew is joining 3 sections of a quilt. Each section has 2 rows with 4 squares in each row. How many squares are in these 3 sections? Find $3 \times 2 \times 4$.

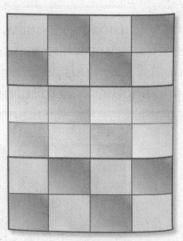

You can multiply to find the total for an array.

B **One Way**

Find 3×2 first.

$(3 \times 2) \times 4$

$\quad\downarrow$

$6 \quad \times 4 = 24$

6 rows, 4 squares in each row

There are 24 squares in all.

C **Another Way**

Find 2×4 first.

$3 \times (2 \times 4)$

$\qquad\downarrow$

$3 \times \quad 8 = 24$

3 sections, 8 squares in each section

There are 24 squares in Drew's quilt.

The Associative (Grouping) Property of Multiplication says that you can change the grouping of the factors and the product will be the same.

Convince Me! **Generalize** Use the Associative Property of Multiplication to show two different ways to find $5 \times 2 \times 3$. Did you get the same answer both ways? What can you generalize?

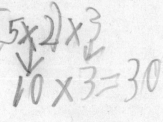

$5 \times (2 \times 3)$

$\quad\downarrow$

$6 \times 5 = 30$

$(5 \times 2) \times 3$

$\quad\downarrow$

$10 \times 3 = 30$

Practice Buddy Tools Assessment

☆ Guided Practice *

Do You Understand?

1. Sarah has 4 pages of stickers in an album. Each page has 3 rows with 2 stickers in each row. How many stickers are in Sarah's album? You may use objects to help.

2. **Critique Reasoning** Billy concludes the product of $(2 \times 3) \times 5$ is not equal to the product of $2 \times (3 \times 5)$. Is Billy correct? Explain.

Do You Know How?

In **3–6**, use the Associative Property of Multiplication to find the missing number. You may use objects or draw a picture to help.

3. $2 \times (4 \times 2) = (2 \times 4) \times$ ____

4. $(3 \times 4) \times 3 = 3 \times ($ **4** $\times 3)$

5. $2 \times (2 \times 3) = (2 \times 2) \times$ ____

6. $(3 \times 2) \times 4 =$ ____ $\times (2 \times 4)$

☆ Independent Practice ☆

In **7–12**, use the Associative Property of Multiplication to find the missing number. You may use objects or draw a picture to help.

7. $8 \times (3 \times 6) = (8 \times 3) \times$ ____

8. $5 \times (6 \times 9) = (5 \times 6) \times$ **9**

9. $5 \times (7 \times 2) = (5 \times 7) \times$ ____

10. $5 \times (2 \times 9) = (5 \times$ ____ $) \times 9$

11. $3 \times (2 \times 5) = (3 \times 2) \times$ ____

12. $4 \times (2 \times 2) = (4 \times$ **2** $) \times 2$

In **13–18**, use the Associative Property of Multiplication to find the product. You may use objects or draw a picture to help.

13. $2 \times 3 \times 2 =$ ____

14. $3 \times 6 \times 2 =$ ____

15. $2 \times 6 \times 2 =$ ____

16. $5 \times 2 \times 4 =$ **40**

17. $5 \times 2 \times 2 =$ ____

18. $3 \times 3 \times 2 =$ ____

Problem Solving

19. Reasoning There are 7 mockingbird nests at a park. What is the greatest number of eggs there could be at this park? What is the least number of eggs there could be?

Mockingbirds lay 3 to 5 eggs.

20. At another park, there are 3 mockingbird nests with 4 eggs in each nest and 1 more nest with 3 eggs. How many eggs are there at this park?

---

21. Critique Reasoning Maria says she can find the product for $2 \times 3 \times 4$ by solving $3 \times 2 \times 4$. Is Maria correct? Explain.

22. Number Sense Anita says the product of $5 \times 2 \times 3$ is less than 20. Do you agree? Explain.

---

23. Algebra Which number makes both equations true?

$4 \times (3 \times 2) = (4 \times \text{?}) \times 2$

$3 \times (5 \times 2) = (\text{?} \times 5) \times 2$

24. Higher Order Thinking How do you know that $4 \times 2 \times 2$ is the same as 4×4? Explain.

$2 \times 2 = 4 \times 4$

is same

✓ **Assessment**

Fill in the blanks to make the equations correct.

Use properties to help multiply.

25. $(7 \times 2) \times 3 = \underline{\hspace{1cm}} \times (\underline{\hspace{1cm}} \times 3)$

$(7 \times 2) \times 3 = \underline{\hspace{1cm}}$

26. $(9 \times 3) \times 3 = \underline{\hspace{1cm}} \times (\underline{\hspace{1cm}} \times 3)$

$(9 \times 3) \times 3 = \underline{\hspace{1cm}}$

Name _____

Help Practice Tools Games
       Buddy

Homework
& Practice 3-7

The Associative
Property: Multiply
with 3 Factors

Another Look!

Use the Associative Property of Multiplication
to find the product of $4 \times 2 \times 5$.

The Associative Property of
Multiplication states that the way
the factors are grouped does not
change the product.

One Way
$4 \times 2 \times 5$
$(4 \times 2) \times 5$
$8 \times 5 = 40$

Another Way
$4 \times 2 \times 5$
$4 \times (2 \times 5)$
$4 \times 10 = 40$

1. Find the product of $4 \times 2 \times 3$ two different ways.

$4 \times 2 \times 3$
$(4 \times 2) \times 3$

_____ $\times 3 =$ _____

$4 \times 2 \times 3$
$4 \times (2 \times 3)$

$4 \times$ _____ $=$ _____

In **2–16**, find each product. You may draw a picture to help.

2. $3 \times 2 \times 1 =$ _____

3. $2 \times 3 \times 5 =$ _____

4. $4 \times 3 \times 2 =$ _____

5. $4 \times 2 \times 7 =$ _____

6. $3 \times 3 \times 2 =$ _____

7. $2 \times 4 \times 5 =$ _____

8. $2 \times 2 \times 6 =$ _____

9. $4 \times 1 \times 5 =$ _____

10. $5 \times 1 \times 3 =$ _____

11. $6 \times 1 \times 5 =$ _____

12. $3 \times 3 \times 4 =$ _____

13. $4 \times 2 \times 6 =$ _____

14. $5 \times 5 \times 2 =$ _____

15. $2 \times 2 \times 5 =$ _____

16. $3 \times 2 \times 2 =$ _____

17. Model with Math Mrs. Stokes bought 3 packages of fruit juice. Each package has 2 rows with 6 boxes in each row. How many boxes of fruit juice did Mrs. Stokes buy? Use equations to solve.

18. Higher Order Thinking Write two different multiplication equations for the arrays shown and find the product.

19. Matt has a block. He uses one of the flat surfaces of the block to trace a triangle. What type of solid figure is Matt's block?

20. A-Z Vocabulary Write an equation that has 20 as the *product* and 4 as a *factor*.

21. Reasoning Amy has 3 bags of marbles, and Ron has 2 bags of marbles. There are 6 marbles in each of their bags. How many marbles do they have in all? Show how you know.

22. Make Sense and Persevere Marco bought 6 sheets of stamps. On each sheet there are 3 rows of stamps with 3 stamps in each row. How many stamps did Marco buy?

✓ **Assessment**

Write numbers to make the equations correct.

23. $(8 \times 2) \times 4 = \underline{\quad} \times (\underline{\quad} \times 4)$

$(8 \times 2) \times 4 = \underline{\quad}$

24. $(6 \times 5) \times 2 = \underline{\quad} \times (\underline{\quad} \times 2)$

$(6 \times 5) \times 2 = \underline{\quad}$

You can solve problems different ways using properties.

Name _____

Solve & Share

You have learned that you can use known facts to find unknown facts. For each of the 4 multiplication facts below, list two multiplication facts from the box that can be added to find the given product. The first solution is completed for you.

What do you notice about the facts you used to find the products when 6 or 7 is a factor?

I can ...
use reasoning to look for and describe general strategies for finding products.

I can also break apart facts.

6×7 6×9

$5 \times 7 + 1 \times 7 = 42$ _____ + _____ $= 54$

7×8 7×9

_____ + _____ $= 56$ _____ + _____ $= 63$

1×9	2×8	1×7
5×8	5×9	1×8
5×7	2×7	2×9

Thinking Habits
Be a good thinker!
These questions can help you.

- Are any calculations repeated?
- Can I generalize from examples?
- What shortcuts do I notice?

Look Back! **Generalize** Use your observations from your work above to complete these facts.

(___ × 6) + (___ × 6) = 36

(___ × 7) + (___ × 7) = 49

Essential Question ## How Can You Use Repeated Reasoning When Multiplying?

A

Ellie wrote the equations below to find the total number of squares in each of these rectangles. Look at the equations. Known facts with which factors are used repeatedly to find the products?

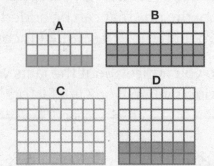

A $3 \times 6 = (2 \times 6) + (1 \times 6) = 12 + 6 = 18$

B $4 \times 9 = (2 \times 9) + (2 \times 9) = 18 + 18 = 36$

C $6 \times 8 = (5 \times 8) + (1 \times 8) = 40 + 8 = 48$

D $7 \times 7 = (5 \times 7) + (2 \times 7) = 35 + 14 = 49$

What do I need to do to complete the task?

I need to see if there are known facts that can be used repeatedly to find other facts.

B

How can I make a generalization from repeated reasoning?

I can

- look for repeated calculations.

- make generalizations about the repeated calculations.

- test whether my generalizations work for other numbers.

C I see that the factors 1, 2, and 5 are used repeatedly. I see two generalizations.

Here's my thinking...

I can break facts with 3 or 4 into 2s and 1s facts.
$3 \times 6 = (2 \times 6) + (1 \times 6)$
$4 \times 9 = (2 \times 9) + (2 \times 9)$

I can break facts with 6 or 7 into 5s, 2s, and 1s facts.
$6 \times 8 = (5 \times 8) + (1 \times 8)$
$7 \times 7 = (5 \times 7) + (2 \times 7)$

I can test this with other facts.
$3 \times 5 = (2 \times 5) + (1 \times 5)$
$6 \times 7 = (5 \times 7) + (1 \times 7)$

Convince Me! **Generalize** Use the generalizations above to complete each of the following. Tell how you decided.

$7 \times 5 = ($ _____ $) + ($ _____ $)$

$7 \times 6 = ($ _____ $) + ($ _____ $)$

☆ **Guided Practice** *

Generalize

Ricardo wrote the equations below.

> When you generalize, you make a statement about a larger group based on examples that are true.

1. Which factors did Ricardo use repeatedly to find the products? Make a generalization.

   $3 \times 8 = (2 \times 8) + (1 \times 8) = 24$

   $3 \times 7 = (2 \times 7) + (1 \times 7) = 21$

   $6 \times 3 = (6 \times 1) + (6 \times 2) = 18$

2. Complete this equation to test whether your generalization is true for other facts. Explain.

   $3 \times 9 = (\_\_ \times \_\_) + (\_\_ \times \_\_) = \_\_\_\_$

☆ **Independent Practice** ☆

Generalize

Mary wrote the equations at the right.

3. Which factors did Mary use repeatedly to find the products? Make a generalization.

   $8 \times 7 = (5 \times 7) + (3 \times 7) = 56$

   $6 \times 8 = (6 \times 5) + (6 \times 3) = 48$

   $8 \times 9 = (3 \times 9) + (5 \times 9) = 72$

4. Complete this equation to test whether your generalization is true for other facts. Explain.

   $8 \times 3 = (\_\_ \times \_\_) + (\_\_ \times \_\_) = \_\_\_\_$

5. What is another way you can use known facts to solve 8×3? What generalization can you make from this way?

*For another example, see Set F on page 160.

Topic 3 | Lesson 3-8   **153**

Baking Pizzas

Adam is baking 4 pizzas. Each pizza is a rectangle. It takes Adam 35 minutes to bake the pizzas. He divides each pizza into the equal-size square slices shown.

Pizza 1   **Pizza 2**

 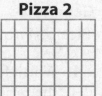

Pizza 3   **Pizza 4**

 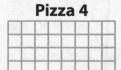

6. **Make Sense and Persevere** Adam multiplies to find the total number of square slices for each pizza. For each pizza, tell the factors Adam multiplies.

7. **Use Structure** Look at the facts you wrote in **6**. Break apart these facts into 1s, 2s, or 5s facts to find the total number of slices for each pizza.

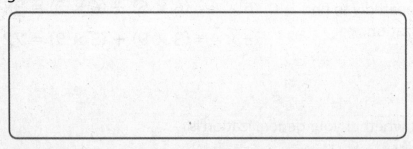

Pizza 1

(__ × __) = (__ × __) + (__ × __) = ____

Pizza 2

(__ × __) = (__ × __) + (__ × __) = ____

Pizza 3

(__ × __) = (__ × __) + (__ × __) = ____

Pizza 4

(__ × __) = (__ × __) + (__ × __) = ____

8. **Generalize** Look at how you used the 1s, 2s, and 5s facts above. What generalizations can you make? Test your generalizations with another fact.

You can test your generalization by checking to see if it is true for other facts.

9. **Critique Reasoning** Look at the model for Pizza 3. Adam says he can use 2s facts to solve 4 × 7 or 7 × 4. Is he correct? Explain.

Another Look!

John used facts he knows to solve 6×7 and 6×5.
He wrote these equations.

$6 \times 7 = (5 \times 7) + (1 \times 7) = 42$

$6 \times 5 = (5 \times 5) + (1 \times 5) = 30$

Tell how you can use repeated reasoning to find multiplication facts.

- I can look for repeated calculations.

- I can make generalizations about the repeated calculations.

Make a generalization.
Test whether this is true for other facts.

I can break facts with 6 into 5s and 1s facts.

This is true for other facts with 6: $6 \times 9 = (5 \times 9) + (1 \times 9) = 54$

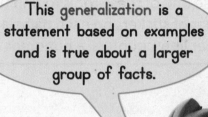

This generalization is a statement based on examples and is true about a larger group of facts.

Generalize

Pam wrote the equations below.

1. Tell how you can use repeated reasoning to find multiplication facts.

2. Which factors did Pam use repeatedly? Make a generalization.

$7 \times 6 = (5 \times 6) + (2 \times 6) = 42$

$7 \times 9 = (5 \times 9) + (2 \times 9) = 63$

$7 \times 7 = (5 \times 7) + (2 \times 7) = 49$

3. Complete this equation to test whether your generalization is true for other facts. Explain.

$7 \times 8 = (\underline{} \times \underline{}) + (\underline{} \times \underline{}) = \underline{}$

Julia puts her stickers into arrays in an album. Some of her stickers are animal stickers. There are a different number of stickers on each page. The table at the right shows information about the stickers in Julia's album.

DATA

Julia's Stickers

Page Number	Animal Stickers	Rows of Stickers	Columns of Stickers
1	7	4	7
2	4	4	6
3	9	8	9
4	9	8	6

4. Use Appropriate Tools Explain how you can use one of these tools to find the number of stickers on each page: a number line, counters, a hundreds chart.

5. Make Sense and Persevere Julia multiplies to find the total number of stickers on each page. For each page, tell the factors that she multiplies.

6. Use Structure Look at the facts you wrote for **5**. Break these facts into 1s, 2s, 3s, and 5s facts to find the total number of stickers on each page.

You can generalize by thinking about the factors that you use repeatedly to solve problems.

Page 1
(__ × __) = (__ × __) + (__ × __) = ____
Page 2
(__ × __) = (__ × __) + (__ × __) = ____
Page 3
(__ × __) = (__ × __) + (__ × __) = ____
Page 4
(__ × __) = (__ × __) + (__ × __) = ____

7. Generalize Look at the 1s, 2s, 3s, and 5s facts above. What generalizations can you make? Test each generalization with another fact.

Name _____

Shade a path from **START** to **FINISH**. Follow the differences that are correct. You can only move up, down, right, or left.

I can ...
subtract within 100.

Start				
75 − 13 62	99 − 63 36	85 − 39 46	70 − 48 32	41 − 31 11
39 − 21 12	24 − 16 10	59 − 37 22	55 − 32 67	91 − 65 47
77 − 38 45	47 − 40 87	46 − 27 19	100 − 62 58	45 − 27 17
69 − 21 47	34 − 29 15	65 − 59 6	81 − 29 52	67 − 19 48
82 − 46 58	38 − 12 23	93 − 34 69	24 − 18 9	78 − 35 43

Finish

A-Z Glossary

Word List

- Associative (Grouping) Property of Multiplication
- Commutative (Order) Property of Multiplication
- Distributive Property
- Identity (One) Property of Multiplication
- factor
- multiple
- product
- Zero Property of Multiplication

Understand Vocabulary

Match the example to the term.

1. $5 \times 0 = 0 \times 5$

2. $(3 \times 8) + (1 \times 8) = 4 \times 8$

3. $(6 \times 2) \times 2 = 6 \times (2 \times 2)$

4. $7 \times 1 = 7$

Associative (Grouping) Property of Multiplication

Commutative (Order) Property of Multiplication

Distributive Property

Identity (One) Property of Multiplication

Write T for *true* or F for *false*.

_____ **5.** 3 and 8 are *multiples* of 24.

_____ **6.** You can multiply *factors* in any order.

_____ **7.** The *product* of zero and any number is that number.

_____ **8.** There are 3 *factors* in the equation $5 \times 3 \times 2 = 30$.

Use Vocabulary in Writing

9. Explain how to use $8 \times 5 = 40$ to find 8×6. Use at least 2 terms from the Word List in your explanation.

Name _____

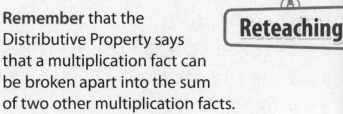

Reteaching

Set A pages 109–114 _____

You can break an array into 2 smaller arrays.

You can write an unknown fact as the sum of 2 known facts.

$8 \times 4 = (8 \times 3) + (8 \times 1)$

Remember that the Distributive Property says that a multiplication fact can be broken apart into the sum of two other multiplication facts.

In **1** and **2**, find the missing value.

1. _____ $\times 4 = (2 \times 4) + (2 \times 4)$

2. $6 \times 5 = (4 \times 5) + ($_____$\times 5)$

Set B pages 115–126 _____

Find 3×4.

You can use a 2s fact to help multiply by 3.

$3 \times 4 \begin{cases} \text{( ) ( ) ( ) ( )} \\ \text{( ) ( ) ( ) ( )} \end{cases} \} 2 \times 4 = 8$
$\quad\quad \text{( ) ( ) ( ) ( )} \} 1 \times 4 = 4$

$8 + 4 = 12$

You can also find 4s facts.
$3 \times 4 = (3 \times 2) + (3 \times 2) = 6 + 6 = 12$

Remember that to find a 3s fact, add a 2s fact and a 1s fact. To find a 4s fact, double the product of a 2s fact.

1. $3 \times 7 =$ _____   2. $4 \times 9 =$ _____

3. $4 \times 10 =$ _____   4. $3 \times 10 =$ _____

5. $3 \times 8 =$ _____   6. $8 \times 4 =$ _____

7. $9 \times 3 =$ _____   8. $10 \times 4 =$ _____

Set C pages 127–132 _____

You can use known facts to help multiply. Find 6×9.

$6 \times 9 = (5 \times 9) + (1 \times 9)$

$6 \times 9 = 45 + 9$

$6 \times 9 = 54$

Find 7×4.

$7 \times 4 = (5 \times 4) + (2 \times 4)$

$7 \times 4 = 20 + 8$

$7 \times 4 = 28$

Remember that you can break a multiplication problem into two smaller problems.

1. $6 \times 6 =$ _____   2. $7 \times 9 =$ _____

3. $7 \times 7 =$ _____   4. $6 \times 8 =$ _____

5. $\begin{array}{r} 6 \\ \times 5 \\ \hline \end{array}$ 6. $\begin{array}{r} 6 \\ \times 3 \\ \hline \end{array}$ 7. $\begin{array}{r} 10 \\ \times 7 \\ \hline \end{array}$

Set D | pages 133–144

Find 8×9.

You can use 2s facts.

$8 \times 9 = (2 \times 9) + (2 \times 9) + (2 \times 9) + (2 \times 9)$

$8 \times 9 = 18 + 18 + 18 + 18$

$8 \times 9 = 72$

You can use skip counting.

8, 16, 24, 32, 40, 48, 56, 64, 72

Remember to use patterns, known facts, or skip counting to find products.

1. $8 \times 6 =$ _____   2. $8 \times 8 =$ _____

3. $8 \times 7 =$ _____   4. $8 \times 10 =$ _____

5. $1 \times 8 =$ _____   6. $0 \times 8 =$ _____

7. $\begin{array}{r} 8 \\ \times\ 5 \\ \hline \end{array}$ 8. $\begin{array}{r} 8 \\ \times\ 3 \\ \hline \end{array}$ 9. $\begin{array}{r} 8 \\ \times\ 2 \\ \hline \end{array}$

Set E | pages 145–150

You can use the Associative Property to group the factors. The product does not change.

Find $4 \times 2 \times 2$.

One Way	Another Way
$4 \times (2 \times 2)$	$(4 \times 2) \times 2$
$4 \times 4 = 16$	$8 \times 2 = 16$

Remember that you can use properties to write unknown facts as known facts.

In **1–3**, find the product. Show how you grouped the factors.

1. $4 \times 5 \times 2 =$ _____ $\times$ _____ $=$ _____

2. $3 \times 7 \times 3 =$ _____ $\times$ _____ $=$ _____

3. $5 \times 5 \times 2 =$ _____ $\times$ _____ $=$ _____

Set F | pages 151–156

Think about these questions to help you use **repeated reasoning**.

Thinking Habits

- Are any calculations repeated?
- Can I generalize from examples?
- What shortcuts do I notice?

Remember that patterns can help you make a generalization.

1. What is repeated in these equations? Use what you see to make a generalization.

$6 \times 6 = (6 \times 3) + (6 \times 3) = 18 + 18 = 36$

$7 \times 6 = (7 \times 3) + (7 \times 3) = 21 + 21 = 42$

$8 \times 6 = (8 \times 3) + (8 \times 3) = 24 + 24 = 48$

2. Solve this equation to test whether your generalization is true.

$10 \times 6 = ?$

_____ $\times$ _____ $= ($ _____ $\times$ _____ $) + ($ _____ $\times$ _____ $)$

$=$ _____ $+$ _____ $=$ _____

1. Krista arranged her buttons in an array. Which shows a way to break Krista's array into two smaller arrays?

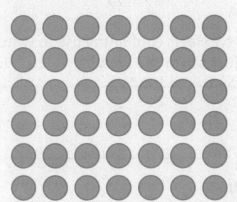

Ⓐ $(3 \times 6) + (3 \times 1)$

Ⓑ $(3 \times 7) + (3 \times 7)$

Ⓒ $(3 \times 6) + (3 \times 6)$

Ⓓ $(3 \times 7) + (4 \times 7)$

2. Choose *Yes* or *No* to tell if 16 is the missing product.

2a. $4 \times 4 = ?$ ○ Yes   ○ No

2b. $2 \times 8 = ?$ ○ Yes   ○ No

2c. $2 \times 4 = ?$ ○ Yes   ○ No

2d. $8 \times 2 = ?$ ○ Yes   ○ No

3. Jeff makes the generalization that a 10s fact can be broken into two 5s facts. Write an equation to test his generalization.

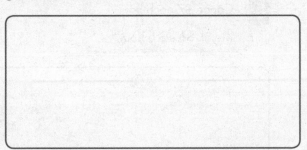

4. June broke up a large array into a 3×4 array and a 5×4 array. What was the large array that June started with?

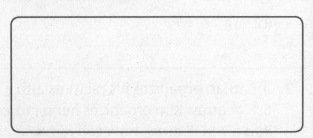

5. Which facts can you use to find 4×8? Choose all that apply.

☐ 2×8 and 2×9

☐ 2×8 and 2×8

☐ 2×4 and 1×8

☐ 4×5 and 4×3

☐ 3×8 and 1×8

6. A bakery uses 3 cups of flour to make each loaf of bread. There are 3 loaves of bread on a tray. There are 6 trays on a cart. How many cups of flour are used to make a full cart of bread? Show your work.

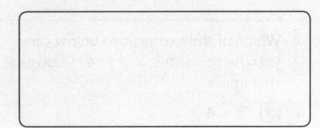

7. What number makes this equation correct?

$(3 \times 4) + (3 \times 4) =$ _____

8. Casey has 3 bags of baseballs. There are 6 baseballs in each bag. How many baseballs does Casey have?

Ⓐ 9

Ⓑ 12

Ⓒ 15

Ⓓ 18

9. Jonathan organizes his pictures into a 6 × 4 array. Kim organizes her pictures into a 7 × 5 array. How can Kim and Jonathan break apart their arrays? Write each pair of facts in the correct space.

6 × 4	7 × 5

5 × 5 and 2 × 5

1 × 4 and 5 × 4

4 × 5 and 3 × 5

1 × 5 and 6 × 5

3 × 4 and 3 × 4

10. Which of the expressions below can you use to solve 3 × 2 × 4? Choose all that apply.

☐ 3 × 4 × 2

☐ 3 × 3 × 3

☐ 4 × 3 × 1

☐ 4 × 2 × 3

☐ 4 × 2 × 4

11. Amy arranged her counters into this array.

Part A

What two facts could Amy use to write an equation for the array?

Part B

If Amy adds one more row of 9 counters to her array, can she still use the facts you wrote in Part A to find the total number? Explain why or why not.

12. Tim's family rented a canoe for 6 hours on Monday and 2 hours on Tuesday. How much did they spend? Show any equations you used.

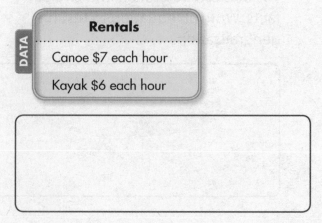

Rentals

Canoe $7 each hour

Kayak $6 each hour

Name _____

School Fair

Kay and Ben are helping to organize the School Fair.
Kay is organizing the school band.
Ben is organizing the bake sale.

The 3 × 7 array at the right shows how chairs
have been set up for the school band.
Use the array to answer Questions 1 and 2.

1. Kay wants to have chairs in a 6 × 7 array.
   Add to the array to show how the new array
   will look.

2. Kay needs a path between two of
   the rows, so she separates the chairs
   into two smaller arrays.

   Part A

   Draw a line to show one way Kay
   can separate the chairs into two
   smaller arrays.

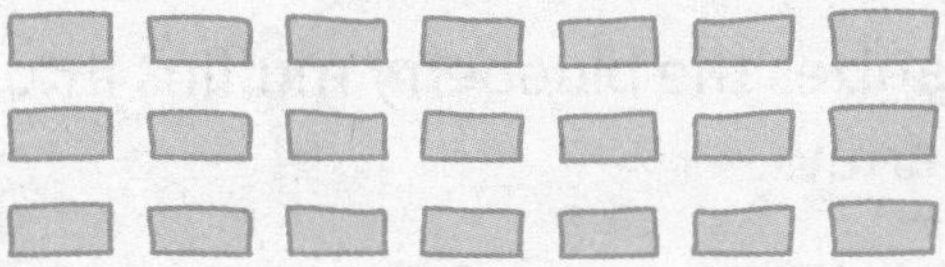

   Part B

   Kay wants to know the number of chairs in each new
   array. Write a multiplication fact for each of the new
   arrays to show how she can find this.

   Part C

   Kay wants to find the total number of chairs that are
   being used. Show how to use the facts in Part B to find
   the total number of chairs.

The **Bake Sale** table shows the baked goods Ben has for sale at the School Fair. Use the **Bake Sale** table to answer Questions 3, 4, and 5.

Bake Sale			
Baked Goods	Number of Trays	Number on Each Tray	Cost per Tray
Blueberry Muffins	4	7	$6
Strawberry Tarts	7	8	$4
Granola Bars	8	6	$3

3. Ben sells 4 trays of granola bars in the morning and 4 trays of granola bars in the afternoon. How much money does this raise? Show your work.

4. Ben organizes the blueberry muffins into a 4 × 7 array.

   Part A

   Ben breaks up the array of blueberry muffins into 2 arrays that look the same. At the right draw the 2 arrays of blueberry muffins.

   Part B

   Ben wants to check the total number of blueberry muffins. He knows 2 × 7 = 14. How can he use this to find the total number of blueberry muffins?

5. 2 friends each bought 3 trays of strawberry tarts. Ben says they spent more than $20 in total. Do you agree? Explain.

Essential Question: How can unknown division facts be found using known multiplication facts?

Digital Resources

Solve · Learn · Glossary · Practice Buddy

Tools · Assessment · Help · Games

To build a better car, people make models or prototypes and then test them.

It takes a lot of testing to make a new car.

Let's see how numbers are used in testing. Here's a project on using tests to review models.

Math and Science Project: Testing Models

Do Research Tests can be done to see if a model works or if a change makes it better. Use the Internet or other sources to find information about a model or prototype that was tested. Identify how the testing was done.

Journal: Write a Report Include what you found. Also in your report:

• Make a chart that includes the model, what changed in the test, and what stayed the same.

• Explain the results of the test.

• Write an equation to show one of the relationships in the test. Explain what the numbers represent.

Name _____

Review What You Know

- division
- equation
- factors
- multiplication

1. _____ are multiplied together to give a product.

2. Use _____ to find how many equal groups or how many are in each group.

3. _____ is an operation that gives the total number when you put together equal groups.

Division

Solve each problem. You can use bar diagrams or counters or draw a picture to help.

4. Stuart has 15 stickers to give to his 3 friends.
   How many stickers can each friend have?

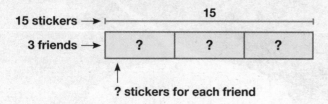

15 stickers → 15
3 friends → | ? | ? | ? |
↑
? stickers for each friend

5. There are 32 muffins. Eight people share them equally.
   How many muffins does each person get?

6. Suzy has 12 granola bars. There are 2 granola bars in each package.
   How many packages of granola bars are there?

Equations

7. Brian has 5 boxes. He puts 8 markers in each box. Which equation shows the total number of markers?

   Ⓐ $5 + 8 = 13$ Ⓑ $5 \times 8 = 40$ Ⓒ $40 \div 5 = 8$ Ⓓ $40 \div 8 = 5$

My Word Cards

Use the examples for each word on the front of the card to help complete the definitions on the back.

fact family

$2 \times 3 = 6$
$3 \times 2 = 6$
$6 \div 2 = 3$
$6 \div 3 = 2$

dividend

$63 \div 9 = 7$
↑
dividend

divisor

$63 \div 9 = 7$
↑
divisor

quotient

$63 \div 9 = 7$
↑
quotient

even number

Even numbers have a 0, 2, 4, 6, or 8 in the ones place.

odd number

Odd numbers have a 1, 3, 5, 7, or 9 in the ones place.

My Word Cards

Complete each definition. Extend learning by writing your own definitions.

The _____ is the number to be divided.

A _____ is a group of related facts using the same numbers.

The _____ is the answer to a division problem.

The number by which another number is divided is called the _____.

A number that is not divisible by 2 is an _____.

A number that is divisible by 2 is an _____.

Name _____

Solve & Share

Use 24 counters to make an array with 3 equal rows. Write a multiplication equation and a division equation to describe the array.

I can ...
use fact families to see how multiplication and division are related.

I can also choose and use a math tool to solve problems.

You can use tools to help you see the relationship between multiplication and division.

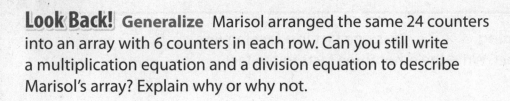

Look Back! **Generalize** Marisol arranged the same 24 counters into an array with 6 counters in each row. Can you still write a multiplication equation and a division equation to describe Marisol's array? Explain why or why not.

A

How Can Multiplication Facts Help You Divide?

This array can show the relationship between multiplication and division.

Multiplication
3 rows of 10 drums
$3 \times 10 = 30$
30 drums

Division
30 drums in 3 equal rows
$30 \div 3 = 10$
10 drums in each row

B A fact family shows how multiplication and division are related.

Fact family for 3, 10, and 30:

$3 \times 10 = 30 \quad 30 \div 3 = 10$

$10 \times 3 = 30 \quad 30 \div 10 = 3$

dividend   divisor   quotient

A fact family is a group of related facts using the same numbers.

C The **dividend** is the number of objects to be divided.

The **divisor** is the number by which another number is divided.

The **quotient** is the answer to a division problem.

Remember, a product is the answer to a multiplication problem.

Convince Me! Reasoning $4 \times 7 = 28$ is one fact in a fact family. Draw an array for this fact. Write the other three facts in the fact family.

☆Guided Practice☆

Do You Understand?

1. Look at the fact family for 3, 10, and 30 on page 170. What do you notice about the products and the dividends?

2. **Generalize** Is 4 × 6 = 24 part of the fact family for 3, 8, and 24? Explain.

Do You Know How?

In **3–5**, complete each fact family.

3. 3 × _____ = 21   7 × _____ = 21

   21 ÷ 3 = _____   21 ÷ 7 = _____

4. 2 × _____ = 18   9 × _____ = 18

   18 ÷ 2 = _____   18 ÷ 9 = _____

5. 2 × _____ = 20   10 × _____ = 20

   20 ÷ 2 = _____   20 ÷ 10 = _____

☆Independent Practice☆

In **6** and **7**, complete each fact family.

6. 2 × _____ = 16
   16 ÷ 2 = _____
   8 × _____ = 16
   16 ÷ 8 = _____

7. 8 × _____ = 56
   56 ÷ 8 = _____
   7 × _____ = 56
   56 ÷ 7 = _____

Some fact families have only 2 facts. The fact family for 2, 2, and 4 has 2 × 2 = 4 and 4 ÷ 2 = 2.

In **8–13**, write the fact family.

8. Write the fact family for 6, 7, and 42.

9. Write the fact family for 9, 10, and 90.

10. Write the fact family for 2, 3, and 6.

11. Write the fact family for 1, 5, and 5.

12. Write the fact family for 3, 8, and 24.

13. Write the fact family for 5, 6, and 30.

Problem Solving

14. Write a multiplication equation and division equation for the array.

$4 \times$ ____ $= 20$

$20 \div$ ____ $= 5$

15. Make Sense and Persevere How many inches shorter is the red fabric than the green and yellow fabrics combined?

Sophia's Fabrics	
Color	Length in Inches
Red	72
Blue	18
Green	36
Yellow	54

16. Higher Order Thinking Anya says that with 24 counters she can make only 6 possible arrays. Todd says he can make 8 arrays. Who is correct? Explain.

17. Algebra Carla picked 9 apples a day for three days. Which number tells you how many apples she picked in three days and makes this equation true?

▢ $\div 3 = 9$

18. **A-Z** **Vocabulary** Can you write a *fact family* for 3, 5, and 7? Explain.

19. Use Structure Lisa, Bret, and Gary harvested apples. Lisa filled 3 carts with apples. Bret also filled 3 carts with apples. Gary filled another 3 carts with apples. Write a multiplication equation and a division equation for this story.

 Assessment

20. Nick made an array that has 10 counters. Draw 4 arrays that he might have made.

Name _____

Another Look!

Multiplication

6 rows of 4 glue sticks

$6 \times 4 = 24$

24 glue sticks

Division

24 glue sticks in 6 equal rows

$24 \div 6 = 4$

4 glue sticks in each row

Look for relationships. Multiplication facts can help you learn division facts!

Here is the fact family for 4, 6, and 24:

$4 \times 6 = 24$ $24 \div 4 = 6$

$6 \times 4 = 24$ $24 \div 6 = 4$

In **1** and **2**, complete each fact family.

1. $2 \times$ ____ $= 14$ $7 \times$ ____ $= 14$

$14 \div 2 =$ ____ $14 \div 7 =$ ____

2. $9 \times$ ____ $= 81$

$81 \div 9 =$ ____

In **3** and **4**, write the fact family.

3. Write the fact family for 4, 7, and 28.

4. Write the fact family for 2, 10, and 20.

5. Model with Math Use the array to write a multiplication equation and a division equation.

6. Higher Order Thinking For every row of objects in an array there are 2 columns. The total number of objects in the array is 18. How many rows and columns does the array have?

---

7. Math and Science Julio's class was making bridges out of balsa wood to see which bridge could hold the most weight. Each person in Julio's group made 2 bridges. What fact family represents the total bridges made by the group?

Name	Bridges Made
Julio	2
Rosa	2
Miguel	2
Clara	2

---

8. Reasoning There are 5 pairs of scissors in one package. Mrs. Hill bought 35 scissors for students in her art classes. How many packages did she buy?

9. Serena has a set of toy trains. She has 3 passenger cars. What is the total length of her passenger cars?

Serena's Train Cars	
Type	**Length in Inches**
Engine	4
Tender	3
Passenger Car	9
Caboose	7

✓ **Assessment**

10. Esther has 15 dimes. She wants to put them in stacks that are the same height. She has already made one stack. Draw the rest of the stacks to show all of Esther's dimes.

Esther has _____ stacks of _____ dimes.

Name _____

Solve & Share

Kara puts 30 toys into 5 party bags. She puts the same number of toys into each bag. How many toys are in each bag? *Solve this problem any way you choose.*

I can ...
divide by 2, 3, 4, and 5 by thinking about how I multiply with those numbers.

I can also look for patterns to solve problems.

You can use structure. How can a fact family that uses 30 and 5 help you solve the problem?

$$30 - 5 = 25 \cdot 1 \quad 5 - 5 = 0 \cdot 6$$
$$25 - 5 = 20 \cdot 2$$
$$20 - 5 = 15 \cdot 3$$
$$15 - 5 = 10 \cdot 4$$
$$10 - 5 = 5 \cdot 5$$

product

Look Back! **Reasoning** Show two pictures you might draw to represent 30 ÷ 5.

Essential Question: **What Multiplication Fact Can You Use?**

A

Dee has 14 noisemakers. She puts the same number on each of 2 tables. How many noisemakers are on each table?

Find 14 ÷ 2.

What You Think	What You Write
2 times what number is 14? $2 \times 7 = 14$	$14 \div 2 = 7$ 7 noisemakers are on each table.

B

Dee has 40 stickers. If she puts 5 stickers on each bag, how many bags can Dee decorate?

Find 40 ÷ 5.

What You Think	What You Write
What number times 5 is 40? $8 \times 5 = 40$	$40 \div 5 = 8$ Dee can decorate 8 bags.

You can use multiplication to help divide.

C

Dee wants to put 15 cups in 3 equal stacks on the table. How many cups will Dee put in each stack?

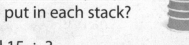

Find 15 ÷ 3.

What You Think	What You Write
3 times what number is 15? $3 \times 5 = 15$	$15 \div 3 = 5$ Dee will put 5 cups in each stack.

Multiplication and division facts form relationships.

Convince Me! **Construct Arguments** How can you use multiplication to help solve 20 ÷ 4? Write the related multiplication fact you use to help solve the problem.

$1 \times 4 = 4$
$2 \times 4 = 8$
$3 \times 4 = 12$
$4 \times 4 = 16$
$5 \times 4 = 20$

Another Example!

Here are two ways to write a division problem.

$$24 \div 4 = 6$$

dividend   divisor   quotient

divisor → 4)24

6 ← quotient
← dividend

☆ Guided Practice*

Do You Understand?

1. How can $5 \times 3 = 15$ help you divide 15 by 3?

2. **Reasoning** Dena has 3 children. She buys 30 pencils to share equally among her children for the school year. How many pencils will each of her children get? Write the answer and the fact family you used.

 10

Do You Know How?

In **3** and **4**, complete each fact family.

3. $3 \times 6 = 18$ _____

   $18 \div 3 = 6$ _____

4. $9 \times 4 = 36$ _____

   $36 \div 4 = 9$ _____

In **5–8**, find each quotient.

5. $36 \div 4 =$ _____

6. $15 \div 5 =$ 3

7. 2)18

8. 5)50 10

☆ Independent Practice ☆

In **9–20**, find each quotient.

9. $12 \div 2 =$ _____

10. $12 \div 3 =$ 4

11. $16 \div 4 =$ _____

12. $35 \div 5 =$ 7

13. $14 \div 2 =$ _____

14. $20 \div 4 =$ 5

15. $24 \div 4 =$ _____

16. $45 \div 5 =$ 9

17. 3)27 10

18. 4)40

19. 5)40

20. 3)21 7

Problem Solving

In **21** and **22**, use the rectangle at the right.

21. Reasoning How many individual squares are inside the rectangle? Write a division equation in which the quotient represents the number of rows.

22. Make Sense and Persevere If Anna arranges the squares into an array with 2 columns, how many rows will there be?

23. Number Sense Joey says, "I can't solve 8 ÷ 2 by using the fact 2 × 8 = 16." Do you agree or disagree? Explain.

24. Miko and Bob want to buy a tablet that is on sale for $99. Miko has $45 and Bob has $52. Do they have enough to buy the tablet? If not, how much more do they need?

25. A-Z Vocabulary Write a division equation. Tell which is the *quotient*, the *dividend*, and the *divisor*.

26. Higher Order Thinking Chris gives 18 pretzels equally to 3 friends. Martha gives 20 pretzels equally to 4 friends. Whose friends got more pretzels? Use equations to justify your answer.

✓ Assessment

27. Which expression can help you divide 12 ÷ 3?

- Ⓐ 2 × 3
- Ⓑ 3 × 3
- Ⓒ 4 × 3
- Ⓓ 5 × 3

28. Mike bought 28 marbles in bags that hold 4 marbles each. How many bags did he buy?

- Ⓐ 7 bags
- Ⓑ 5 bags
- Ⓒ 4 bags
- Ⓓ 3 bags

Name _____

Homework & Practice 4-2

Use Multiplication to Divide with 2, 3, 4, and 5

Another Look!

You can think multiplication to find division facts.

Example 1

Darren and Molly have 16 sheets of paper to share. Each will get the same number of sheets of paper. How many sheets will Darren and Molly each get?

Find 16 ÷ 2.

What You Think	What You Write
2 times what number equals 16? $2 \times 8 = 16$	$16 \div 2 = 8$ Darren and Molly will each get 8 sheets of paper.

Example 2

Peter has 24 pennies. He puts the pennies into 4 equal rows. How many pennies are in each row?

Find 24 ÷ 4.

What You Think	What You Write
4 times what number equals 24? $4 \times 6 = 24$	$24 \div 4 = 6$ Peter has 6 pennies in each row.

In **1–16**, find each quotient.

1. 14 ÷ 2 = _____

2. 35 ÷ 5 = _____

3. 15 ÷ 3 = _____

4. 32 ÷ 4 = _____

5. 9 ÷ 3 = _____

6. 18 ÷ 2 = _____

7. 16 ÷ 2 = _____

8. 21 ÷ 3 = _____

9. 2)$\overline{12}$

10. 3)$\overline{27}$

11. 5)$\overline{25}$

12. 4)$\overline{20}$

13. 5)$\overline{30}$

14. 5)$\overline{45}$

15. 2)$\overline{10}$

16. 4)$\overline{28}$

17. Be Precise You have 18 erasers and use 3 erasers each month. How many months will your erasers last? Identify the quotient, dividend, and divisor.

18. Use Structure Write a fact family using the numbers 5, 6, and 30.

19. Paul drew two different polygons. One shape has 4 sides. The other shape has fewer than 4 sides. What could be the two shapes Paul drew?

20. Model with Math Megan arranges 25 chairs into 5 equal rows. Write and solve an equation to find how many chairs are in each row.

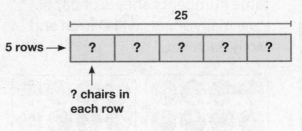

21. Higher Order Thinking Carl has 16 rubber balls to share with his 2 brothers and 1 sister. If Carl and his brothers and sister each get the same number of rubber balls, how many rubber balls will each of them get?

Think about what you know and what you need to find.

✓ **Assessment**

22. Franklin says that if he divides 40 by 5, he will get 8. Jeff says that 40 divided by 5 is 9. Who is correct?

Ⓐ Franklin is correct.

Ⓑ Jeff is correct.

Ⓒ Both are correct.

Ⓓ Neither is correct.

23. 16 divided by what number is 4?

Ⓐ 2

Ⓑ 4

Ⓒ 8

Ⓓ 12

Name _____

Solve & Share

There are 18 children in a ballet class. They are standing in rows of 6 for a dance recital. How many rows of children are there? *Solve the problem any way you choose.*

I can ...
divide by 6 and 7 by thinking about how I multiply with those numbers.

I can also reason about math.

$6 + 12 = 18$
$6 + 6 = 12$

3

You can use reasoning. How are the numbers in this problem related?

Look Back! **Model with Math** Draw a bar diagram to represent the problem.

Essential Question How Do You Divide with 6 and 7?

A

There are 48 dogs entered in a dog show. The judge wants 6 dogs in each group. How many groups will there be?

You can divide to find how many groups of dogs there will be.

B Find 48 ÷ 6.

What You Think	What You Write
What number times 6 is 48? $8 \times 6 = 48$	$48 \div 6 = 8$ There will be 8 groups.

Use a multiplication problem to make sense of a division problem.

C Another dog was entered in the show. There will now be 7 dogs in each group. How many groups will there be?

Find 49 ÷ 7.

What You Think	What You Write
What number times 7 is 49? $7 \times 7 = 49$	$49 \div 7 = 7$ There will be 7 groups.

Convince Me! **Model with Math** Draw a bar diagram using the numbers 36, 6, and 6. Write the division fact and the related multiplication fact that your bar diagram shows.

$$36 \div 6 = 6$$
$$6 \times 6 = 36$$

Name _____

☆Guided Practice☆

Do You Understand?

1. Reasoning How can you tell without dividing that $42 \div 6$ will be greater than $42 \div 7$?

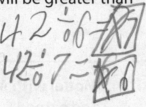

2. How can $8 \times 6 = 48$ help you divide 48 by 6?

Do You Know How?

In **3–8**, write the related multiplication fact, and then find each quotient.

3. $36 \div 6 = \underline{6}$

4. $42 \div 6 = \underline{}$

5. $42 \div 7 = \underline{6}$

6. $18 \div 6 = \underline{}$

7. $6\overline{)24}$ _(4)_

8. $6\overline{)30}$

☆Independent Practice☆

Leveled Practice In **9–20**, use related multiplication and division facts to find the quotient.

9. $12 \div 6 = ?$
What number times 6 is 12?
$6 \times \boxed{2} = 12$
$12 \div 6 = \boxed{2}$

10. $21 \div 3 = ?$
What number times 3 is 21?
$3 \times \boxed{} = 21$
$21 \div 3 = \boxed{}$

11. $30 \div 6 = ?$
What number times 6 is 30?
$6 \times \boxed{5} = 30$
$30 \div 6 = \boxed{5}$

12. $2\overline{)14}$

13. $7\overline{)49}$ _(7)_

14. $6\overline{)60}$

15. $6\overline{)54}$ _(9)_

16. $6\overline{)6}$

17. $7\overline{)28}$ _(4)_

18. Find 49 divided by 7.

19. Divide 54 by 6.

20. Find 35 divided by 7.

_(9)_

Problem Solving

21. A pizza parlor made 88 deep-dish pizzas. It made 10 more thin-crust pizzas than deep-dish pizzas. How many thin-crust pizzas did the parlor make?

98

22. **Higher Order Thinking** There are 35 new tires. Each truck will get 6 tires plus 1 tire for a spare. How many trucks will get new tires?

23. **Make Sense and Persevere** Explain the mistake in the fact family below. Give the correct fact.

$$4 \times 7 = 28 \qquad 7 \times 4 = 28$$
$$7 \div 4 = 28 \qquad 28 \div 7 = 4$$

$28 \div 4 = 7$

24. **Model with Math** Gloria mowed 7 lawns and earned $56. She was paid the same amount for each lawn. How much money did Gloria earn for mowing each lawn? Write an equation to represent this problem.

✓ Assessment

1 package of 7 red beads

1 package of 6 green beads

1 package of 5 gold beads

25. Andy bought 35 beads. He bought only one color of beads. Which shows the beads he could have bought? Choose all that apply.

- ☐ 5 packages of red beads
- ☐ 6 packages of green beads
- ☑ 7 packages of gold beads
- ☑ 7 packages of red beads
- ☑ 7 packages of green beads

26. Cassidy buys only green beads to make a necklace. She buys the exact number of beads that she needs. Which of the following bead amounts could she have bought? Choose all that apply.

- ☐ 46 beads
- ☐ 36 beads
- ☐ 26 beads
- ☐ 24 beads
- ☐ 16 beads

Name _____

Another Look!

Martha has 63 pine trees to plant on a plot of land. The owner wants 7 rows of trees. How many trees should Martha plant in each row?

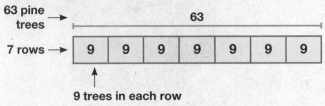

63 pine trees → 63

7 rows → 9 9 9 9 9 9 9

↑ 9 trees in each row

Find 63 ÷ 7.

You can divide to find how many trees in each row.

What You Think	What You Write
What number times 7 is 63?	$63 \div 7 = 9$
$9 \times 7 = 63$	There will be 9 trees in each row.

In **1** and **2**, draw a bar diagram to find the quotient.

1. Find 56 ÷ 7.

2. Find 36 ÷ 6.

In **3–13**, find the quotient.

3. 30 ÷ 6 = _____

4. 28 ÷ 7 = _____

5. 42 ÷ 6 = _____

6. 54 ÷ 6 = _____

7. 6)48

8. 7)56

9. 7)70

10. 7)49

11. Divide 60 by 6.

12. Divide 7 by 7.

13. Find 21 divided by 7.

14. Willa is building birdhouses. Each side of the birdhouse will need 9 nails. How many nails does Willa need for each birdhouse?

15. Number Sense If Willa uses only 7 nails on each side, how will the total number of nails she uses change?

There are 7 sides on the birdhouse.

16. Model with Math 24 students are going to the zoo. They are going in 4 equal groups. Write and solve an equation to find how many students are in each group.

24

4 groups → | ? | ? | ? | ? |

↑
? students in each group

17. Higher Order Thinking There are 42 roses in the garden. Diane picks 7 roses for each bouquet of flowers. How many bouquets can she make? How many more bouquets can Diane make if she uses 6 roses in each bouquet?

✔ **Assessment**

18. Juanita read 48 pages. All chapters are the same length. Choose all the possible pages Juanita could have read.

☐ 6 chapters with 6 pages in each chapter

☐ 6 chapters with 8 pages in each chapter

☐ 8 chapters with 6 pages in each chapter

☐ 8 chapters with 8 pages in each chapter

☐ 8 chapters with 9 pages in each chapter

19. Manny has 28 chapters in a book to read. He reads 7 chapters each week. Choose all of the facts that can help you find how long it will take Manny to read the book.

☐ $28 + 7 = 35$

☐ $4 \times 7 = 28$

☐ $2 \times 2 = 4$

☐ $28 \div 7 = 4$

☐ $7 \times 4 = 28$

Name _____

★ ☆ ★
Solve & Share

An art teacher has 72 crayons. The crayons came in boxes with 8 crayons in each box. How many boxes of crayons were there? *Solve this problem any way you choose.*

I can ...
divide by 8 and 9 by thinking about how I multiply with those numbers.

I can also reason about math.

You can use reasoning. Which fact family uses the numbers 72 and 8 and could help you solve the problem?

$816 - 8 = 8$
$98 - 8 = 0$

$72 - 8 = 64\ 9$
$64 - 8 = 56\ 2$
$56 - 8 = 48\ 3$
$48 - 8 = 40\ 4$
$40 - 8\ 32\ 5$
$32 = 8 = 24\ 6$
$24 - 8 = 16\ 7$

9 boxes

Look Back! **Model with Math** Draw a picture you could use to help solve the problem above.

What Multiplication Fact Can You Use?

A

John has 56 straws. He needs 8 straws to make a spider. How many spiders can John make? Find 56 ÷ 8.

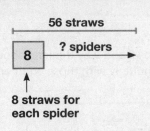

56 straws

| 8 | ? spiders → |

8 straws for each spider

7 × 8 = 56

John can make 7 spiders.

What number times 8 is 56?

To make each spider, you need 8 straws.

B

Luz made 9 animals. She used 54 straws. She used the same number of straws for each animal. How many straws did Luz use for each animal?

Find 54 ÷ 9.

You can divide to find the number of straws Luz used for each animal.

54 straws

| ? | ? | ? | ? | ? | ? | ? | ? | ? |

? straws for one animal

What You Think	What You Write
9 times what number is 54?	54 ÷ 9 = 6
9 × 6 = 54	Luz used 6 straws for each animal.

Convince Me! **Look for Relationships** Write the related multiplication fact that can be used to complete each division fact.

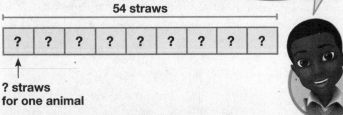

Division Fact	Related Multiplication Fact
72 ÷ 8 = 9	8 × 9 = 72
48 ÷ 8 = 6	8 × 6 = 48
63 ÷ 9 = 7	9 × 7 = 63

Name _____

☆ Guided Practice ☆

Do You Understand?

1. What multiplication fact can you use to find $18 \div 9$?

2. **Construct Arguments** Carla and Jeff each use 72 straws. Carla makes animals with 9 legs. Jeff makes animals with 8 legs. Who makes more animals? Explain.

Do You Know How?

In **3** and **4**, use the multiplication equation to help find each quotient.

3. $16 \div 8 = ?$
What number times 8 is 16?
____ $\times 8 = 16$
So $16 \div 8 =$ ____.

4. $64 \div 8 = ?$
What number times 8 is 64?
__8__ $\times 8 = 64$
So $64 \div 8 =$ _8_.

☆ Independent Practice ☆

Leveled Practice In **5–7**, use the multiplication equation to help find each quotient.

5. $24 \div 8 = ?$
What number times 8 is 24?
____ $\times 8 = 24$
$24 \div 8 =$ ____

6. $45 \div 9 = ?$
What number times 9 is 45?
____ $\times 9 = 45$
$45 \div 9 =$ ____

7. $27 \div 9 = ?$
What number times 9 is 27?
____ $\times 9 = 27$
$27 \div 9 =$ ____

In **8–16**, find each quotient.

8. $48 \div 8 =$ _6_

9. $72 \div 9 =$ ____

10. $8 \div 8 =$ ____

11. $54 \div 9 =$ ____

12. $72 \div 8 =$ _9_

13. $90 \div 9 =$ ____

14. $8\overline{)80}$

15. $8\overline{)32}$

16. $9\overline{)9}$

Problem Solving

17. Model with Math Callie biked 27 miles on Saturday. She biked 9 miles every hour. How many hours did Callie bike? Draw a picture to represent the problem.

18. Math and Science 8 friends decide to test how far 40 paper airplanes with different shapes will fly. If each friend tests the same number of airplanes, how many airplanes does each friend test?

19. Reasoning What other equations are in the same fact family as $18 \div 9 = 2$?

20. Higher Order Thinking Jeremy had 30 gummy bears. He ate 6, then gave the rest to 8 friends. Each friend got the same number of gummy bears. How many did each friend get?

3

21. What is the value of the 1 in 491? What is the value of the 4? What is the value of the 9?

22. Christopher started with $52. He buys 4 snacks that are $3 each. How much money does Christopher have left?

✓ Assessment

23. Mr. Stern spends $36 on tickets. He buys only one type of ticket.

Playhouse Ticket Prices

Type of Ticket	Price of Ticket
Child	$4
Youth	$8
Adult	$9

Part A

Which types of ticket could he be buying?

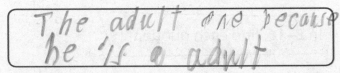

The adult one because he 'is a adult

Part B

Which type of ticket could Mr. Stern **NOT** be buying? Explain why not.

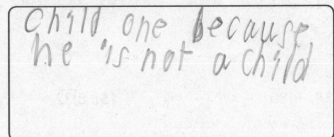

Child one because he 'is not a child

Name _____

Another Look!

Multiplication facts can help you to find division facts when 8 or 9 is the divisor.

There are 32 counters. There are 8 rows of counters. How many counters are in each row?

Think about multiplication facts you know.

Find 32 ÷ 8.

What You Think	What You Write
8 times what number equals 32? 8 × 4 = 32	32 ÷ 8 = 4 There are 4 counters in each row.

There are 45 counters. There are 9 equal groups. How many counters are in each group?

Find 45 ÷ 9.

What You Think	What You Write
9 times what number equals 45? 9 × 5 = 45	45 ÷ 9 = 5 There are 5 counters in each group.

In **1–3**, use the multiplication equation to help find each quotient.

1. 54 ÷ 9 = ?

9 × ____ = 54

So, 54 ÷ 9 = ____.

2. 24 ÷ 8 = ?

8 × ____ = 24

So, 24 ÷ 8 = ____.

3. 56 ÷ 8 = ?

8 × ____ = 56

So, 56 ÷ 8 = ____.

In **4–12**, find each quotient.

4. 36 ÷ 9 = ____

5. 63 ÷ 9 = ____

6. 80 ÷ 8 = ____

7. 9)‾72‾

8. 8)‾48‾

9. 9)‾81‾

10. 8)‾8‾

11. 9)‾90‾

12. 9)‾27‾

13. Reasoning Maluwa has 9 identical tiles. When she counts the total number of sides on the tiles, she gets 72. Draw a picture of what her tile could look like, and name that shape.

14. Each month Bailey deposits money in her savings account. Over 8 months, she has added $48. If Bailey deposited the same amount every month, how much is one deposit?

15. Construct Arguments The table at the right shows prices for matinee and evening movies. With $63, would you be able to buy more matinee tickets or evening tickets? Explain.

Movie Prices	
Matinee	$7
Evening Movie	$9

DATA

16. Model with Math Teri scored 64 points in the first 8 basketball games she played in. She scored the same number of points in each game. Write and solve an equation to find the number of points Teri scored in each game.

17. Higher Order Thinking Adam made 19 paper cranes on Monday and 8 more on Tuesday. He gave all the cranes away to 9 friends so that all the friends had an equal number of cranes. How many cranes did each friend receive? Explain your answer.

 Assessment

18. Andy earns money washing cars on Monday and Tuesday. He earns $8 for each car that he washes.

Part A

On Monday, Andy earned $40. How can you figure out how many cars Andy washed that day?

Part B

On Tuesday, Andy earned $56. Did he wash more cars on Monday than on Tuesday? Explain how you know without computing.

Name _____

Solve

☆ ☆
Solve & Share

Prizes for a school fair are packaged with 2 prizes in each package. Which of the prizes listed below can be packaged with none left over? Tell how you decided.

Prize Type	cars	hats	balls	boats	books
Number of Prizes	6	15	23	18	36

I can ...
find and explain patterns for even and odd numbers.

I can also reason about math.

You can reason. Think about numbers that can be separated into two equal groups.

Look Back! **Look for Relationships** What do you notice about the numbers for the prizes that can be packaged in 2s with none left over? What do you notice about the numbers for the other prizes?

How Can You Explain Multiplication Patterns for Even and Odd Numbers?

A

Nita says that the product of an even number and an odd number is always even. Is she correct?

Even numbers have 0, 2, 4, 6, or 8 in the ones place.

Even numbers are whole numbers that can be divided by 2 with none left over.

Odd numbers are whole numbers that cannot be divided by 2 with none left over.

1	2	3	4	5	6	7	8	9	10
11	12	13	14	15	16	17	18	19	20
21	22	23	24	25	26	27	28	29	30
31	32	33	34	35	36	37	38	39	40

B Even numbers greater than 0 can be shown as two equal groups.

Think about 2×3 and 2×5.

2 is an even number.

2×3 means 2 equal groups of 3. $2 \times 3 = 6$

2×5 means 2 equal groups of 5. $2 \times 5 = 10$

There are always 2 equal groups, so the product of 2 times any number is even.

C You can **generalize**.

All even numbers are multiples of 2.

Think about 4×3.

You can think of 4 as 2 groups of 2.

Using properties you can write
$4 \times 3 = (2 \times 2) \times 3$ as
$4 \times 3 = 2 \times (2 \times 3)$.

So, $4 \times 3 = 2 \times 6$.

There are 2 equal groups of 6. So, the product will be even.

You can write any even number as 2 equal groups. So, Nita is correct: even $\times$ odd = even.

Convince Me! Generalize Does multiplying by 8 also always result in an even product? Explain.

Another Example!

An odd number cannot be divided by 2 with none left over.

Think about 3×5.
3 cannot be divided by 2 with none left over.
5 cannot be divided by 2 with none left over.

$3 \times 5 = 15$

15 is odd.

Both factors are odd. Odd numbers cannot be divided into 2 equal groups with none left over. So: odd $\times$ odd = odd.

✩ Guided Practice*

Do You Understand?

1. **Reasoning** If you multiply two even numbers, will the product be even or odd? Explain with an example.

Do You Know How?

Write or circle to complete the sentences. Explain whether the product is even or odd. Then solve.

2. $4 \times 6 = ?$

Can 4 be divided by 2? _____

Can 6 be divided by 2? _____

So 4×6 is   even / odd .

$4 \times 6 =$ _____

Independent Practice ✩

In **3–5** circle the factors that can be divided by 2.
Then write *even* or *odd* to describe the product and solve the equation.

3. $9 \times 5 = ?$

   9×5 is _____.

   $9 \times 5 =$ _____

4. $8 \times 7 = ?$

   8×7 is _____.

   $8 \times 7 =$ _____

5. $4 \times 8 = ?$

   4×8 is _____.

   $4 \times 8 =$ _____

*For another example, see Set E on page 227.   **Topic 4** | Lesson 4-5   195

Problem Solving

In **6–8**, use the table at the right. Look at the factors. Write *even* or *odd* to describe the product. Then solve.

Distances Bicycled Per Day

Cyclist	Miles Bicycled per Day
Riaz	5
Caitlin	6
Joseph	3
Maria	4

6. How many miles did Joseph bicycle in 6 days?

The product is _____.

7. How many miles did Caitlin bicycle in 8 days?

The product is _____.

8. Make Sense and Persevere
How many miles did Maria and Riaz bicycle in 3 days?

The total is _____.

9. Critique Reasoning Ryan says that the following patterns are true:
even $\times$ odd = even
odd $\times$ even = odd

Is he correct? Explain.

10. Draw a shape with an odd number of sides. Then write the name of the shape.

11. Higher Order Thinking The bakery has 84 muffins. Ms. Craig buys 5 packs of 6 muffins. Did Ms. Craig purchase an even number of muffins or an odd number of muffins? Is the number of muffins left over even or odd? Explain your answer.

✓ Assessment

12. Choose all of the equations with even products.

☐ $7 \times 9 = ?$ ☐ $1 \times 6 = ?$
☐ $9 \times 2 = ?$ ☐ $7 \times 5 = ?$
☐ $5 \times 3 = ?$

13. Choose all of the equations that do **NOT** have even products.

☐ $5 \times 1 = ?$ ☐ $8 \times 8 = ?$
☐ $2 \times 7 = ?$ ☐ $6 \times 4 = ?$
☐ $3 \times 9 = ?$

Name _____

Another Look!

Even numbers have 0, 2, 4, 6, or 8 in the ones place. Odd numbers have 1, 3, 5, 7, or 9 in the ones place.

Think about the numbers 0, 2, 4, 6, and 8. When you divide these numbers by 2, nothing is left over.
These numbers are even.

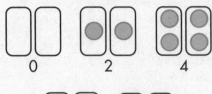

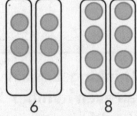

All even numbers can be shown as two equal groups. When multiplying, if one factor is even, the product will be even.

$4 \times 5 = (2 \times 2) \times 5$
$4 \times 5 = 2 \times (2 \times 5)$.

So, $4 \times 5 = 2 \times 10$.
The product is 2 equal groups of 10.

Think about the numbers 1, 3, 5, 7, and 9. When you divide these numbers by 2, there is 1 left over.
These numbers are odd.

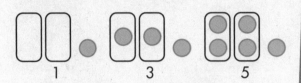

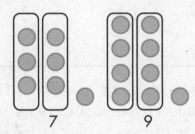

You cannot think of odd numbers as 2 equal groups with none left over. When multiplying, if both factors are odd, the product will be odd.

$7 \times 5 = 35$
$1 \times 9 = 9$

In **1–4**, circle the digit in the ones place. Then write *even* or *odd*.

1. 36 is _____.

2. 18 is _____.

3. 83 is _____.

4. 40 is _____.

In **5–7**, circle the factors that can be divided by 2.
Then write *even* or *odd* to describe the product and solve.

5. $7 \times 4 = ?$

7×4 is _____.

$7 \times 4 = 28$

6. $6 \times 6 = ?$

6×6 is _____.

$6 \times 6 = 36$

7. $5 \times 9 = ?$

5×9 is _____.

$5 \times 9 = 45$

8. Ted bought 1 box of whistles, 1 box of streamers, and 1 box of stickers. How many party favors did he buy in all? Show your work.

Party Favors	
Item	**Number per Box**
Whistles	12
Hats	24
Streamers	48
Stickers	36

9. Critique Reasoning Don says that 9×9 is even. Is he correct? Explain.

10. Generalize Explain why the product of 2 times any number is an even number.

11. Model with Math Sandra has 18 bags of peanuts to hand out to 9 friends. How many bags can she give each friend? Draw a bar diagram to help you solve.

12. Higher Order Thinking Explain whether the product of an **even number × odd number × odd number** is even or odd.

✓ **Assessment**

13. Choose all of the equations with odd products.

☐ $7 \times 3 = ?$
☐ $6 \times 2 = ?$
☐ $1 \times 3 = ?$
☐ $5 \times 7 = ?$
☐ $9 \times 6 = ?$

14. Choose all of the equations with products that are **NOT** odd.

☐ $1 \times 3 = ?$
☐ $3 \times 5 = ?$
☐ $7 \times 1 = ?$
☐ $8 \times 2 = ?$
☐ $6 \times 6 = ?$

Name _____

☆ ☆
Solve & Share

Find 5 ÷ 1, 0 ÷ 5, and 5 ÷ 5. Explain how you found each quotient. You can use counters to help.

I can ...
understand the patterns of division with 0 and 1.

I can also look for patterns to solve problems.

Look for relationships. Think about the relationship between division and multiplication. *Show your work in the space below!*

Look Back! **Use Structure** Use your understanding of multiplying by 0 to find 0 ÷ 7, 0 ÷ 4, and 0 ÷ 10. Describe the patterns you see.

Essential Question **How Do You Divide with 1 or 0?**

A

Neil has 3 goldfish. He puts 1 goldfish in each bowl. How many bowls did Neil use? Find 3 ÷ 1.

Any number divided by 1 is itself.

What number times 1 is 3?

$3 \times 1 = 3$
So, $3 \div 1 = 3$.

Neil used 3 bowls.

3 put into groups of 1

B **1 as a Quotient**

Find $3 \div 3$.

3 times what number equals 3?

$3 \times 1 = 3$

So, $3 \div 3 = 1$.

Rule: Any number (except 0) divided by itself is 1.

C **Dividing 0 by a Number**

Find $0 \div 3$.

3 times what number equals 0?

$3 \times 0 = 0$

So, $0 \div 3 = 0$.

Rule: 0 divided by any number (except 0) is 0.

D **Dividing by 0**

Find $3 \div 0$.

0 times what number equals 3?

There is no such number. So, $3 \div 0$ can't be done.

Rule: You cannot divide any number by 0.

Convince Me! **Be Precise** Sue wrote 9 invitations. She put 1 invitation in each mailbox on her street. How many mailboxes got invitations? Which equation shows the problem and the solution? Explain your thinking.

$0 \div 9 = 0$ $9 \div 1 = 9$

Name _____

☆ Guided Practice *

Do You Understand?

1. How can you tell, without dividing, that $375 \div 375 = 1$?

2. Describe how you can find $0 \div 1$.

Do You Know How?

In **3** and **4**, solve the multiplication equation to find each quotient.

3. Find $8 \div 8$.

$8 \times \underline{\quad} = 8$

So, $8 \div 8 = \underline{\quad}$.

4. Find $0 \div 9$.

$9 \times \underline{\quad} = 0$

So, $0 \div 9 = \underline{\quad}$.

Remember, you cannot divide any number by 0.

Independent Practice ☆

Leveled Practice In **5–7**, solve the multiplication equation to find each quotient.

5. Find $0 \div 7$.

$7 \times \underline{\quad} = 0$

So, $0 \div 7 = \underline{\quad}$.

6. Find $4 \div 4$.

$4 \times \underline{\quad} = 4$

So, $4 \div 4 = \underline{\quad}$.

7. Find $6 \div 1$.

$1 \times \underline{\quad} = 6$

So, $6 \div 1 = \underline{\quad}$.

In **8–18**, find each quotient.

8. $3 \div 3 = \underline{\quad}$

9. $0 \div 8 = \underline{\quad}$

10. $5 \div 5 = \underline{\quad}$

11. $7 \div 1 = \underline{\quad}$

12. $6\overline{)6}$

13. $1\overline{)5}$

14. $25\overline{)25}$

15. $1\overline{)13}$

16. Find 0 divided by 8.

17. Find 9 divided by 1.

18. Find 10 divided by 10.

Problem Solving

In **19–22**, use the picture at the right.

19. Reasoning Addie hiked 3 different trails for a total distance of 11 miles. Which trails did she hike?

20. Construct Arguments Marty hikes one of the trails 4 times. In all, he hikes more than 10 miles but less than 16 miles. Which trail does he hike? Explain your answer.

21. Reasoning Four teams are tidying the Green trail. They will each tidy an equal distance. How many miles does each team tidy?

22. Fiona hiked on Wednesday and Sunday. Each day she hiked all of the trails. How many miles did Fiona hike?

23. Anthony divided 0 by 6. Jessica used a different equation with even numbers, but got the same answer. What could be an equation Jessica used?

24. Higher Order Thinking Yvonne says that 0 ÷ 21 and 21 ÷ 0 both have a quotient of 0. Is Yvonne correct? Explain.

✔ Assessment

25. Bella had 12 crayons. She used one crayon for each picture she drew. How many pictures did Bella draw? Write the equation that shows the problem and the solution.

26. A group shares 9 stickers equally among 9 friends. Write an equation and solve to show the number of stickers each friend receives.

Name _____

Help   Practice   Tools   Games
       Buddy

Another Look!

There are special rules to follow when dividing with 0 or 1.

Rule	Example	What You Think	What You Write
When any number is divided by 1, the quotient is that number.	$7 \div 1 = ?$	1 times what number is 7? $1 \times 7 = 7$ So, $7 \div 1 = 7$.	$7 \div 1 = 7$ or $1\overline{)7}$ with quotient 7
When any number (except 0) is divided by itself, the quotient is 1.	$8 \div 8 = ?$	8 times what number is 8? $8 \times 1 = 8$ So, $8 \div 8 = 1$.	$8 \div 8 = 1$ or $8\overline{)8}$ with quotient 1
When zero is divided by a number (except 0), the quotient is 0.	$0 \div 5 = ?$	5 times what number is 0? $5 \times 0 = 0$ So, $0 \div 5 = 0$.	$0 \div 5 = 0$ or $5\overline{)0}$ with quotient 0
You cannot divide a number by 0.	$9 \div 0 = ?$	0 times what number is 9? There is no number that works, so $9 \div 0$ cannot be done.	$9 \div 0$ cannot be done

In **1–8**, write the quotient.

1. $5 \div 1 =$ _____   **2.** $9 \div 9 =$ _____   **3.** $0 \div 8 =$ _____   **4.** $6 \div 6 =$ _____

5. $4 \div 1 =$ _____   **6.** $1\overline{)7}$ **7.** $8\overline{)8}$ **8.** $7\overline{)0}$

In **9** and **10**, use the sign at the right.

9. **Be Precise** Aiden has $20. He spends all of his money on ride tickets. How many ride tickets does Aiden buy?

RIDE TICKETS
$1 each

10. Tanji spends $8 on ride tickets and gives an equal number of tickets to 8 friends. How many tickets does each friend get?

11. Explain which of these has the greatest quotient. $6 \div 6, 5 \div 1, 0 \div 3, 8 \div 8$

12. **Number Sense** Place the numbers 0, 1, 3, and 3 in the blanks so that the number sentence is true.

_____ ÷ _____ > _____ ÷ _____

13. The number of students at Netherwood Elementary School is an odd number between 280 and 300. List all the possible numbers of students there could be.

14. **Higher Order Thinking** Write and solve a story problem that goes with $6 \div 6$.

 Assessment

15. Lamaar shares 6 pencils equally with himself and 5 friends. Write an equation and solve to show the number of pencils each friend receives.

16. There are 7 ducklings. They sleep in 1 large nest. Write and solve an equation that shows how many ducklings sleep in the nest.

Name _____

Solve

☆ ✦ ☆
Solve & Share

A tour bus to a national park holds 56 people. There are 7 tour guides at the park to lead equal groups of people from the bus. How many people are in each tour group? Each person in a group pays a $2 entrance fee to a tour guide. How much does 1 tour guide collect? **Solve these problems any way you choose.**

Model with math. Use any strategies you know to solve. *Show your work in the space below!*

I can ...
use patterns and related facts to solve multiplication and division problems.

I can also model with math to solve problems.

$56 \div 7 = 8$ people

$8 \times 2 = \$16$ in each group

Look Back! **Reasoning** How can 7 × ? = 56 help you find 56 ÷ 7 = ?

Essential Question **What Fact Can You Use?**

A

Sabrina has 28 quarters in her bank. She wants to trade all of them for one-dollar bills. How many one-dollar bills will Sabrina get?

There are 4 quarters in one dollar.

B **One Way**

How many groups of 4 are in 28?

You can draw a bar diagram to help solve the problem.

28 quarters

| 4 | ? |

↑
4 quarters in one dollar

$28 \div 4 = 7$

There are 7 groups of 4 in 28. Sabrina can trade 28 quarters for 7 one-dollar bills.

C **Another Way**

What number times 4 equals 28?

You can use multiplication facts to help solve the problem.

$? \times 4 = 28$

$7 \times 4 = 28$

Sabrina can trade 28 quarters for 7 one-dollar bills.

Convince Me! **Construct Arguments** Why can both $28 \div 7 = ?$ and $? \times 7 = 28$ be used to solve the problem above?

28 and 7 is in the fact family

$28 \div 7 = 4$ $4 \times 7 = 28$
$28 \div 4 = 7$ $7 \times 4 = 28$

4 one dollar bills

☆ Guided Practice ☆

Do You Understand?

1. Look back at the problem on page 206. Suppose Sabrina put 8 more quarters in her bank. How many one-dollar bills can she trade for the quarters in her bank now?

2. **Number Sense** Calvin solves the equation $49 \div 7 = \boxed{}$. How does this help him complete the equation $7 \times \boxed{} = 49$?

Do You Know How?

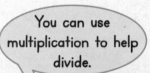

In **3–7**, use a multiplication or a division fact to complete the equations.

3. $45 \div 5 = 9$
   $5 \times 9 = 45$

4. $3 \times 7 = 21$
   $21 \div 3 = 7$

5. $6 \times 5 = 30$
   $30 \div 6 = 5$

6. $24 \div 6 = 4$
   $6 \times 4 = 24$

7. $6 \times 2 = 12$
   $12 \div 6 = 2$

You can use multiplication to help divide.

Independent Practice ☆

Leveled Practice In **8–10**, use fact families to complete the equations.

8. $42 \div 7 = \underline{\hphantom{00}}$
   $7 \times \underline{\hphantom{00}} = 42$

9. $6 \times \underline{\hphantom{00}} = 18$
   $18 \div 6 = \underline{\hphantom{00}}$

10. $9 \times \underline{\hphantom{00}} = 72$
    $72 \div 9 = \underline{\hphantom{00}}$

In **11–19**, find the product or quotient.

11. $36 \div 4 = \underline{\hphantom{00}}$

12. $\underline{\hphantom{00}} = 8 \times 8$

13. $15 \div 3 = 5$

14. $6\overline{)36}$

15. $9\overline{)63}$

16. $9\overline{)54}$

17. Multiply 8 times 5. ____

18. Divide 18 by 9. ____

19. Divide 27 by 3. ____

Problem Solving

In **20–22**, use the recipe at the right.

20. Model with Math How many cups of peanuts would Eric need to make 5 batches of trail mix?
Write an equation to show your thinking.

Eric's Trail Mix
Makes one batch
Ingredients:
4 cups peanuts
3 cups raisins
2 cups walnuts

21. Reasoning How many batches of trail mix can Eric make with 16 cups of peanuts, 15 cups of raisins, and 8 cups of walnuts?

22. Reasoning Eric spends $30 to buy the ingredients for 5 batches of trail mix. Find the cost of the ingredients Eric needs for one batch. How much would Eric need for 2 batches?

23. Emilia drew lines to divide these squares into parts. What is a way to name these parts?

24. Higher Order Thinking Wilson is thinking of 2 one-digit numbers. When he multiplies them, the product is 27. What is the sum of the two numbers? Explain your answer.

✓ Assessment

25. Erin made 32 rings. She gives rings to 8 of her friends. Which two equations could be used to find the number of rings each friend gets?

Ⓐ $32 \div 1 = 32$ and $1 \times 32 = 32$

Ⓑ $8 + 32 = 40$ and $40 - 32 = 8$

Ⓒ $8 \div 2 = 4$ and $4 \times 2 = 8$

Ⓓ $32 \div 8 = 4$ and $8 \times 4 = 32$

26. A tray has 10 plants and costs $7. Jed has $42. How many trays can he buy? How many plants?

Ⓐ 4 trays; 40 plants

Ⓑ 5 trays; 50 plants

Ⓒ 6 trays; 60 plants

Ⓓ 7 trays; 70 plants

Homework & Practice 4-7

Practice Multiplication and Division Facts

Another Look!

A class is making popcorn for a carnival. 10 students each made 3 cups of popcorn. The students put the popcorn in bags that hold 6 cups each. Find the total number of cups. Then find how many bags of popcorn the students made.

You can solve the problems using multiplication and division.

Multiplication

How many total cups of popcorn did they make?

$$10 \times 3 = ?$$

Number of students | Cups each student made | Total number of cups

$$10 \times 3 = 30$$

The students made a total of 30 cups of popcorn.

Division

How many groups of 6 are in 30?

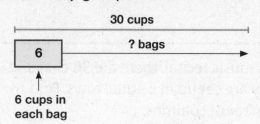

30 cups

6 | ? bags

6 cups in each bag

Divide the total number of cups by the number of cups in each bag:

$$30 \div 6 = 5 \leftarrow \text{Number of bags}$$

The students made 5 bags of popcorn.

In **1–9**, use multiplication and division to complete the fact family.

1. $21 \div 3 =$ _____

$3 \times$ _____ $= 21$

$21 \div$ _____ $= 3$

_____ $\times 3 = 21$

2. $36 \div 6 =$ _____

$6 \times$ _____ $= 36$

3. $18 \div 9 =$ _____

$9 \times$ _____ $= 18$

$18 \div$ _____ $= 9$

_____ $\times 9 = 18$

4. $54 \div 9 =$ _____

$9 \times$ _____ $= 54$

$54 \div$ _____ $= 9$

_____ $\times 9 = 54$

5. $18 \div 6 =$ _____

$6 \times$ _____ $= 18$

$18 \div$ _____ $= 6$

_____ $\times 6 = 18$

6. $40 \div 5 =$ _____

$5 \times$ _____ $= 40$

$40 \div$ _____ $= 5$

_____ $\times 5 = 40$

7. $14 \div 2 =$ _____

$2 \times$ _____ $= 14$

$14 \div$ _____ $= 2$

_____ $\times 2 = 14$

8. $25 \div 5 =$ _____

$5 \times$ _____ $= 25$

9. $32 \div 4 =$ _____

$4 \times$ _____ $= 32$

$32 \div$ _____ $= 4$

_____ $\times 4 = 32$

In **10** and **11**, use the chart at the right.

10. **Make Sense and Persevere** Ellis asks some classmates to name their favorite color. He records the information in this chart. How many classmates answered the question?

11. Suppose Ellis asked more classmates to name their favorite color. If 4 more classmates named blue this time, how many classmates named blue in all?

Favorite Color

DATA		
Red	ꟷꟷ	卌 卌 /
Blue	ꟷꟷ	卌 ////
Green	ꟷꟷ	卌 卌 ///

12. At a music recital, there are 30 chairs. They are set up in 6 equal rows. Find the number of columns.

13. A music teacher has 4 drum kits. Each kit has 2 drumsticks. Each drumstick costs $3. How many drumsticks does she have? What is the cost to replace them all?

14. **Higher Order Thinking** A chessboard has 8 rows of squares with 8 squares in each row. Two players each put 16 chess pieces on the board, with each piece on its own square. How many squares are empty now? Explain your answer.

✔ **Assessment**

15. Tolen has 18 dog treats. He gives the same number of treats to 6 dogs at the animal shelter. Which two equations could be used to find the number of treats each dog gets?

Ⓐ $18 + 6 = 24$ and $24 - 6 = 18$

Ⓑ $18 \div 6 = 3$ and $6 \times 3 = 18$

Ⓒ $18 \div 18 = 1$ and $1 \times 18 = 18$

Ⓓ $6 \div 3 = 2$ and $6 \div 2 = 3$

16. A pack of pens costs $3. Lynn spent $12 on pens. Each pack has 5 pens. How many packs did she buy? How many pens does she have?

Ⓐ 3 packs; 15 pens

Ⓑ 4 packs; 20 pens

Ⓒ 5 packs; 20 pens

Ⓓ 6 packs; 30 pens

Name _____

Solve & Share

24 ÷ 4 is on the right side of the balance below. What can you write on the left side that will have the same value as the right side? Write 5 different multiplication or division problems that will keep the pans balanced.

I can ...
use multiplication and division facts to find unknown values in an equation.

I can also generalize from examples.

You can generalize to find 5 problems that keep the pans balanced. What part of the problem is repeated? *Show your work in the space below!*

? = 24 ÷ 4

$2 \times 3 = 6$ $18 \div 3 = 6$

$6 \times 1 = 6$

$48 \div 8 = 6$

$36 \div 6 = 6$

$72 \div 12 = 6$

Look Back! **Construct Arguments** Would the problem $1 \times 3 \times 2 \times 1$ keep the pans above balanced? Explain.

Essential Question: How Do Multiplication and Division Equations Work?

A The pan balance shows $35 \div 7 = 5$.

Remember, in an equation, the symbol = means "is equal to." It tells you the value on the left is the same as the value on the right.

B These are other examples of equations.

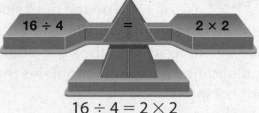

$$16 \div 4 = 2 \times 2$$

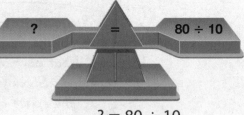

$$? = 80 \div 10$$
$$8 = 80 \div 10$$

C Frank has some tubes of tennis balls. Each tube has 4 tennis balls. Frank has 8 tennis balls in all. How many tubes of tennis balls does he have?

You can write an equation to represent the problem.

$$8 = ? \times 4$$

D Some equations have symbols to represent unknowns. The ? represents the number of tubes of tennis balls Frank has.

$$8 = ? \times 4$$

A multiplication fact that matches this is $8 = 2 \times 4$.

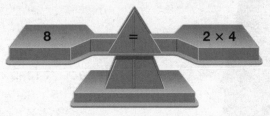

The value of ? is 2. So, ? = 2.

Convince Me! **Reasoning** Use the value of ? in the multiplication equation to write and solve two division equations.

$$7 \times \underset{6}{?} = 42 \qquad 42 \div ? = \boxed{7} \qquad 42 \div \boxed{7} = ?$$

$$42 \div 6 = 7 \qquad 42 \div 7 = 6$$

☆Guided Practice☆

Do You Understand?

1. Write an equation that represents the following problem:
Walt makes some sandwiches. Each sandwich uses 2 slices of bread. He uses 16 slices of bread. How many sandwiches does Walt make? Use ? to represent the number of sandwiches.

Do You Know How?

In **2–5**, find the value for ? that makes the equation true.

2. $9 \times ? = 27$

3. $8 = 40 \div ?$

4. $32 = ? \times 8$

5. $? \div 3 = 6$

Independent Practice☆

In **6–9**, find the value for ? that makes the equation true.

6. $? \div 4 = 7$

7. $25 = 5 \times ?$
5

8. $72 = ? \times 9$

9. $4 = 20 \div ?$

In **10–13**, write and solve an equation that represents the problem.

10. Sasha has 21 dimes. She puts them in stacks with the same number of dimes in each stack. In all, she has 3 stacks. How many dimes are in each stack? Use ? to represent the number of dimes in each stack.

11. There were some sheep in a barnyard. Each sheep had 4 legs. There were 24 legs in the barnyard. How many sheep were in the barnyard? Use ? to represent the number of sheep in the barnyard.

12. A football team scored 48 points. The team only scored on touchdowns, worth 6 points each. How many touchdowns did the team score? Use ? to represent the number of touchdowns.

13. There were 6 ladybugs on a leaf. Each ladybug had the same number of spots. There were 36 spots. How many spots were on each ladybug? Use ? to represent the number of spots on each ladybug.

Problem Solving

14. A baker is decorating 5 cakes. He uses 9 chocolate flowers to decorate each cake. How many flowers will he need to decorate all the cakes?

Write an equation to represent the problem, using ? to represent the missing information. Then solve your equation.

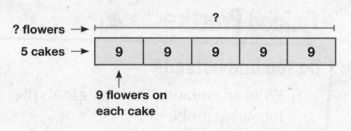

? flowers →
5 cakes →

| 9 | 9 | 9 | 9 | 9 |

↑
9 flowers on each cake

---

15. Be Precise Hal asked 20 people to name their favorite sport. The tally chart shows how many people answered *baseball* and *swimming*. All the other people he asked said their favorite sport was football. Complete the tally chart to show how many people chose football.

Favorite Sport	
Baseball	///
Swimming	ℍℍ ////
Football	

---

16. Higher Order Thinking A building has more than 2 stories but fewer than 10 stories. Each story of the building has the same number of windows. The building has 25 windows. Complete the sentence. Then explain how you found your answer.

The building has __5__ stories, and each story has __5__ windows.

---

17. Claire has 18 strawberries. She wants to give an equal number of strawberries to her 6 friends. How many strawberries should she give to each friend?

Claire says she can write a division equation and a multiplication equation using ? for the unknown value.

Part A

Write and solve a division equation to find the number of strawberries each friend should receive.

$$18 \div 6 = 3$$

Part B

Write and solve a multiplication equation to find the number of strawberries each friend should receive.

$$6 \times 3 = 18$$

Name _____

Another Look!

Remember that an equation uses an equal sign (=) to show the value on the left is the same as the value on the right.

Some equations have unknown numbers. These numbers may be represented by question marks.

$$10 = 40 \div ?$$

This equation means 10 is equal to 40 divided by some number. You know $40 \div 4 = 10$, so $? = 4$.

You can write equations to represent math problems.

1. Frankie has some nickels. His nickels have a value of 45 cents. How many nickels does Frankie have? Complete the table to write an equation to represent the problem.

Use a ? to represent the number of nickels Frankie has.	?
Nickels are worth 5 cents. You can multiply the number of nickels by 5 to find the total value of the coins.	? × _____
Frankie's nickels are worth 45 cents.	? × 5 = _____

To solve the problem, find the value of ? that makes the equation true: _____ × 5 = 45. Frankie has _____ nickels.

In **2–5**, find the value of ? that makes the equation true.

2. $? \div 5 = 6$ **3.** $36 = 6 \times ?$ **4.** $14 = ? \times 2$ **5.** $81 \div ? = 9$

In **6** and **7**, write and solve an equation for each problem.

6. A restaurant has 24 chairs and some tables. There are 4 chairs at each table. How many tables are there?

7. Suzanne buys 6 paint sets. Each set contains the same number of brushes. She buys 18 brushes. How many brushes are in each paint set?

8. Carlos has a string that is 24 inches long. He wants to divide it into 3 equal parts. Write an equation to find how long each part will be. Use ? to represent the unknown number. Then solve your equation.

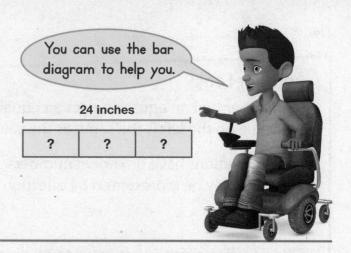

You can use the bar diagram to help you.

24 inches

| ? | ? | ? |

9. **Higher Order Thinking** Hector spent from Sunday to the following Saturday at the beach. Each day he found an equal number of shells. If Hector found 63 shells, how many shells did he find on Tuesday? Explain your answer.

10. **Make Sense and Persevere** Ella solves the equation 32 ÷ ? = 8. She says the value of ? is 4. Does Ella's answer make sense? Explain.

11. **Reasoning** Do points A and B represent the same number, or do they represent different numbers? Explain.

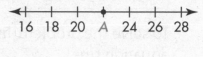

16 18 20 A 24 26 28

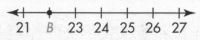

21 B 23 24 25 26 27

12. Bruce arranges 35 pencils on his desk into equal groups of 7. How many groups of pencils are on Bruce's desk?

Bruce says he can write a multiplication equation and a division equation using ? for the unknown value.

Part A

Write and solve a multiplication equation to find the number of groups of pencils.

Part B

Write and solve a division equation to find the number of groups of pencils.

Name _____

Solve & Share

Two girls and two boys went to the festival. The total cost of their tickets was $20. Each child paid the same amount for a ticket. What was the cost of each ticket? *Solve this problem any way you choose.*

I can ...
make sense of problems and keep working if I get stuck.

I can also solve multi-step problems.

Thinking Habits

Be a good thinker!
These questions can help you.

- What do I need to find?
- What do I know?
- What's my plan for solving the problem?
- What else can I try if I get stuck?
- How can I check that my solution makes sense?

Look Back! **Make Sense and Persevere** How did you find how many children bought tickets? How did this plan help you solve the problem?

How Can You Make Sense of a Problem and Persevere in Solving It?

A

A store has boxes of video games for sale. In each box, the video games are in 2 rows with 3 video games in each row.

Each video game costs the same amount.

What is the cost of each video game?

To persevere you can check your strategy and your work.

What do I need to do?

I need to make sense of the problem before I can solve it. If I get stuck, I need to persevere until I find the cost of each video game.

$54   VIDEO GAMES

B How can I make sense of and solve this problem?

I can

- identify what is known from the problem.

- look for and answer hidden questions in the problem.

- make a plan to solve the problem.

- check to make sure my work and answer make sense.

C

Here's my thinking...

I know a box costs $54.
There are 2 rows of 3 games in a box.

First, I need to find the total number of games in a box.

I will **multiply** the number of rows by the number of games in each row.

$2 \times 3 = 6$ 6 games are in a box.

Then I will **divide** the cost of a box by the total number of games to find the cost of each game.

$54 \div 6 = 9$ Each game costs $9.

Convince Me! Make Sense and Persevere How can you check to make sure the work and answer given above make sense?

Name _____

☆ Guided Practice *

Make Sense and Persevere

Twelve friends went camping. All except 4 of them went on a hike. The hikers carried 32 water bottles. Each hiker carried the same number of water bottles. How many water bottles did each hiker carry?

1. Tell what you know. Then explain what you need to find first to solve the problem.

   If you are stuck, you can persevere. Think: Does the strategy I am using make sense?

2. Tell which operations you will use. Then solve the problem.

☆ Independent Practice ☆

Make Sense and Persevere

Four students went bowling. They bowled 2 games each. The cost was $5 per game. How much money did the students spend on bowling? Explain.

3. Tell what you know. Then explain what you need to find first to solve the problem.

4. Tell which operations you will use. Then solve the problem.

5. How can you check that your work is correct?

Problem Solving

County Fair

The table shows costs at the county fair.
Mr. Casey spent $24 on admission tickets
for himself and the children in his group.
How many children are in his group? Answer
Exercises 6–9 to solve the problem.

DATA	County Fair		
	Kind of Ticket	**Adult**	**Child**
	Admission	$8	$4
	Boat Rides	$2	$1

6. **Make Sense and Persevere** What do you know? What
   are you asked to find?

7. **Be Precise** Why is it important to know which kind of
   tickets Mr. Casey bought?

As you make sense
of a problem, you can
think about whether you
have solved a problem
like it before.

8. **Critique Reasoning** Dan says there are 6 children in
   Mr. Casey's group because $24 ÷ $4 = 6. Does Dan's
   reasoning make sense? Explain.

9. **Use Reasoning** Solve the problem. Write an equation for
   each step and explain.

Name _____

Another Look!

To solve a two-step problem, you may need to find the answer to a hidden question first. Then you can use that answer to solve the problem.

Sandra has $22 to spend on school supplies. She buys a backpack and spends the rest of her money on notebooks. How many notebooks does Sandra buy?

Tell how to make sense of the problem.

- I can identify what is known from the problem.

- I can look for and answer any hidden questions.

- I can make a plan to solve the problem.

Tell which operations you will use. Then solve the problem.

I will use subtraction and division.

A backpack costs $10. $22 − $10 = $12.

Sandra now has $12 to spend on notebooks. Each notebook costs $3.

$12 ÷ $3 = 4. Sandra can buy 4 notebooks.

If you are stuck, you can persevere by trying a different strategy.

Make Sense and Persevere

There are 5 players on a basketball team. In a game, 4 players scored 6 points each. The team scored a total of 34 points. How many points did the other player score?

1. Tell how to make sense of the problem.

2. Tell the quantities you know. Then explain what you need to find first to solve the problem.

3. Tell which operations you will use. Then solve the problem.

Performance Assessment

Zoo Field Trip

The third-grade class at Thomas Elementary School goes on a trip to the zoo. Students are in groups of 6. Mr. Bell's and Ms. Ridley's classes are combined.

Classroom Teacher	Number of Students
Mr. Bell	18
Ms. Ridley	24
Ms. Holtz	17

4. **Make Sense and Persevere** The teachers want to know how many groups will be in the combined classes. What do you need to know to solve?

5. **Use Reasoning** Find the number of groups in the combined classes. Write an equation for each step. Explain how the quantities are related.

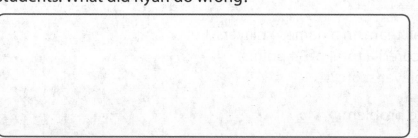

Make sense of the information in the problem by identifying the quantities. Think: Is there a hidden question I need to solve first?

6. **Critique Reasoning** Ryan solved the problem above. He says there are 6 groups of 6 students and 1 group of **5** students. What did Ryan do wrong?

7. **Generalize** If you wanted to find the number of groups of 6 students if Mr. Bell's and Ms. Holtz's classes were combined, could you use the same strategy you used in **5**? Explain.

Find a Match

Work with a partner. Point to a clue.

Read the clue.

Look below the clues to find a match. Write the clue letter in the box next to the match.

Find a match for every clue.

I can ...
add and subtract within 100.

Clues

A Is equal to 59 + 19	**E** Is equal to 72 − 24	**I** Is equal to 39 − 17
B Is equal to 13 − 6	**F** Is equal to 35 + 15	**J** Is equal to 29 + 44
C Is equal to 48 + 38	**G** Is equal to 100 − 19	**K** Is equal to 56 − 47
D Is equal to 57 − 18	**H** Is equal to 65 + 33	**L** Is equal to 16 + 35

☐ 73 − 64	☐ 24 + 26	☐ 19 − 12
☐ 37 + 14	☐ 56 − 8	☐ 52 + 26
☐ 47 + 39	☐ 65 − 43	☐ 72 + 26
☐ 48 + 25	☐ 92 − 11	☐ 66 − 27

Vocabulary Review

Word List

- dividend
- divisor
- even number
- fact family
- odd number
- product
- quotient

Understand Vocabulary

1. Circle the *divisor* in each equation.

$30 \div 6 = 5$ $24 \div 3 = 8$ $14 \div 2 = 7$ $45 \div 5 = 9$

2. Circle the *dividend* in each equation.

$63 \div 7 = 9$ $4 \div 1 = 4$ $0 \div 5 = 0$ $8 \div 4 = 2$

3. Circle the *quotient* in each equation.

$21 \div 3 = 7$ $54 \div 9 = 6$ $15 \div 5 = 3$ $16 \div 8 = 2$

4. Circle the *even numbers*.

19   24   45   68

5. Circle the *odd numbers*.

21   36   13   47

6. Look at the equations below. Write **Y** if the *product* is 6. Write **N** if the *product* is NOT 6.

$4 \times 6 = 24$ _____ $2 \times 3 = 6$ _____ $6 = 3 \times 2$ _____

7. Look at the equations below. Write **Y** if the group shows a *fact family*. Write **N** if the group does NOT show a *fact family*.

$3 \times 9 = 27$ _____ $12 \div 6 = 2$ _____ $56 \div 8 = 7$ _____
$27 \div 9 = 3$ $2 \times 6 = 12$ $56 \div 7 = 8$
$9 \times 3 = 27$ $12 \div 3 = 4$ $8 \times 7 = 56$
$27 \div 3 = 9$ $6 \times 2 = 12$ $7 \times 8 = 56$

Use Vocabulary in Writing

8. Explain how to find the fact family for 2, 4, and 8. Use at least 2 terms from the Word List in your explanation.

Set A pages 169–174

Monica has 24 chairs to arrange equally in 3 rows. You can use an array to find the number of chairs in each row.

This array shows the relationship between multiplication and division.

3 rows of 8   24 in 3 equal rows
  $3 \times 8 = 24$ $24 \div 3 = 8$

A fact family shows how multiplication and division are related.

Fact family for 3, 8, and 24:

$3 \times 8 = 24$ $24 \div 3 = 8$
$8 \times 3 = 24$ $24 \div 8 = 3$

Remember that a fact family is a group of related facts using the same numbers.

In **1–4**, write the other three facts in the fact family.

1. $3 \times 7 = 21$

2. $5 \times 3 = 15$

3. $8 \times 6 = 48$

4. $4 \times 5 = 20$

Set B pages 175–180

You can use multiplication to solve division problems.

Hector has 24 oranges. He puts 4 oranges in each basket. How many baskets does Hector need for all the oranges?

What number times 4 is 24?

$6 \times 4 = 24$
$24 \div 4 = 6$

Hector needs 6 baskets.

Remember that you can use multiplication to help divide.

In **1** and **2**, solve each problem. Write the multiplication fact and division fact you use to solve the problem.

1. Sally has 32 flowers. She puts 8 flowers in each vase. How many vases does Sally need for all the flowers?

2. Jon has 18 peaches. He uses 3 peaches to make a peach tart. How many peach tarts does Jon make if he uses all the peaches?

Set C pages 181–186

Brent is putting 42 books on shelves. He puts 6 books on each shelf. How many shelves will Brent need?

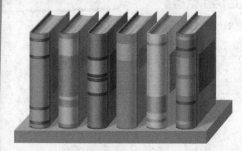

What number times 6 is 42?

$7 \times 6 = 42$
$42 \div 6 = 7$

Brent will need 7 shelves.

How many shelves would Brent need if he put 7 books on each shelf?

What number times 7 is 42?

$6 \times 7 = 42$
$42 \div 7 = 6$

Brent would need 6 shelves.

Remember that you can use multiplication facts for 6s and 7s to help you divide by 6s and 7s.

In **1–3**, solve each problem. Write the multiplication fact and division fact you use to solve the problem.

1. There are 36 runners entered in a marathon. They run in groups of 6. How many groups are there?

2. Lani has 35 bird stickers. There are 5 stickers on each sheet. How many sheets of bird stickers does she have?

3. Jake has 18 remote-controlled boats for 6 friends to share equally. How many boats will each friend get?

Set D pages 187–192

Lu made 9 bracelets. He used 72 beads. He used the same number of beads for each bracelet. How many beads did Lu use for each bracelet?

72 beads

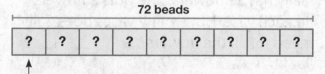

↑
**? beads for
one bracelet**

9 times what number is 72?

$9 \times 8 = 72$
$72 \div 9 = 8$

Lu used 8 beads for each bracelet.

Remember that you can use multiplication facts for 8s and 9s to help you divide by 8s and 9s.

In **1–5**, write the related multiplication fact that can be used to complete each division fact. Then find the quotient.

1. $54 \div 9 =$ _____   _____ $\times$ _____ $=$ _____

2. $64 \div 8 =$ _____   _____ $\times$ _____ $=$ _____

3. $36 \div 9 =$ _____   _____ $\times$ _____ $=$ _____

4. $56 \div 8 =$ _____   _____ $\times$ _____ $=$ _____

5. $72 \div 8 =$ _____   _____ $\times$ _____ $=$ _____

Name _____

Set E pages 193–198

A whole number is **even** if it can be divided by 2 with none left over.

A whole number is **odd** if it cannot be divided by 2 with none left over.

Which product is even? Which is odd?

$3 \times 7 =$ odd $5 \times 8 =$ even
          product   product

All even numbers can be thought of as 2 equal groups.

When at least one factor is even, the product is even.

Remember that you can think about dividing by 2 to tell whether a number is even or odd.

In **1–3**, circle the factors that can be divided by 2. Then circle even or odd to describe the product.

1. $6 \times 4 = ?$ **even**   **odd**

2. $9 \times 1 = ?$ **even**   **odd**

3. $8 \times 7 = ?$ **even**   **odd**

Set F pages 199–204

Find $5 \div 1$. Five groups of 1.

What number times 1 is 5?

$5 \times 1 = 5$ So, $5 \div 1 = 5$.

Find $0 \div 8$.

$8 \times 0 = 0$ So, $0 \div 8 = 0$.

Remember that any number divided by 1 is itself. Any number (except 0) divided by itself is 1. Zero divided by any number (except 0) is 0.

In **1–3**, use division to solve.

1. $0 \div 16 =$ _____

2. $10 \div 10 =$ _____

3. Leroy had 4 oranges. He gave one orange to each of his 4 friends. How many oranges did each friend get? Write an equation to show your answer.

Set G pages 205–210

How many groups of 4 are in 24?

24

4 in each group → 4   ?

You can use multiplication facts.

$? \times 4 = 24$ $6 \times 4 = 24$

There are 6 groups of 4 in 24.

Remember that you can use bar diagrams or multiplication facts to help solve a division problem.

In **1** and **2**, use related multiplication and division facts to solve.

1. $21 \div 7 =$ _____   **2.** $5 \times$ _____ $= 45$

$7 \times$ _____ $= 21$ $45 \div 5 =$ _____

Set H | pages 211–216

Look at the equation $3 \times ? = 15$.

The **?** stands for an unknown number.

Read the equation like this:

"Multiply 3 by a number. The result is 15."
Then find the value of the unknown.
Think of a fact that uses the numbers in
the equation.

$3 \times 5 = 15$, so the unknown number is 5.

Remember that you can use multiplication
and division facts to find the value of
an unknown.

In **1–6**, find the value of the unknown.

1. $? \div 2 = 6$ **2.** $7 \times ? = 42$

3. $20 = 4 \times ?$ **4.** $9 = ? \div 3$

5. $16 \div ? = 2$ **6.** $24 \div ? = 6$

Set I | pages 217–222

Think about these questions to help you
**make sense of problems and persevere in
solving them.**

Thinking Habits

- What do I need to find?

- What do I know?

- What's my plan for solving
  the problem?

- What else can I try if I get stuck?

- How can I check that my
  solution makes sense?

Remember to use the information in each
step to solve the problem.

In **1** and **2**, answer to solve a two-step
problem.

Fourteen friends went to the county fair. All
except 6 of them bought a hot dog. Each
hot dog costs $3. How much did the friends
spend on hot dogs?

1. Tell what you know. Then explain what
you need to find first to solve the problem.

2. Tell which operations you will use.
Then solve the problem.

Name _____

1. Heather wrote a multiplication fact and a division fact for the array below. Choose all of the equations that show a fact Heather could have written.

☐ 5 × 9 = 45

☐ 5 × 5 = 25

☐ 45 ÷ 5 = 9

☐ 10 × 5 = 50

☐ 50 ÷ 5 = 10

2. Colin wrote three equations. What number will make all of Colin's equations true?

14 = ? × 2

56 ÷ 8 = ?

? × ? = 49

3. Betsy and Carlos are sharing a bowl of cherries. They divide the cherries into 2 equal groups. There is 1 cherry left in the bowl. Which number below could be the number of cherries they started with in the bowl?

Ⓐ 37

Ⓑ 48

Ⓒ 24

Ⓓ 18

4. Mrs. Raspa wrote four number sentences. For questions 4a–4d, choose *Yes* or *No* to tell if the equations are true.

4a. 0 ÷ 8 = 0   ○ Yes ○ No

4b. 5 ÷ 1 = 5   ○ Yes ○ No

4c. 7 ÷ 7 = 1   ○ Yes ○ No

4d. 4 ÷ 0 = 0   ○ Yes ○ No

5. Mr. Vargas is buying used computer equipment. He buys 3 keyboards and 4 mice. He spends $42. If the items are all the same price, how much does each item cost?

6. Look at the counters below.

Part A

Draw lines around the counters to show 12 ÷ 6.

Part B

Find a different multiplication fact where the product is 12. Explain how you can group the counters for the fact.

7. Draw lines to connect equal expressions.

8 ÷ 8		9 ÷ 1
0 × 7		0 ÷ 3
24 ÷ 4		1 × 6
27 ÷ 3		7 ÷ 7

8. Peter wrote five numbers. Which of Peter's numbers can be divided into 7 equal groups with 0 left over? Choose all that apply.

☐ 56
☐ 52
☐ 42
☐ 35
☐ 27

9. Crystal drew this bar diagram to model a division problem. Write a multiplication equation Crystal could use to help solve the problem.

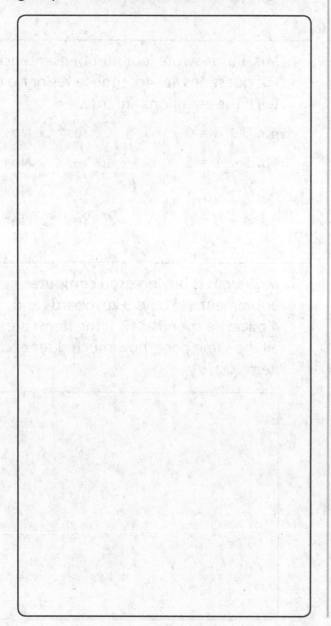

35

| ? | ? | ? | ? | ? |

10. Xavier divided his action figure collection into 2 equal groups. There was 1 figure left over. Xavier said he has an even number of action figures. Is he correct? Explain.

11. Mandy is trying to find $6 \div 0$. She says the answer is 6 because $6 \times 0 = 6$. Is Mandy correct? Explain.

12. Luz has 36 pencil toppers. She sorts her pencil toppers into 6 groups. How many are in each group?

13. Kira has 63 sheets of recycled paper. She gives the same number of sheets to each of 9 friends. How many sheets does Kira give to each friend?
Use the bar diagram to help.

63 sheets

| ? | ? | ? | ? | ? | ? | ? | ? | ? |

(A) 6

(B) 7

(C) 8

(D) 9

14. Write the fact family for 1, 4, and 4.

15. Gennaro wrote 4 true statements about even and odd products. Choose all of the true statements.

☐ An even number times an even number has an even product.

☐ An even number times an odd number has an even product.

☐ An odd number times an odd number has an odd product.

☐ An odd number times an even number has an odd product.

☐ If one factor is even, then the product is even.

16. Which number makes both equations true?

$$18 \div 9 = ? \qquad ? \times 9 = 18$$

17. Anna drew the bar diagram below. Which equations could be used to represent the problem shown in Anna's bar diagram? Choose all that apply.

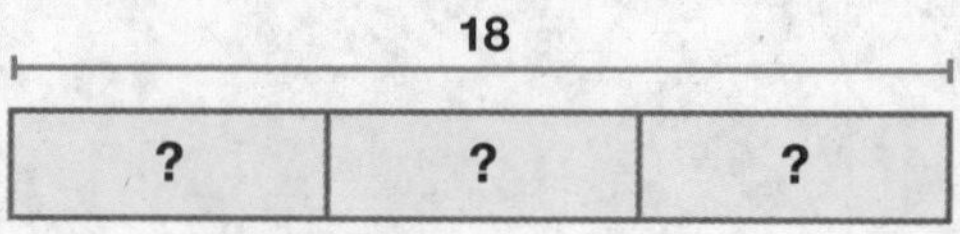

18		
?	?	?

☐ $18 \times 3 = ?$

☐ $3 \div ? = 18$

☐ $18 \div 3 = ?$

☐ $? \div 3 = 18$

☐ $3 \times ? = 18$

18. A balloon artist wants to make 6 different kinds of balloon animals. She needs 4 balloons to make each animal. If the balloons come in packs of 8, how many packs will she need to buy?

Part A

Explain what you need to find first to solve the problem.

Part B

Tell which operations you will use. Then solve the problem.

Name _____

Relay Race

Mrs. Achilles teaches Physical Education. She is planning a relay race for her school. Each grade forms teams. Each student is on 1 team.

Race Details
- The field is 40 feet wide.
- Each runner gets 1 lane.
- Mrs. Achilles has 7 trophies.

Use the **Race Details** list to answer the following question.

1. Each lane must be an equal width. Mrs. Achilles wants to use the entire width of the field for lanes. How wide will each lane be if Mrs. Achilles sets out 10 lanes? 5 lanes? Use multiplication facts to help you.

Grade Size	
Grade	**Students**
K	24
1	28
2	27
3	24
4	30
5	25
6	32

Use the **Race Details** list and **Grade Size** table to answer the following question.

2. Each grade gets an equal number of trophies. How many trophies does each grade get? Write a division fact and a related multiplication fact you can use to solve this problem.

Use the **Grade Size** table to answer the following question.

3. Mrs. Achilles wonders whether each team can have exactly 2 people. Explain whether or not this is possible.

Use the **Grade Size** and **Grade 3 Possible Team Sizes** tables to answer the following question. Use related multiplication facts to help you.

4. Mrs. Achilles puts more than 2 students on each team. Each team must have an equal number of students.

Grade 3 Possible Team Sizes	
Number of Students on Team	Number of Teams
4	
3	

Part A

Complete the table to show the 4 different ways Mrs. Achilles can form teams for Grade 3.

Part B

Mrs. Achilles tries to make teams of 4 students each. She can do this for some grades but not for all. Which grades can have equal teams of 4?

Team Size			
Grade	Number of Students	Number of Students on Team	Number of Teams
K	24		
1	28		
2	27		
3	24		
4	30		
5	25		
6	32		

Fill out the table for the grades written above. Use the same-size team for each of these grades.

Part C

In the **Team Size** table, write the grades that you did **NOT** fill out in Part B.

Choose team sizes that let everyone in these grades participate. Use different sizes for each of these grades. Fill out the rest of the table.

Fluently Multiply and Divide within 100

Essential Question: What are strategies to solve multiplication and division facts?

> The weather changes from day to day and from place to place.

> Scientists look for patterns in the weather. These patterns help them understand different climates!

> I predict there will be math in the forecast! Here is a project on weather information and basic facts.

Math and Science Project: Weather Information

Do Research Use the Internet or other sources to find the weather in different places on Earth. Find the weather at different times of day. Write down the temperature for each place. Also write down any conditions such as rain or snow.

Journal: Write a Report Include what you found. Also in your report:

- Tell how many places you checked.

- Tell how many times you checked the weather in one day.

- Write a multiplication or division story using your information. Then find an answer for your story.

Review What You Know

A-Z Vocabulary

Choose the best term from the box.
Write it on the blank.

• dividend	• product
• divisor	• quotient
• factor	

1. The answer to a division problem is the _____ .

2. A _____ is the answer to a multiplication problem.

3. The _____ is the number in a division problem that is divided into equal groups.

4. Multiply a factor by a _____ to solve a multiplication problem.

Multiplication

5. $6 \times 2 =$ ___   **6.** $5 \times 1 =$ ___   **7.** $4 \times 10 =$ ___

8. $7 \times 5 =$ ___   **9.** $4 \times 4 =$ ___   **10.** $9 \times 3 =$ ___

11. The oranges in a store are in 7 rows and 8 columns. How many oranges are there?

Division

12. $60 \div 6 =$ ___   **13.** $25 \div 5 =$ ___   **14.** $12 \div 3 =$ ___

15. $30 \div 6 =$ ___   **16.** $14 \div 2 =$ ___   **17.** $9 \div 3 =$ ___

18. If 28 stamps are arranged into an array with 4 columns, how many rows are there?

The Distributive Property

19. Explain how to use 2s facts to find 4×9.

Name _____

Max found $6 \times 8 = 48$. He noticed that $(6 \times 4) + (6 \times 4)$ also equals 48.

Use the multiplication table to find two other facts whose sum is 48.
Use facts that have a 6 or 8 as a factor. What pattern do you see?

I can ...
use structure and properties to explain patterns for multiplication facts.

I can also look for patterns to solve problems.

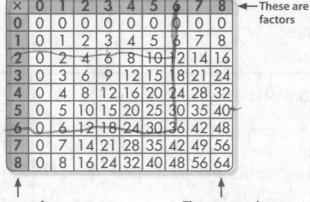

These are factors

These are factors   These are products

You can look for relationships. Use the multiplication table to make connections.

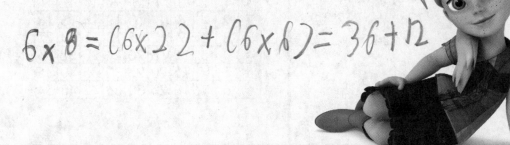

$6 \times 8 = (6 \times 2) + (6 \times 6) = 36 + 12$

Look Back! **Generalize** How can a multiplication table help you find products that equal 48 when added together?

Essential Question **How Can You Explain Patterns in the Multiplication Chart?**

A

Yolanda noticed that 4 × 6 is double 2 × 6. How can you explain this?

You can use a multiplication table to find patterns.

×	1	2	3	4	5	6	7	8	9
1	1	2	3	4	5	6	7	8	9
2	2	4	6	8	10	12	14	16	18
3	3	6	9	12	15	18	21	24	27
4	4	8	12	16	20	24	28	32	36
5	5	10	15	20	25	30	35	40	45
6	6	12	18	24	30	36	42	48	54

B

4 is the double of 2.

So, 4 × 6 is double 2 × 6.

You can use the Distributive Property of Multiplication to explain.

$4 \times 6 = (2 \times 6) + (2 \times 6)$
$4 \times 6 = \quad 12 \quad + \quad 12$
$4 \times 6 = \qquad 24$

C

Look at the highlighted rows.

The product of any number multiplied by 4 will be double the product of that number multiplied by 2.

×	1	2	3	4	5	6	7	8	9
1	1	2	3	4	5	6	7	8	9
2	2	4	6	8	10	12	14	16	18
3	3	6	9	12	15	18	21	24	27
4	4	8	12	16	20	24	28	32	36
5	5	10	15	20	25	30	35	40	45
6	6	12	18	24	30	36	42	48	54

Properties can be used to understand a pattern and check if it is always true.

Convince Me! **Look for Relationships** Look at the highlighted rows of numbers multiplied by 2 or 4. What pattern do you see across the rows?

I know the top row is a duoble of two fromthe bottom row. The bottom row is a double of 4.

Name _____

☆ Guided Practice *

Do You Understand?

1. How are 3 × 7 and 6 × 7 related?

   3×7 is a double

2. **Construct Arguments** In the table on page 238, is the pattern that Yolanda found also true for factors that are multiplied by 3 and 6? Explain.

Do You Know How?

In **3** and **4**, use the multiplication table shown below.

3. What pattern do you see in the columns and rows that have 0 as a factor?

   0 is the product

4. Explain why this pattern is true.

   0 × 9 = 0
   0 × 1 = 0

☆ Independent Practice ☆

In **5–8**, use the multiplication table shown at the right.

5. Look at the shaded products. What pattern do you see?

   even numbers

6. Write the equation for each shaded product.

   8 + 6 = 14

×	0	1	2	3	4	5	6	7	8	9
0	0	0	0	0	0	0	0	0	0	0
1	0	1	2	3	4	5	6	7	8	9
2	0	2	4	6	8	10	12	14	16	18
3	0	3	6	9	12	15	18	21	24	27
4	0	4	8	12	16	20	24	28	32	36
5	0	5	10	15	20	25	30	35	40	45
6	0	6	12	18	24	30	36	42	48	54
7	0	7	14	21	28	35	42	49	56	63
8	0	8	16	24	32	40	48	56	64	72
9	0	9	18	27	36	45	54	63	72	81

7. Look at the factors you wrote. Explain why the pattern for the products is true.

   if an numbers ones is 0,2,4,6,8

A multiplication table helps you see lots of products at the same time.

8. Shade a line in the multiplication table to show how this pattern is true for other products.

For another example, see Set A on page 287.

Topic 5 | Lesson 5-1   **239**

Problem Solving

9. **Math and Science** How many arms do 9 starfish have if…

   a each starfish has 6 arms? Write a multiplication equation to solve.

   $9 \times 6 = 54$

   b each starfish has 7 arms? Write a multiplication equation to solve.

   $9 \times 7 = 63$

   | 6 arms | | 7 arms |

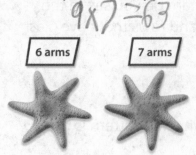

10. **Higher Order Thinking** Karen found a pattern on the multiplication table. What pattern did she find? Explain why it is true.

×	1	2	3	4	5	6	7	8
3	3	6	9	12	15	18	21	24
6	6	12	18	24	30	36	42	48

Every number is even

11. **Number Sense** The distance from Tom's house to his brother's house is 200 miles. Tom drove 38 miles in the morning and 57 miles in the afternoon. Estimate how much farther Tom has to drive to reach his brother's house.

127

12. **Look for Relationships** Describe a pattern you see in the 9s row of the multiplication table.

the pattern Is see is even odd

 Assessment

13. Shade the 1s row and the 1s column on the multiplication table below.

×	0	1	2	3	4	5	6	7	8	9
0	0	0	0	0	0	0	0	0	0	0
1	0	1	2	3	4	5	6	7	8	9
2	0	2	4	6	8	10	12	14	16	18
3	0	3	6	9	12	15	18	21	24	27
4	0	4	8	12	16	20	24	28	32	36
5	0	5	10	15	20	25	30	35	40	45
6	0	6	12	18	24	30	36	42	48	54
7	0	7	14	21	28	35	42	49	56	63
8	0	8	16	24	32	40	48	56	64	72
9	0	9	18	27	36	45	54	63	72	81

Part A

What pattern do you see?

equels the number moltiplied.

Part B

Explain why the pattern is true.

$1 \times 9 = 9$
$1 \times 10 = 10$

240 **Topic 5** | Lesson 5-1

Another Look!

You can find and explain multiplication patterns.

×	1	2	3	4	5	6	7	8	9
6	6	12	18	24	30	36	42	48	54

You can see that the products of 6 increase by 6 as the other factor increases.

So, you know that 4 groups of 6 is the same as 3 groups of 6 plus 1 more group of 6. You can use the Distributive Property to explain.

$$4 \times 6 = (3 + 1) \times 6$$
$$= (3 \times 6) + (1 \times 6)$$
$$= 18 + 6$$
$$= 24$$

To find patterns, look for things that repeat or are the same.

In **1–5**, use the multiplication table shown at the right.

1. Find the column which has products that are the sum of the yellow shaded numbers in each row. Shade this column.

2. What pattern do you see?

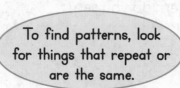

×	1	2	3	4	5	6	7	8	9
1	1	2	3	4	5	6	7	8	9
2	2	4	6	8	10	12	14	16	18
3	3	6	9	12	15	18	21	24	27
4	4	8	12	16	20	24	28	32	36
5	5	10	15	20	25	30	35	40	45
6	6	12	18	24	30	36	42	48	54
7	7	14	21	28	35	42	49	56	63
8	8	16	24	32	40	48	56	64	72
9	9	18	27	36	45	54	63	72	81

3. Explain why this pattern is true.

4. Find a similar pattern using different products. Shade the columns on the multiplication table.

5. Explain how you choose which columns to shade.

6. **Make Sense and Persevere** Teresa bought 3 boxes of chocolate. Each box has 9 pieces of chocolate inside. Teresa gave away 15 pieces of chocolate. How many pieces of chocolate does she have left?

7. **A-Z Vocabulary** Margie divided 24 by 3. The *dividend* is _____. The *quotient* is _____.

8. **Look for Relationships** Look at the multiples of 2. What pattern do you see?

×	1	2	3	4	5	6	7	8	9	10
2	2	4	6	8	10	12	14	16	18	20

9. **Construct Arguments** Look at the table on page 241. Does this table have more even products or more odd products? Explain.

10. **Higher Order Thinking** Chris needs to find the product of two numbers. One of the numbers is 11. The answer also needs to be 11. How will Chris solve this problem? Explain.

✓ **Assessment**

11. Look at the shaded products in the multiplication table shown below.

×	1	2	3	4	5	6	7	8	9
1	1	2	3	4	5	6	7	8	9
2	2	4	6	8	10	12	14	16	18
3	3	6	9	12	15	18	21	24	27
4	4	8	12	16	20	24	28	32	36
5	5	10	15	20	25	30	35	40	45
6	6	12	18	24	30	36	42	48	54
7	7	14	21	28	35	42	49	56	63
8	8	16	24	32	40	48	56	64	72
9	9	18	27	36	45	54	63	72	81

Part A

What pattern do you notice?

Part B

Explain why the pattern works.

Name _____

Solve & Share

Find 18 ÷ 3 any way you choose.

I can ...

use reasoning and the relationship between multiplication and division to find basic facts.

I can also reason about math.

You can use reasoning. Think about how the quantities in the problem are related.

×	0	1	2	3	4	5	6	7	8	9	10
0	0	0	0	0	0	0	0	0	0	0	0
1	0	1	2	3	4	5	6	7	8	9	10
2	0	2	4	6	8	10	12	14	16	18	20
3	0	3	6	9	12	15	18	21	24	27	30
4	0	4	8	12	16	20	24	28	32	36	40
5	0	5	10	15	20	25	30	35	40	45	50
6	0	6	12	18	24	30	36	42	48	54	60
7	0	7	14	21	28	35	42	49	56	63	70
8	0	8	16	24	32	40	48	56	64	72	80
9	0	9	18	27	36	45	54	63	72	81	90
10	0	10	20	30	40	50	60	70	80	90	100

6

3

$3 - 3 = 0$ 6

$18 ÷ 3 = 15$ 1

$15 - 3 = 12$ 2

$12 - 3 = 9$ 3

$9 - 3 = 6$ 4

$6 - 3 = 3$ 5

$18 ÷ 3 = 3$

$18 ÷ 3 = 6$

Look Back! Make Sense and Persevere Describe another way you can find 18 ÷ 3.

Essential Question

How Can You Use a Multiplication Table to Solve Division Problems?

A

Write a missing factor equation and then use the multiplication table to find 15 ÷ 3.

Look at where rows and columns intersect in a multiplication table to solve a division problem.

×	0	1	2	3	4	5
0	0	0	0	0	0	0
1	0	1	2	3	4	5
2	0	2	4	6	8	10
3	0	3	6	9	12	15

$15 \div 3 = ?$

$3 \times ? = 15$

3 times what number equals 15?

B ## Step 1

You know one factor is 3. Find the 3 in the first column of this multiplication table.

×	0	1	2	3	4	5
0	0	0	0	0	0	0
1	0	1	2	3	4	5
2	0	2	4	6	8	10
3	0	3	6	9	12	15

C ## Step 2

You know the product is 15. Follow the row the 3 is in until you come to 15.

×	0	1	2	3	4	5
0	0	0	0	0	0	0
1	0	1	2	3	4	5
2	0	2	4	6	8	10
3	0	3	6	9	12	15

D ## Step 3

Look straight up to the top of that column of the table. The number on the top of the column is 5. The missing factor is 5.

$3 \times 5 = 15$ $15 \div 3 = 5$

×	0	1	2	3	4	5
0	0	0	0	0	0	0
1	0	1	2	3	4	5
2	0	2	4	6	8	10
3	0	3	6	9	12	15

Convince Me! **Reasoning** Write a missing factor equation and use the multiplication table above to solve each division problem.

$6 \div 3 = ?$ $12 \div 3 = ?$ $9 \div 3 = ?$

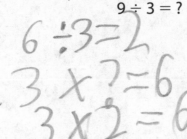

$6 \div 3 = 2$

$3 \times ? = 6$

$3 \times 2 = 6$

Name _____

☆Guided Practice*

Do You Understand?

1. Where in a multiplication table do you find the two factors in a multiplication problem?

2. How can you rephrase $35 \div 7$ so you can solve using a multiplication table?

3. Explain how to use a multiplication table to solve a missing factor equation.

Do You Know How?

In **4–11**, find the value that makes the equation correct. Use a multiplication table to help.

4. $24 \div 6 =$ _____

   $6 \times$ _____ $= 24$

5. $63 \div 9 =$ _____

   $9 \times$ _____ $= 63$

6. $25 \div 5 = \underline{5}$

   $5 \times \underline{5} = 25$

7. $42 \div 7 =$ _____

   $7 \times$ _____ $= 42$

8. $45 \div 5 =$ _____

   $5 \times$ _____ $= 45$

9. $15 \div 3 = \underline{5}$

   $3 \times \underline{5} = 15$

10. $12 \div 6 =$ _____

    $6 \times$ _____ $= 12$

11. $40 \div 5 =$ _____

    $5 \times$ _____ $= 40$

☆Independent Practice☆

Leveled Practice In **12–23**, find the value that makes the equations correct. Use a multiplication table to help.

12. $45 \div 9 = \underline{5}$

    $9 \times \underline{5} = 45$

13. $21 \div 3 =$ _____

    $3 \times$ _____ $= 21$

14. $36 \div 6 =$ _____

    $6 \times$ _____ $= 36$

15. $32 \div 4 = \underline{8}$

    $4 \times \underline{8} = 32$

16. $20 \div 5 =$ _____

    $5 \times$ _____ $= 20$

17. $21 \div 7 =$ _____

    $7 \times$ _____ $= 21$

18. $18 \div 9 = \underline{9}$

19. $35 \div 5 =$ _____

20. $56 \div 8 =$ _____

21. $28 \div 4 = \underline{7}$

22. $14 \div 7 =$ _____

23. $40 \div 5 =$ _____

Problem Solving

24. Some members of the Bird Club used a tally chart to record how many different birds they each saw one day. Fill in the blanks below to make the sentence correct. _____

saw 4 more birds than _____.

25. Complete the chart to show that Mr. Molina saw 5 fewer birds than Mr. Dobbs and Miss Simmons combined.

Number of Different Birds Seen	
Ms. Chester	ЖЖ II
Mr. Dobbs	IIII
Miss Simmons	ЖЖ ЖЖ I
Mr. Molina	_____

---

26. Critique Reasoning Bill used a multiplication table to find the value of $12 \div 6$. His answer was 3. Do you agree? Why or why not?

27. Algebra Find the value that makes the equation correct.

$$30 \div ? = 5$$
$$? = \underline{\quad}$$

---

28. Higher Order Thinking Brit uses a multiplication table to multiply 2 different factors. She notices that the product is in the same column as the number 35. What is one of the factors in Brit's multiplication problem? Explain your answer.

> Think about what you know and what you need to find.

 Assessment

29. Which of the following is the missing number in $21 \div \boxed{} = 7$?

    Ⓐ 1

    Ⓑ 3

    Ⓒ 7

    Ⓓ 9

×	0	1	2	3	4	5	6	7
0	0	0	0	0	0	0	0	0
1	0	1	2	3	4	5	6	7
2	0	2	4	6	8	10	12	14
3	0	3	6	9	12	15	18	21
4	0	4	8	12	16	20	24	28
5	0	5	10	15	20	25	30	35
6	0	6	12	18	24	30	36	42
7	0	7	14	21	28	35	42	49
8	0	8	16	24	32	40	48	56
9	0	9	18	27	36	45	54	63

Solve

Solve & Share

What are the missing factors and products in the table below? Fill in each missing number. *Solve these problems any way you choose.*

You can use reasoning about factors, products, and quotients to find basic facts.

I can ...
use reasoning and the relationship between multiplication and division to find basic facts.

I can also reason about math.

×	7	3	6	8	4	9
5	35	15	30	40	20	45
6	42	18	36	48	24	54
2	14	6	12	16	8	18
7	49	21	42	56	28	63
4	28	12	24	32	16	36
1	7	3	6	8	4	9

Look Back! **Construct Arguments** How did you find the missing factors in the top row and the first column? Explain using an example.

A

Essential Question **How Can You Find Multiplication and Division Basic Facts?**

The table at the right has some missing factors and some missing products. What are the missing numbers in the table?

You can use strategies and reasoning to find missing factors.

×	8	5	
2			
9	72		36
		20	
7			

← These are factors

↑ These are factors   ↑ These are products

B Think multiplication or division to find missing factors.

$36 ÷ 9 = 4$, so $9 × 4 = 36$

×	8	5	4
2			
9	72		36
4		20	
7			

$4 × 5 = 20$
$20 ÷ 5 = 4$

C Complete the table.

$2 × 8 = 16$ $2 × 5 = 10$ $2 × 4 = 8$
$4 × 8 = 32$ $9 × 5 = 45$ $4 × 4 = 16$
$7 × 8 = 56$ $7 × 5 = 35$ $7 × 4 = 28$

×	8	5	4
2	16	10	8
9	72	45	36
4	32	20	16
7	56	35	28

Convince Me! **Be Precise** Suppose one factor is 0 and the product is 0. What is the other factor? Tell how you decided.

It dose not matter because 0×1×0 0×2=0 It can by any number.

Name_____

☆ Guided Practice *

Do You Understand?

1. Reasoning When completing a multiplication table, how do you know when you can use division?

Do You Know How?

In **2**, find the missing factors and products.

2.

×	4	7	9
3	12	21	27
6	24	42	54
8	32	56	72
9	36	63	81

☆ Independent Practice ☆

In **3–6**, find the missing factors and products.

3.

×	8	5	7
2	16	10	14
5	40	25	35
6	48	30	42
9	72	45	63

4.

×	3	☐	9
4	12		
6	18		54
3	9	6	
☐			72

5.

×	☐	☐	9
2	12		
☐			54
3	18	9	
☐			45

6.

×	☐	7	4
8	16		32
☐		42	
☐	10		

*For another example, see Set C on page 288.

Topic 5 | Lesson 5-3   **251**

Problem Solving

7. Higher Order Thinking Which missing number do you find first in the multiplication table at the right: *A*, *B*, or *C*? Explain why.

×		B
5		35
A		14
1		C

---

8. Algebra What value of ? makes the equation $5 \times ? = 30$ true?

9. What division equations are in the same fact family as 7×4?

---

10. Model with Math Last week Toby practiced the drums 2 hours each day for 5 days. This week he practiced the drums for 12 hours in all. How many hours did he practice both weeks? Write equations to represent this problem.

11. Jordan is inviting 8 friends to his party. He wants to give each friend 2 maracas and have 2 for himself. Maracas come in boxes of 6. How many boxes does he need to buy?

---

12. Number Sense Fill in the blanks to make the equation correct.

_____ $\times 7 =$ _____ $\times 9$

> Think about how multiplication facts are related.

✓ **Assessment**

13. Complete the sentences below.

Robin has 24 eggs. She wants to put them in 3 baskets with the same number of eggs in each basket. How many eggs should she put in each basket?

$24 \div 3 =$ ☐ because $3 \times$ ☐ $= 24$.

Robin should put ☐ eggs in each basket.

14. Find the missing factors and products.

×	☐	4
2		
☐	63	36

---

252   **Topic 5** │ Lesson 5-3

Help Practice Tools Games
        Buddy

Another Look!

What are the missing factors and products in the table?

×	5	9	6
3	15	27	18
2	10	18	12
1	5	9	6
8	40	72	48

$12 \div 2 = 6$

$3 \times 5 = 15, 3 \times 6 = 18$

$2 \times 9 = 18$

$9 \div 9 = 1, 1 \times 5 = 5, 1 \times 6 = 6$

$8 \times 5 = 40, 8 \times 9 = 72, 8 \times 6 = 48$

Use the given numbers to find the missing numbers. Think multiplication or division.

In **1–4**, find the missing factors and products.

1.

×	☐	6	☐
0			
☐		30	
9	45		63
☐		42	

2.

×	☐	☐	9
2	8		
☐			81
3		9	
☐			72

3.

×	☐	☐	6
5	10		
☐			48
2	4	0	
☐			36

4.

×	3	☐	☐
4			20
☐	18		
1		8	
☐			35

5. **Model with Math** Leah has the flowers shown. She wants to put them in 4 vases with the same number in each vase. How many flowers does she need to put in each vase? Tell how you know.

6. **Higher Order Thinking** Bradley is trying to find a missing factor. A product of that factor has a 3 in the ones digit. Is the missing factor even or odd? Explain.

A chart can help you find relationships.

7. **Construct Arguments** George has 7 boxes of 5 pencils. Julio has 3 boxes of 8 pencils. One of the boys arranges all his pencils equally into 2 groups. Was this George or Julio? How many are in each group? Explain.

8. **Critique Reasoning** Ned says he cannot use division to solve a missing factor problem because factors are part of multiplication equations. Do you agree? Explain why or why not.

9. Complete the sentences below.

Jamal took 72 pictures with his digital camera while on vacation. He wants to put them in 8 folders on his computer. How many pictures should he put in each folder?

$72 \div 8 = \boxed{}$ because $8 \times \boxed{} = 72$.

Jamal should put $\boxed{}$ pictures in each folder.

10. Find the missing factors and products.

×	□	5
3		
□	48	40

Name _____

Solve

Alfredo has 3 bags of oranges in each hand. Each bag contains 5 oranges. How many oranges does Alfredo have? *Solve this problem any way you choose.*

I can ...
use different strategies to solve multiplication problems.

I can also look for patterns to solve problems.

You can use structure. Look for relationships when using counters, drawings, skip counting, arrays, or known facts to help solve the problem. *Show your work in the space below!*

$(2 \times 3) \times 5$

$6 \times 5 = 30$

oranges

2 hands
3 bags
5 oranges in each bag

Look Back! **Make Sense and Persevere** How do strategies such as skip counting, using known facts, and making arrays help you solve multiplication facts?

Essential Question **How Do You Use Strategies to Multiply?**

A

A scientist on a boat is studying hammerhead sharks. The length of 6 hammerhead sharks lined up nose to tail without gaps is equal to the length of the boat. How long is the boat?

An adult hammerhead shark is 5 yards long.

Drawings, skip counting, tools, and properties of operations are strategies you can use to multiply equal groups.

B **One Way**

Use a bar diagram to find 6×5.

6×5 means 6 groups of 5.
Skip count by 5s.

| ? |
| 5 | 5 | 5 | 5 | 5 | 5 |
 5   10   15   20   25   30

So, $6 \times 5 = 30$.

The boat is 30 yards long.

C **Another Way**

Use counters and properties to find 6×5.

The Distributive Property says you can break the problem into smaller parts. Use 2s facts and 4s facts to help.

$\}$ $2 \times 5 = 10$

$\}$ $4 \times 5 = 20$

Then add the two products: $10 + 20 = 30$.
The boat is 30 yards long.

Convince Me! **Use Structure** How can knowing the product of 5×6 help you solve 6×5?

are in the because 5x6 and 6x5 sam fact family

Practice Buddy   Tools   Assessment

☆Guided Practice*

Do You Understand?

1. What two known facts can you use to find 3×5?

   15

2. How could knowing $7 \times 5 = 35$ help you find 9×5?

Do You Know How?

In **3–8**, multiply.

3. $6 \times 4 = $ 24   4. $4 \times 5 = $ ____

5. $9 \times 3 = $ 27   6. $3 \times 2 = $ ____

7. $\begin{array}{r} 1 \\ \times\,4 \\ \hline \end{array}$ 4   8. $\begin{array}{r} 9 \\ \times\,8 \\ \hline \end{array}$

☆Independent Practice☆

In **9–25**, use strategies to find the product.

9. $5 \times 5 = $ 25   10. $9 \times 2 = $ ____   11. $5 \times 9 = $ 45

12. $8 \times 7 = $ ____   13. $3 \times 6 = $ 18   14. $8 \times 4 = $ ____

15. $\begin{array}{r} 10 \\ \times\,4 \\ \hline \end{array}$ 40   16. $\begin{array}{r} 7 \\ \times\,6 \\ \hline \end{array}$ 17. $\begin{array}{r} 6 \\ \times\,5 \\ \hline \end{array}$ 30   18. $\begin{array}{r} 2 \\ \times\,8 \\ \hline \end{array}$

19. $\begin{array}{r} 9 \\ \times\,0 \\ \hline \end{array}$ 0   20. $\begin{array}{r} 10 \\ \times\,6 \\ \hline \end{array}$ 21. $\begin{array}{r} 4 \\ \times\,9 \\ \hline \end{array}$ 36   22. $\begin{array}{r} 9 \\ \times\,7 \\ \hline \end{array}$

23. What is 4×6? 24   24. What is 5×8? ____   25. What is 10×1? 10

Problem Solving

In **26** and **27**, use the pictures below.

26. Make Sense and Persevere
Mr. Marks is studying 3 blacktip sharks and 4 tiger sharks. What is the total length of the 7 sharks? Show your strategy.

27. Critique Reasoning Kent says the total length of 4 blacktip sharks can be found using addition. Is he correct? Explain your thinking.

addition *yes, reppted*

Blacktip Shark
2 yards long

Tiger Shark
4 yards long

28. Cecilia buys two gifts. One gift costs $57. Cecilia spends $82 in all. How much money does the second gift cost?

$82

$57	$?

29. Higher Order Thinking Show how you can use known facts to find 11 × 9. Explain how you chose the known facts.

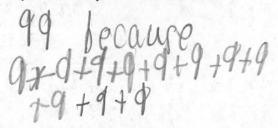

99 because
9×9+9+9+9+9+9
+9+9+9

✓ **Assessment**

30. Hal counted the number of fish in 3 fish tanks. There were 7 fish in each. How many fish were in the 3 fish tanks?

Ⓐ 21 fish
Ⓑ 24 fish
Ⓒ 27 fish
Ⓓ 37 fish

31. Bob is starting a sports card collection. He buys 5 packages of sports cards with 9 cards in each package. Which of the following does **NOT** show a way to find how many cards Bob has?

Ⓐ 9 + 9 + 9 + 9 + 9
Ⓑ (4 × 5) + (5 × 5) = 20 + 25
Ⓒ 5 × 9 = 45, so 9 × 5 = 45
Ⓓ 9 × (2 × 5)

Help Practice Tools Games
Buddy

Homework & Practice 5-4
Use Strategies to Multiply

Another Look!
Find 6 × 4.

You can use different strategies to find 6 × 4.

One Way
Draw a bar diagram and use skip counting.

6 × 4 means 6 groups of 4.

Each section of the bar diagram is 1 group of 4.

?

4	4	4	4	4	4
4	8	12	16	20	24

Skip count by 4s to solve.

So, 6 × 4 = 24.

Another Way
Using the Distributive Property is another way to solve this problem. Use 3s facts to help.

3 × 4 = 12

3 × 4 = 12

12 + 12 = 24

So, 6 × 4 = 24.

In **1** and **2**, show two different ways to find the product.

1. 3 × 5 = ?

?

5	5	
5	10	

2 × 5 = _____

1 × 5 = _____

3 × 5 = _____

10 + _____ = _____

2. 3 × 4 = ?

?

4	4	
4	8	

2 × 4 = _____

1 × 4 = _____

3 × 4 = _____

8 + _____ = _____

In **3–8**, multiply.

3. 7 × 2 = _____

4. 8 × 5 = _____

5. 6 × 8 = _____

6. 9 × 7 = _____

7. 4 × 8 = _____

8. 7 × 3 = _____

9. **Make Sense and Persevere** The home team scored 3 touchdowns. The visiting team scored 4 field goals. Which team scored more points? Show your strategy.

DATA

Football Points

Type	Points
Touchdown	6 points
Field Goal	3 points
Safety	2 points

10. **Critique Reasoning** Rick says, "To find 2 × 5, I can skip count by 5s: 5, 10, 15, 20, 25. The product is 25." Explain what Rick did wrong.

11. **Algebra** Write the symbols to make the equations correct.

$81 = 9 \boxed{} 9$

$9 \boxed{} 6 = 54$

$9 = 72 \boxed{} 8$

12. **Higher Order Thinking** Jill has 4 bags of marbles. There are 3 red, 5 green, 2 yellow, and 6 black marbles in each bag. How many marbles does Jill have? Show how you found the answer.

13. Mr. Roberts plans to drive a total of 56 miles. He has 29 more miles to go. How many miles has he driven so far?

56 miles	
?	29 miles

✔ **Assessment**

14. Tia counted the campers and beds in 7 cabins. Each cabin had 9 campers and 12 beds. How many campers were in the 7 cabins?

  Ⓐ 84 campers   Ⓒ 63 campers

  Ⓑ 72 campers   Ⓓ 35 campers

15. Which of the following does **NOT** show a way to find the product of 2 × 5?

  Ⓐ 5 × 2

  Ⓑ 5 + 5 + 5

  Ⓒ 2 + 2 + 2 + 2 + 2

  Ⓓ (2 × 2) + (3 × 2) = 4 + 6

Name _____

Solve

Lesson 5-5
Solve Word
Problems:
Multiplication and
Division Facts

Solve & Share

At the Fall Fest parade, members of the Cat Lovers Club and the Dog Lovers Club will march in equal rows. There will be 6 members in each row. How many rows of dog lovers will march in the parade? How many total cat lovers will march in the parade?

Complete the table. **Solve the problem any way you choose.**

I can ...
use strategies to solve word problems that involve multiplication and division.

I can also choose and use a math tool to solve problems.

Think about how you can use appropriate tools to help solve the problem.

Pet Club	Number of Members at the Parade	Number of Rows at the Parade
Dog Lovers	24	4
Cat Lovers	30	5

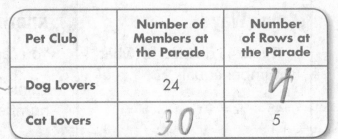

$24 \div 6 = 4$

$5 \times 6 = 30$

Look Back! Reasoning What operations did you use to solve the problem? Explain your reasoning.

A

Essential Question: How Can You Solve Word Problems Using Multiplication and Division?

Gina has 45 hats. She is packing them by putting 9 hats in each of several boxes. How many boxes will she fill?

Drawing pictures and writing equations can help you when solving multiplication and division problems.

B

45 hats

? boxes

9

9 hats in a box

You can use a bar diagram to show how the numbers are related.

C **One Way**

Think: 45 divided by what number equals 9?

$45 \div 5 = 9$

There are 5 groups of 9 in 45.

Gina can divide 45 hats into 5 boxes of 9 hats each.

D **Another Way**

You can use a related fact.

Think: 9 times what number equals 45?

$9 \times 5 = 45$

So, $45 \div 9 = 5$.

Gina can divide 45 hats into 5 boxes of 9 hats each.

Convince Me! **Generalize** Gina instead has 42 hats. She is putting 6 hats in each of several boxes. Can you find how many boxes she needs using the same strategies as in the example above? Explain.

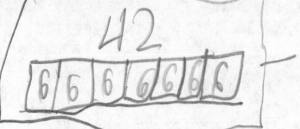

42

6 6 6 6 6 6 6 = 7 boxes

☆ Guided Practice ☆

Do You Understand?

1. Why can you use division to model the problem on page 262?

2. Casey gives 27 stickers to 3 friends. She writes the equation $27 \div 3 = 9$. What does the 9 represent in this problem?

   ✗ q u s o n t

Do You Know How?

In **3**, represent the problem with an equation or a bar diagram. Then solve.

3. A checkerboard has 64 squares. It has 8 rows. How many columns does it have?

Independent Practice ☆

In **4** and **5**, draw a bar diagram to represent the problem. Then solve.

4. There are 5 pancakes in a stack. Elise makes 40 pancakes. How many stacks does Elise make?

   8

5. A park has 4 swing sets. Each of the sets has 7 swings. How many swings are in the park?

In **6** and **7**, write an equation with an unknown to represent the problem. Then solve.

6. Mrs. Jameson plants 30 tulips in rows. Each row has 6 tulips. How many rows did Mrs. Jameson plant?

   5

7. Bonnie buys 6 paperback books every month. She buys 2 hardcover books every month. How many books does she buy in 4 months?

Problem Solving

8. Model with Math Jodie has 24 flowers in her garden. She wants to give an equal number of flowers to 4 families in her neighborhood. How many flowers will each family get? Complete the bar diagram and write an equation to help you solve this problem.

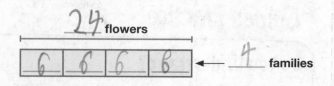

24 flowers

| 6 | 6 | 6 | 6 | ← 4 families

---

9. Model with Math Casey has 2 sisters. He gave each sister 2 pages of stickers. Each page had 9 stickers on it. How many stickers did Casey give in all? Explain what math you used to solve.

10. Jane is thinking about a shape with more than 5 sides. Draw a picture to show which shape Jane could be thinking about.

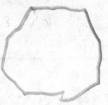

---

11. Higher Order Thinking 25 students are working in groups on a science project. Each group can have either 2 or 3 students in it. What is the fewest number of groups there could be?

A picture can help you solve a problem!

 Assessment

12. 8 vans are going to the zoo. There are 6 children in each van.

Part A

How many children are going to the zoo? Write an equation that could be used to find the answer to this problem. Solve that equation.

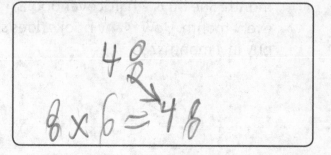

$$8 \times 6 = 48$$

Part B

If instead 9 vans go to the zoo, explain how you can use what you know from Part A to find how many children are going to the zoo.

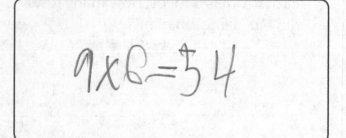

$$9 \times 6 = 54$$

Help   Practice   Tools   Games
Buddy

Another Look!

Rico has 32 pine cones. He uses 8 pine cones to make a sculpture in art class. If Rico makes more sculptures with 8 pine cones for each, how many total sculptures can he make?

Draw a bar diagram to represent the problem.

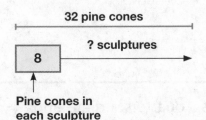

32 pine cones

? sculptures

8

Pine cones in each sculpture

Multiply or divide to solve: $8 \times 4 = 32$ or $32 \div 4 = 8$.

So, Rico can make 4 sculptures.

A bar diagram can help you see there is more than one way to think about this problem.

In **1** and **2**, draw a bar diagram to represent the problem. Then solve.

1. Victor buys some six-packs of soda for a party. He buys 42 cans in all. How many six-packs of soda did Victor buy?

2. Lester listens to 8 songs every time he does his exercise routine. He did his exercise routine 3 times this week. How many songs did Lester listen to while exercising this week?

In **3** and **4**, write an equation with an unknown to represent the problem. Then solve.

3. There are 9 players on a baseball team. A club has 9 baseball teams. How many baseball players are in the club?

4. Megan earned $4 for an hour of babysitting. On Saturday, she earned $16. How many hours did she babysit?

---

5. Model with Math Andre is setting up folding chairs for a school assembly. He sets up 4 rows of chairs. Each row has 7 chairs. How many chairs does Andre set up? Complete the bar diagram and write an equation to solve.

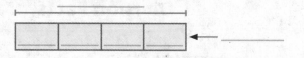

6. Higher Order Thinking 36 students ride a school bus route home. The same number of students get off at each stop. Harriet knows how many students got off at one stop. How could she find how many stops the bus made?

7. Mr. Ameda has 4 children. He gives each of them 2 cookies. He spends $40 on the cookies. How much did each cookie cost?

8. Yogesh has 3 quarters, 1 dime, and 2 pennies. How much money does he have?

9. Critique Reasoning Neville and Anthony are solving this problem: Barbara bought 3 boxes of pencils with 6 pencils in each box. How many pencils did she buy in all?

Neville says, "I add because of the words *in all*. The answer is 9 pencils." Anthony says, "I multiply because there are equal groups. The answer is 18 pencils." Who is correct? Explain.

 Assessment

10. Garrett uses 5 apples to bake an apple pie. On Sunday, he bakes 2 pies.

Part A

How many apples does Garrett need on Sunday? Write an equation that could be used to find the answer to this problem. Solve that equation.

Part B

On each of the next three days, Garrett will bake the same number of apple pies that he baked on Sunday. Explain how you can use what you know from Part A to find how many apples Garrett needs for those three days.

Name _____

☆ **Solve & Share** ☆

Write and solve a multiplication story about 4 × 5. Choose one of the phrases below to use in your multiplication story.

Phrases

• 4 equal groups of 5
• 4 rows of 5
• 4 rows and 5 columns

I can ...
write and solve math stories for multiplication equations.

I can also make sense of problems.

In a math book it said 4 rows of 5 but Mike could not understand what the math book was telling. You will have to figer out

You can make sense of problems. You can write multiplication stories about objects in your classroom.

Look Back! **Reasoning** Why is the answer to your classmate's story the same as the answer to your story?

Essential Question **How Can You Describe a Multiplication Fact?**

A

Write a multiplication story for 3×6.

Stories can be written to describe multiplication facts.

You can draw pictures and use objects to represent joining equal groups.

B **Equal Groups**

Randy has 3 packs of 6 buttons. How many buttons does he have?

$3 \times 6 = 18$

Randy has 18 buttons.

C **An Array**

Eliza planted 6 lilies in each of 3 rows. How many lilies did she plant?

$3 \times 6 = 18$

Eliza planted 18 lilies.

D **Bar Diagram**

A rabbit eats an equal amount of carrots each day for 3 days. If the rabbit eats 6 carrots each day, how many carrots does it eat in all?

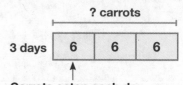

? carrots

3 days | 6 | 6 | 6

Carrots eaten each day

$3 \times 6 = 18$

The rabbit eats 18 carrots.

Convince Me! **Reasoning** Write a multiplication story for $10 \times 3 = \square$.

James has 10 bags in each bag there are 3 marbels. How many marbels are there in all?

☆ Guided Practice *

Do You Understand?

In **1–3**, use the stories on page 268.

1. How would the story about Randy change if $2 \times 6 = \boxed{}$ were used instead?

2. Could the story about the carrots be written as an addition story? Explain.

Yes

3. What equation could be written if Eliza planted 6 lilies in each of 2 rows?

Do You Know How?

In **4** and **5**, write a multiplication story for the equation. Then find the product.

4. $3 \times 5 =$ *15*

5. $2 \times 4 =$ ____

☆ Independent Practice ☆

Leveled Practice In **6–9**, write a multiplication story for each picture or equation. Then find the product.

6.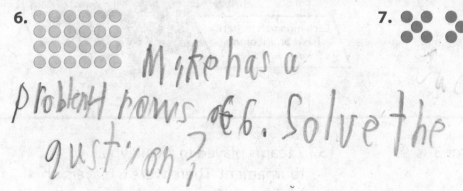

Mike has a problent rows of 6. Solve the question? gurs

7.

8. $7 \times 3 =$ *21*

Mikeis solveing 7x3 but he does not understand. Help him?

9. $5 \times 5 =$ ____

Problem Solving

10. **Reasoning** Write a multiplication story about these pencils. Write an equation for your story.

Think about how many equal groups will be in your story.

11. **Number Sense** Brian said $42 + 35 + 16$ is greater than 150. Explain why his answer is not reasonable.

12. A soccer team traveled to a game in 4 vans. Each van held 6 players. Two of the players are goalkeepers. How many of the players are not goalkeepers?

24 players

13. **Higher Order Thinking** A group of 9 monarch butterflies is getting ready to migrate. Write a multiplication story involving this group. Explain what fact you are using and find the product.

Each monarch butterfly has 4 bright orange wings and 6 legs.

14. Write a multiplication story for 3×9. Then find the product.

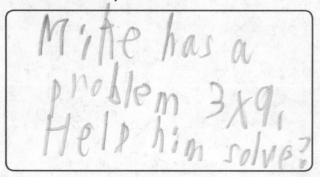

Mike has a problem 3x9, Help him solve?

15. 7 teams played in a volleyball tournament. There were 6 players on each team. Draw a picture and write a multiplication equation for this story.

Name _____

☆ **Solve & Share** ☆

Write a real-world division story for 28 ÷ 4. Then write another real-world story that shows a different way to think about 28 ÷ 4.

You can generalize. What is the same in both of your stories?

Look Back! **Model with Math** Draw a bar diagram and write an equation to represent and solve one of your division stories.

Essential Question

What Is the Main Idea of a Division Story?

A

Mrs. White asked her students to write a division story for 15 ÷ 3.

Mike and Kia decided to write stories about putting roses in vases.

B Mike's Story

I have 15 roses. I want to put an equal number of roses in each of 3 vases. How many roses should I put in each vase?

Find $15 \div 3 = \square$.

The main idea is "How many are in each group?"

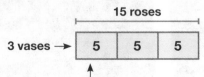

15 roses

3 vases → | 5 | 5 | 5 |

↑
5 roses in each vase

$15 \div 3 = 5$

I should put 5 roses in each vase.

C Kia's Story

I have 15 roses to put into vases. I want to put 3 roses in each vase. How many vases will I need?

The main idea is "How many groups are there?"

Find $15 \div 3 = \square$.

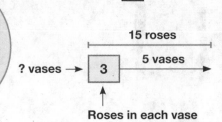

15 roses

? vases → | 3 | 5 vases →

↑
Roses in each vase

$15 \div 3 = 5$

I will need 5 vases.

Convince Me! Generalize How are Mike's and Kia's stories alike? How are the two stories different?

Name _____

☆ Guided Practice *

Do You Understand?

1. When you write a division story, what two pieces of information do you need to include?

2. When you write a division story, what kind of information do you ask for?

Do You Know How?

In **3,** plan and write a division story for the equation. Then solve.

3. $8 \div 4 =$ _____

I will write about 8 _____.
They will be in 4 equal groups.

☆ Independent Practice ☆

Leveled Practice In **4–7**, plan and write a division story for each equation. Then use counters or draw a picture to solve.

4. $18 \div 3 =$ _____

I will write about 18 _____.
I will put them in 3 equal groups.

5. $14 \div$ _____ $= 2$

I will write about 14 _____.
I will put them in groups of 2.

6. $24 \div 8 =$ _____

7. $30 \div$ _____ $= 3$

Problem Solving

In **8–11**, use the table at the right. There are 36 third graders who want to play on different teams.

8. **Model with Math** If all the third graders want to play baseball, how many teams will there be? Write a division equation to represent the problem.

9. **Use Appropriate Tools** Explain how you could use a tool to solve **8**.

	Sports Team	Players per Team
DATA	Baseball	9 players
	Basketball	5 players
	Doubles Tennis	2 players

10. Suppose that 20 third graders went swimming and the rest played doubles tennis. How many doubles tennis teams would there be?

11. **Be Precise** Could all 36 third graders play in basketball games at the same time? Explain your answer.

12. **Higher Order Thinking** Hector wrote this division story for 24 ÷ 4:

"There are 24 bears in the woods. Each bear has 4 legs. How many legs are on all the bears in the woods?"

Explain whether you agree with Hector. If so, find the answer. If not, write a correct division story.

13. Kara has 40 activity books. She keeps 25 books and gives the rest to friends as gifts. Each friend gets the same number of books. How many friends get activity books?

COLORING BOOK

5 books for each friend

✓ **Assessment**

14. Write a division story for 35 ÷ ? = 7. Draw a picture to represent your story. Then solve.

Help Practice Tools Games
Buddy

Another Look!

Eddie was asked to write a division story using $12 \div 4 =$ ☐

This is Eddie's story:

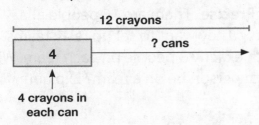

Cami has 12 crayons and some cans.
She put 4 crayons in each can.
How many cans did Cami use?

You can draw a bar diagram to represent Eddie's story.

12 crayons

4

? cans

4 crayons in each can

$12 \div 4 = 3$. So, Cami used 3 cans.

In **1** and **2**, write the missing information to plan a division story for each equation. Write the story. Use counters or draw a picture to solve.

1. $10 \div \underline{\hspace{0.5cm}} = 5$

I will write about 10 _____.
I will put them in groups of 5.

2. $21 \div 7 = \underline{\hspace{0.5cm}}$

I will write about 21 _____.
I will put them in 7 equal groups.

In **3** and **4**, write a division story for each equation. Use counters or draw a picture to solve.

3. $48 \div 6 = \underline{\hspace{0.5cm}}$

4. $56 \div \underline{\hspace{0.5cm}} = 8$

5. **Make Sense and Persevere** Sheila wrote a division story. She wrote about how to divide 24 flowers into equal groups. What information must she give about the groups?

6. **A-Z Vocabulary** Jean wrote the numbers 0, 6, 12, 18, 24, and 30 on a piece of paper. Complete the sentence to describe what each of these numbers has in common with the number 6.

They are all _____ of 6.

7. Vera uses place-value blocks to add two numbers. What addition equation can Vera use?

8. **Be Precise** There are 16 people at a party. They want to set up relay teams with exactly 3 people on each team. Will each person be on a team? Explain.

9. **Higher Order Thinking** Complete the sentences with numbers that make sense. Do not use the number 1. Then write the division equation that matches the story, and draw a picture to solve.

"There are 35 rabbits at the fair. The rabbits are kept in _____ hutches with _____ rabbits in each hutch."

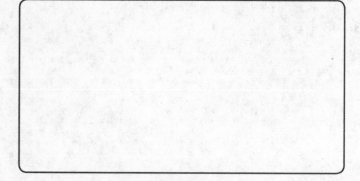

✔ **Assessment**

10. Write a division story for 49 ÷ 7. Draw a picture to represent your story. Then solve.

Name _____

Solve & Share

Jacob has started the pattern below. Fill in the blanks to make correct equations and continue the pattern. Explain your thinking.

$6 \times 1 = 3 \times 2$

$6 \times 2 = 3 \times 4$

$6 \times 3 = 3 \times \boxed{}$

$6 \times \boxed{} = 3 \times \boxed{}$

$\boxed{} \times \boxed{} = \boxed{} \times \boxed{}$

I can ...
use the structure of multiplication and division to compare expressions.

I can also compare without computing.

Thinking Habits

Be a good thinker!
These questions can help you.

• What patterns can I see and describe?

• How can I use the patterns to solve the problem?

• Can I see expressions and objects in different ways?

Look Back! **Use Structure** Jacob starts this new pattern. Fill in the blank to make the equation true. What do you notice about this pattern compared to the pattern above?

$3 \times 2 = 6 \times 1$

$3 \times 4 = 6 \times 2$

$3 \times \boxed{} = 6 \times 3$

Essential Question | How Can You Use the Structure of Mathematics?

A

How can you tell without computing whether the symbol
> , < , or = should be placed in each circle below?

1. 4 × 5 × 2 ◯ 4 × 3 × 5
2. 6 × 7 ◯ 7 × 6

You do not have to compute. You can use the structure of the number system to compare.

What do I need to do to complete the task?

I need to compare the expressions. Instead of doing any calculations, I will look at the values of the factors in each expression.

Here's my thinking...

B **How can I make use of structure to solve this problem?**

I can

- think about properties I know.

- look for patterns and use them as needed.

C

Some factors in the expressions are the same and some are different. I will use this to help me compare.

1. I know that I can group factors in any way, so I can rewrite one expression.

$$2 < 3$$

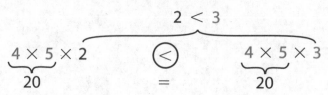

$\underbrace{4 \times 5}\, \times 2 \qquad \textcircled{<} \qquad \underbrace{4 \times 5}\, \times 3$

20 $\qquad\qquad$ = $\qquad\qquad$ 20

2. I see the factors are the same on both sides. I know this means the products are the same.

6 × 7 ◯= 7 × 6

Convince Me! **Use Structure** Dario says, "I can find $9 \times 0 < 3 \times 1$ without computing. I can think about properties that I know." What could he mean?

Name _____

☆Guided Practice☆

Use Structure

Hakeem and Nicole each have 48 stickers. Hakeem shared his stickers among 8 friends. Nicole shared her stickers among 6 friends. These expressions show how Hakeem and Nicole shared their stickers.

Use structure to compare the values on each side of the circle.

$48 \div 8 \bigcirc 48 \div 6$

1. Look at the expressions. Explain how you can use what you see to compare without computing.

2. Whose friends each received more stickers? Write the correct symbol $>$, $<$, or $=$ in the circle above.

Independent Practice ☆

Use Structure

Dan has saved $10 each week for 7 weeks. Misha has saved $7 each week for 9 weeks. These expressions show how they saved.

$7 \times \$10 \bigcirc 9 \times \$7$

3. Look at the expressions. Explain how you can use what you see to compare without computing.

4. Who saved more money? Write the correct symbol $>$, $<$, or $=$ in the circle above.

5. Can you use the same symbol you wrote in **4** to compare $\$10 \times 7$ and $\$7 \times 9$? Explain.

Selling Necklaces

Trina wants to find the cheapest way to buy 24 necklaces. She wants to buy only the same type of packages. She has $48. The table shows the number of necklaces in a package and the cost of each package.

Number of Necklaces in a Package	Number of Packages Trina Should Buy	Cost per Package
3	24 ÷ 3 = 8	$4
4	___ ÷ ___ = ___	$5
6	___ ÷ ___ = ___	$6

6. **Model with Math** Complete the table to find the number of packages Trina would need to buy.

7. **Use Structure** Trina can use 8 × $4 to find the cost of enough $4 packages.
Write a similar expression that shows a way to find how much it costs Trina to buy enough $5 packages.

Write a similar expression that shows a way to find how much it costs Trina to buy enough $6 packages.

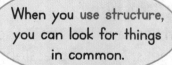

When you use structure, you can look for things in common.

8. **Construct Arguments** Compare the cost of buying the $5 packages to the $6 packages. Which package type costs less if Trina wants to buy 24 necklaces? Explain how to solve without computing.

9. **Construct Arguments** Compare the costs of buying the $4 packages to the $6 packages. Which package type costs less if Trina wants to buy 24 necklaces? Explain how to solve without computing.

Another Look!

How can you tell without computing which of the symbols >, <, or = should be placed in the circle below?

$4 \times 6 \times 2 \bigcirc 6 \times 2 \times 4$

Tell how you can use the structure of mathematics to complete the task.

- I can think about properties I know.

- I can look for patterns and use them as needed.

Look at the expressions. Explain how you can use the factors you see to compare without computing.

The same 3 factors are on each side of the circle. I know that the same factors grouped in a different way have the same product. So, the expressions are equal.

$4 \times (6 \times 2) \, \textcircled{=} \, (6 \times 2) \times 4$

You can use the structure of the number system to compare the values on each side.

Use Structure

Maria wrote the expression at the left of the circle below. Riaz wrote the expression at the right of the circle below. Find without computing which of the symbols >, <, or = should be placed in the circle.

Maria   **Riaz**

$4 \times 8 \times 3 \bigcirc 2 \times 3 \times 8$

1. Tell how you can use the structure of mathematics to complete the task.

2. Look at the expressions. Explain how you can use the factors you see to compare without computing.

3. Whose expression has the greater value? Write the correct symbol >, <, or = in the circle above.

Baseball League

Ms. Bush manages a baseball league. She buys the bucket of baseballs shown to share among the teams. She wants to use all the baseballs. The league will have either 6 or 9 teams. There are 14 players on each team. Ms. Bush is trying to decide whether to charge $3 or $4 for each baseball.

36 baseballs in a bucket

4. **Make Sense and Persevere** What information do you know from the problem?

5. **Use Structure** Ms. Bush says each team will get more baseballs if there are 6 teams in the league. Mr. Rosin says each team will get more baseballs if there are 9 teams in the league. Who is correct?

Compare by writing the symbol $>$, $<$, or $=$. Tell how to decide without computing.

$36 \div 6 \bigcirc 36 \div 9$

6. **Use Structure** Suppose Ms. Bush charges $4 per baseball. Would each team pay more if there are 6 teams or 9 teams?

Compare by writing the symbol $>$, $<$, or $=$. Tell how to decide without computing.

$(36 \div 6) \times \$4 \bigcirc (36 \div 9) \times \$4$

You can use structure to compare information from different problems.

7. **Construct Arguments** Ms. Bush wants to set up the league so that each team pays the least amount. Should there be 6 or 9 teams? Should each baseball cost $3 or $4? Explain.

Point & Tally

Find a partner. Get paper and a pencil. Each partner chooses a different color: light blue or dark blue.

Partner 1 and Partner 2 each point to a black number at the same time. Both partners multiply those numbers.

If the answer is on your color, you get a tally mark. Work until one partner has seven tally marks.

I can ...
multiply within 100.

Partner 1

9

5

6

8

4

63	24	40
42	81	28
36	35	56
16	72	30
54	20	48
25	45	32

Partner 2

7

4

5

6

9

Tally Marks for Partner 1

Tally Marks for Partner 2

A-Z
Glossary

Word List
- column
- equation
- even
- fact family
- odd
- row

Understand Vocabulary

For each of these terms, give an example and a non-example.

	Example	Non-example
1. equation	_____	_____
2. odd number	_____	_____
3. even number	_____	_____
4. fact family	_____	_____
	_____	_____

Write *always*, *sometimes*, or *never*.

5. An *even* number can _____ be divided by 2 with none left over.

6. A *fact family* _____ has *odd* numbers.

7. An array _____ has the same number of *rows* and *columns*.

8. The product of an *odd* number times an *odd* number is _____ an *even* number.

Use Vocabulary in Writing

9. Explain the pattern in the green squares. Use at least 2 terms from the Word List in your explanation.

×	0	1	2	3	4	5
0	0	0	0	0	0	0
1	0	1	2	3	4	5
2	0	2	4	6	8	10
3	0	3	6	9	12	15
4	0	4	8	12	16	20
5	0	5	10	15	20	25

Set A | pages 237–242

You can see patterns in a multiplication table.

×	0	1	2	3	4	5	6	7
0	0	0	0	0	0	0	0	0
1	0	1	2	3	4	5	6	7
2	0	2	4	6	8	10	12	14
3	0	3	6	9	12	15	18	21
4	0	4	8	12	16	20	24	28
5	0	5	10	15	20	25	30	35
6	0	6	12	18	24	30	36	42
7	0	7	14	21	28	35	42	49
8	0	8	16	24	32	40	48	56

In each row, the sum of the green shaded numbers equals the purple shaded number.

$0 + 0 = 0$ $1 + 6 = 7$

$2 + 12 = 14$ $3 + 18 = 21$

This is because of the Distributive Property.

A 1s fact plus a 6s fact equals a 7s fact.

Example: $(1 \times 5) + (6 \times 5) = (7 \times 5)$

Remember that properties can help to explain patterns.

In **1** and **2**, use the multiplication table to answer the questions.

×	0	1	2	3	4	5	6	7	8
0	0	0	0	0	0	0	0	0	0
1	0	1	2	3	4	5	6	7	8
2	0	2	4	6	8	10	12	14	16
3	0	3	6	9	12	15	18	21	24
4	0	4	8	12	16	20	24	28	32
5	0	5	10	15	20	25	30	35	40
6	0	6	12	18	24	30	36	42	48
7	0	7	14	21	28	35	42	49	56
8	0	8	16	24	32	40	48	56	64

1. Find the column which has products that are the sum of the green shaded numbers in each row. Shade this column.

2. Explain why this pattern is true.

Set B | pages 243–248

Use a multiplication table to find $20 \div 4$.

×	0	1	2	3	4	5	6	7
0	0	0	0	0	0	0	0	0
1	0	1	2	3	4	5	6	7
2	0	2	4	6	8	10	12	14
3	0	3	6	9	12	15	18	21
4	0	4	8	12	16	20	24	28
5	0	5	10	15	20	25	30	35
6	0	6	12	18	24	30	36	42
7	0	7	14	21	28	35	42	49
8	0	8	16	24	32	40	48	56
9	0	9	18	27	36	45	54	63

Find 4 in the first column of the table.

Follow the 4s row until you come to 20.

Then look to the top of that column to find the missing factor: 5. $20 \div 4 = 5$

Remember how multiplication and division are related.

In **1–12**, use the multiplication table to find each product or quotient.

1. $2 \times 7 =$ _____   2. $5 \times 8 =$ _____

3. $2 \times 10 =$ _____   4. $5 \times 4 =$ _____

5. $3 \times 5 =$ _____   6. $6 \times 5 =$ _____

7. $63 \div 9 =$ _____   8. $56 \div 8 =$ _____

9. $45 \div 9 =$ _____   10. $40 \div 8 =$ _____

11. $35 \div 7 =$ _____   12. $36 \div 6 =$ _____

You can use basic facts and properties to find missing numbers in a multiplication table.

×	4	5	☐	7
3	12	15	18	21
4	16	20	24	28
5	20	25	30	35
6	24	30	36	42
7	28		42	49
8	32	40	48	56

Use multiplication or division to find missing factors.

$42 \div 7 = 6$, so $7 \times 6 = 42$

Use strategies to find products.

$3 \times 5 = 15$ $4 \times 5 = 20$

$5 \times 5 = 25$ $6 \times 5 = 30$

So, $7 \times 5 = 35$

Remember that you can use strategies and reasoning to find missing numbers.

Use multiplication and division strategies to complete the multiplication table. Show your work.

×	☐	5	6	☐
☐	12	15	18	
☐	16	20		28
5	20	25	30	35
6	24	30		42
7		35	42	49
8	32	40	48	

Find 4×7.

> There are different strategies you can use when multiplying.

You can use skip counting:
7, 14, 21, 28

You can use known facts:

$2 \times 7 = 14$

$4 \times 7 = (2 \times 7) + (2 \times 7)$

$4 \times 7 = 14 + 14 = 28$

Remember that you can use patterns, known facts, or skip counting to find products.

In **1–8**, use strategies to find the product.

1. $5 \times 9 =$ _____

2. $8 \times 10 =$ _____

3. $4 \times 10 =$ _____

4. $9 \times 8 =$ _____

5. $6 \times 9 =$ _____

6. $7 \times 3 =$ _____

7. $6 \times 5 =$ _____

8. $4 \times 9 =$ _____

Set E   pages 261–266

You can solve word problems using multiplication and division.

Aaron has 49 books. His bookcase has 7 shelves. He wants to display an equal number of books on each shelf. How many books can he put on each shelf?

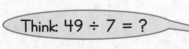

Think: 49 ÷ 7 = ?

You can use a related multiplication fact:

$7 \times 7 = 49$

$49 \div 7 = 7$

Aaron can put 7 books on each shelf.

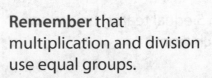

Reteaching
Continued

Remember that multiplication and division use equal groups.

Solve each problem. Show your work.

1. Oksana's dad has 36 batteries in his desk drawer. The batteries come in packs of 4. How many packs of batteries does he have?

2. Every time Lee wins the ring toss at the carnival, he gets 3 prize tickets. Lee needs to win the ring toss 9 times to have enough prize tickets for 1 toy. How many prize tickets does Lee need for 2 toys?

Set F   pages 267–272

Write a multiplication story for 4×7.

You can think of multiplication as equal groups.

Tim has 4 bunches of flowers. Each bunch has 7 flowers. How many flowers does Tim have?

Tim has 28 flowers.

Remember that rows and columns can also represent multiplication.

Write a multiplication story for each equation. Then solve.

1. $3 \times 9 =$ _____

2. $5 \times 6 =$ _____

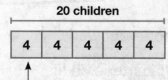

Write a division story for 20 ÷ 5.

If 20 children form 5 equal teams, how many children are on each team?

20 children

4	4	4	4	4

↑
Children on each team

20 ÷ 5 = 4

There are 4 children on each team.

Remember that division stories can ask for the number in each group, or the number of equal groups.

> Write a division story for each equation. Then solve.

1. 60 ÷ 10 = _____

2. 32 ÷ 4 = _____

Set H pages 279–284

Think about these questions to help you **look for and make use of structure.**

Thinking Habits

- What patterns can I see and describe?

- How can I use the patterns to solve the problem?

- Can I see expressions and objects in different ways?

Remember that properties can help you understand patterns.

Leroy earns $7 each hour that he works. He works for 8 hours. Rebecca earns $8 each hour that she works. She works for 7 hours. These expressions show the money they earned.

8 × $7 ◯ 7 × $8

1. Look at the expressions. Explain how you can use what you see to compare without computing.

2. Who earned more money? Write the correct symbol >, <, or = in the circle above.

1. Write and solve a division story for $48 \div 6$.

3. Jesse has 45 apple slices. He bakes 5 apple tarts. How many apple slices are used in each tart? Draw a bar diagram to represent the problem. Then solve the problem.

2. Look at the multiplication table below.

×	☐	☐	8
0			
☐		7	8
2			16
3	18		
☐		28	

Part A

Fill in the missing factors and products.

Part B

What pattern do you see in the first row of products in the table? Explain why this pattern is true.

4. Is the product of the following problems greater than 5×7? Choose *Yes* or *No*.

4a. $2 \times 2 \times 7$　　○ Yes ○ No

4b. $7 \times 1 \times 5$　　○ Yes ○ No

4c. $2 \times 5 \times 7$　　○ Yes ○ No

4d. $8 \times 5 \times 0$　　○ Yes ○ No

5. Nate has 4 pages of stickers arranged in arrays. The table shows the number of rows and columns on each page. Which page has the most stickers?

Page	Rows	Columns
1	3	5
2	5	4
3	4	3
4	5	3

Ⓐ Page 1　　　Ⓒ Page 3

Ⓑ Page 2　　　Ⓓ Page 4

6. Which of the following strategies can help you solve 4 × 6? Choose all that apply.

- ☐ (6 × 6) + (6 × 6)
- ☐ (4 × 3) + (4 × 3)
- ☐ (5 × 5) + (4 × 1)
- ☐ (5 × 4) + (1 × 4)
- ☐ (2 × 4) + (2 × 6)

7. What number is missing from this multiplication table?

×	5	6
2	10	?
3	15	18

- Ⓐ 8
- Ⓑ 9
- Ⓒ 11
- Ⓓ 12

8. Draw lines to match each product or quotient on the left with the equation it solves on the right.

56	54 ÷ 6 = ?
7	8 × 7 = ?
36	49 ÷ 7 = ?
9	6 × 6 = ?

9. Beverly notices a pattern in the multiplication table. She shades some squares orange to show her pattern.

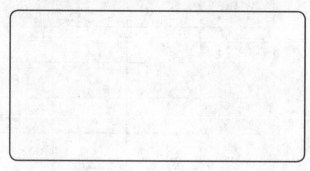

×	4	5	6	7
4	16	20	24	28
5	20	25	30	35
6	24	30	36	42
7	28	35	42	49
8	32	40	48	56

Part A

What pattern could Beverly have seen?

Part B

Explain why this pattern is true.

Name _____

10. Freddy has 70 books. He puts 7 books in a stack. How many stacks can he make this way?

11. Which of the following stories is about 8 × 4? Choose all that apply.

☐ Billy has 4 columns and 8 rows of stamps. How many stamps does Billy have?

☐ Billy gives away 8 stamps. Each of 4 friends gets the same number of stamps. How many stamps does each friend get?

☐ Billy has 8 stamps. They are in 4 equal rows. How many stamps are in each row?

☐ Billy has a row of 4 stamps and a row of 8 stamps. How many stamps does Billy have in all?

☐ Billy has 8 rows of stamps. Each row has 4 stamps. How many stamps are there in all?

12. Maya has 12 pens that she wants to put into equal groups. Can she put the pens in groups of the following numbers with none left over?

12a. 2 ○ Yes ○ No

12b. 3 ○ Yes ○ No

12c. 4 ○ Yes ○ No

12d. 5 ○ Yes ○ No

13. Look at these two expressions.

$40 \div 4 \bigcirc 40 \div 8$

Part A

Explain how you can use what you see to compare the expressions without computing.
Then write the correct symbol >, <, or = in the circle above.

Part B

Check your answer by computing both quotients. Write the quotients and the correct symbol >, <, or = below.

___ ◯ ___

14. A kennel has 9 dogs. Each dog gets 3 dog treats. How many treats do all the dogs get together? Write an equation to solve the problem.

15. Which shows a way to solve 5 × 5?

   Ⓐ Skip count 5 times by numbers that end in 5: 5, 15, 25, 35, 45

   Ⓑ Use the Distributive Property: (4 × 5) + (1 × 5)

   Ⓒ Look at a multiplication table: Find the 5s row. Go across until you find 5. The product is the number at the top of that column, 1.

   Ⓓ Use repeated addition: 5 + 5 + 5 + 5

16. Write and solve a multiplication story for 9 × 7.

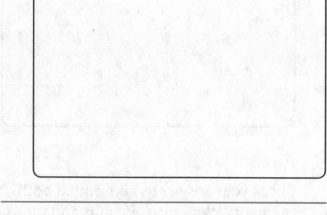

17. On Saturday, Toni biked to and from the pool. The distance from Toni's house to the pool is 7 miles. How many miles did Toni bike on Saturday?

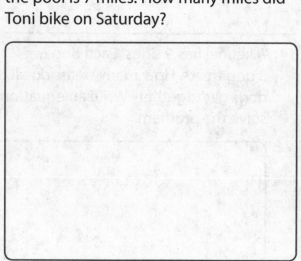

18. Look at the multiplication table below.

×	4	5	6	7
3	12	15	18	21
4	16	20	24	28
5	20	25	30	35
6	24	30	36	42
7	28	35	42	49
8	32	40	48	56

Part A

Shade the products in the 5s column of the table. What pattern do you see there?

Part B

Explain the pattern you found.

Photograph Gallery

Riley is setting up a display. She is hanging photographs on two walls. The photographs are hung in arrays. Riley has to decide how to arrange the photographs. She makes tables to decide which arrangement to use.

1. Use the **Left Wall** table to answer the questions.

   Part A

   Which arrangement on the left wall has the most photographs?

   [   ]

   Part B

   Explain how Riley could find the answer to Part A without calculating the size of each arrangement.

   [   ]

Left Wall				
Arrangement	A	B	C	D
Rows	3	3	7	8
Columns	7	9	2	3

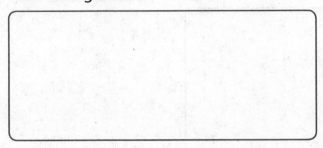

Right Wall

×	☐	☐	6	7	☐	← Rows
4					36	
☐		30		42		
☐	28		42			
☐				63		

Columns

Use the **Right Wall** table to answer questions 2 and 3.

2. Fill in the missing columns, rows, and numbers of photographs so that Riley's table is complete.

3. Riley has 42 on her table twice. Is this reasonable? Explain why or why not.

   [   ]

Use the **Right Wall** table to answer questions 4–6.

4. Some of the photographers were men, and some were women. Riley wants the number of photographs taken by men to be equal to the number of photographs taken by women. Shade the squares in the table to show the arrangements that let Riley do this. Explain what pattern you find.

5. Riley shares this table with her friend Leo. Leo is working on a different project. He is **NOT** hanging photographs. For what project could Leo use the table? Explain what 7×4 means for Leo's project.

6. Riley also shares this table with her mother. Riley's mother is working on a different project. She is also **NOT** hanging photographs. For what project could Riley's mother use the table? Explain what $30 \div 6$ means for Riley's mother's project.

Connect Area to Multiplication and Addition

Essential Question: How can area be measured and found?

Some designs can help protect buildings from unsafe weather.

This lightning rod on top of the building is connected to the ground. It can direct the electrical current from a lightning strike safely to the ground.

This helps protect the building from being damaged by lightning! Here's a project on building designs and area.

Math and Science Project: Design Solutions

Do Research There are different designs that help protect against weather, such as as lightning rods, flood-defense barriers, and wind-resistant roofs. Use the Internet or another source to gather information about these kind of designs and how they work.

Journal: Write a Report Include what you found. Also in your report:

- Tell how some window or door designs can help protect against weather.

- Use a grid to draw one of the window or door designs. Count the number of unit squares your design measures. Label your drawing to show how the design works to protect against weather.

Review What You Know

A-Z Vocabulary

Choose the best term from the box.
Write it on the blank.

- addend
- array
- equal groups
- multiply

1. When you skip count to get the total number, you _____.

2. Dividing apples so everyone gets the same amount is an example of making _____.

3. When you display objects in rows and columns, you make a(n) _____.

Division as Sharing

4. Chen has 16 model cars. He puts them in 4 rows. Each row has an equal number of cars. How many columns are there?

5. Julie has 24 glass beads to give to 4 friends. Each friend gets an equal share. How many glass beads does each friend get?

Arrays

6. Write an addition equation and a multiplication equation for the array shown at the right.

Relating Multiplication and Division

7. There are 12 team members. They line up in 3 equal rows. Which multiplication equation helps you find how many are in each row?

   Ⓐ $2 \times 6 = 12$ Ⓑ $1 \times 12 = 12$ Ⓒ $3 \times 4 = 12$ Ⓓ $3 \times 12 = 36$

8. There are 20 bottles of juice lined up in 4 equal rows. Explain how you can use a multiplication equation to find out how many bottles of juice are in each row.

My Word Cards

Use the examples for each word on the front of the card to help complete the definitions on the back.

A-Z
Glossary

area

You can measure area by counting unit squares.

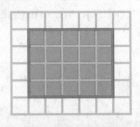

unit square

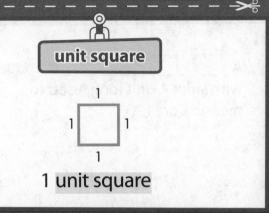

1 unit square

square unit

The area of this shape is 9 square units.

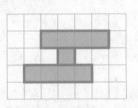

estimate

The area of the circle is about 20 square units.

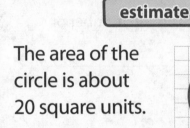

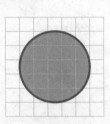

My Word Cards

Complete the definition. Extend learning by writing your own definitions.

A _____ is a square with sides 1 unit long, used to measure area.

_____ is the number of unit squares needed to cover a region.

To give an approximate number or

answer is to _____.

A unit square has

1 _____ of area.

Name _Adhrit B._

Solve & Share

Look at Shapes A–C on Area of Shapes Teaching Tool. How many square tiles do you need to cover each shape? Show your answers below. Explain how you decided.

I can ...
count unit squares to find the area of a shape.

I can also choose and use a math tool to solve problems.

Shape	Number of Square Tiles
Shape A	
Shape B	
Shape C	

Use tools. Think about how to place your tiles to cover each shape completely.

Look Back! **Be Precise** Can you be sure you have an exact answer if there are gaps between the tiles you used? Explain.

Essential Question **How Do You Measure Area?**

A

Emily made a collage in art class. She cut shapes to make her design. What is the area of this shape?

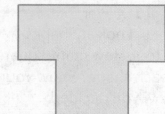

Area is the number of unit squares needed to cover a region with no gaps or overlaps.

A unit square is a square with sides that are each 1 unit long. It has an area of 1 square unit.

This is the unit square for this lesson.

B Count the unit squares that cover Emily's shape. The exact count is the area of the shape.

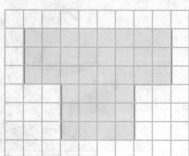

36 unit squares cover the shape. The area of the shape is 36 square units.

C Sometimes you can estimate the area. You can combine partially filled squares to estimate full squares.

Count the unit squares that cover this shape.

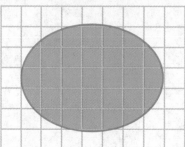

About 27 unit squares cover the shape.

The area of the shape is about 27 square units.

Convince Me! **Construct Arguments** Karen says these shapes each have an area of 12 square units. Do you agree with Karen? Explain.

red shape I think no, For the because I has song blank

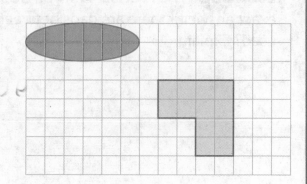

Another Example!

Emily wants to cover this octagon.

If she tries to cover it using unit squares, there will be gaps or overlaps.

Emily can break the square into two triangles. She can cover the shape completely using this triangle:

14 triangles cover the octagon. The area of the octagon is 7 square units.

☆ Guided Practice*

Do You Understand?

1. **Reasoning** How do you know the area of the octagon is 7 square units?

2. **Be Precise** Explain how finding the area of a shape is different from finding the length of a shape.

Do You Know How?

In **3** and **4**, count to find the area. Tell if the area is exact or an estimate.

3.

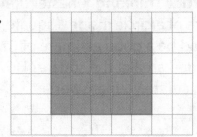

4.

estimate

☆ Independent Practice ☆

In **5–7**, count to find the area. Tell if the area is exact or an estimate.

5.
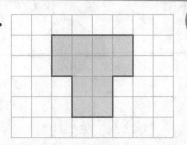

6.
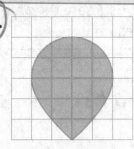

7.
estim...
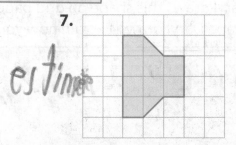

Problem Solving

8. Maggie buys 4 sketch pads. She pays with a 20-dollar bill. How much change does Maggie get back?

5

$3 each

9. **Critique Reasoning** Janet covers the red square with square tiles. She says, "I covered this shape with 12 unit squares, so I know it has an area of 12 square units." Do you agree with Janet? Explain.

10. **Higher Order Thinking** Chester drew this picture of a circle inside a square. What would be a good estimate of the green shaded area of the square? How did you calculate your answer?

   NO

11. **Number Sense** Arthur puts 18 erasers into equal groups. He says there are more erasers in each of 2 equal groups than in each of 3 equal groups. Is Arthur correct? Explain.

✓ **Assessment**

12. Daryl draws this shape on grid paper. Estimate the area of the shape Daryl draws. Explain how you estimated.

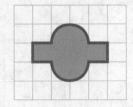

12 saupe unit

Help Practice Tools Games
     Buddy

Homework & Practice 6-1
Cover Regions

Another Look!

You can find the exact area of the rectangle below by counting the number of unit squares that cover it.

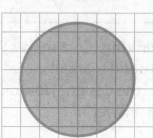

8 unit squares cover the rectangle.

So, the area of the rectangle is 8 square units.

Sometimes you need to estimate area. You can combine partially filled squares to approximate full squares.

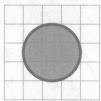

About 28 unit squares cover the shape.

So, the area of the shape is about 28 square units.

Area is the number of unit squares used to cover a region with no gaps or overlaps.

In **1–6**, count to find the area of the shapes. Tell if the area is exact or an estimate.

1.

2.

3.

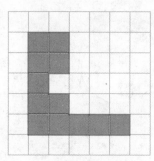

4.

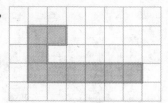

5.

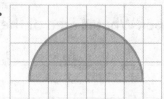

6.

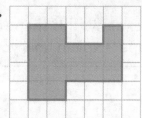

In **7–9**, use the diagram at the right.

7. What is the area of the soccer section of the field?

Use the diagram to help make a plan.

Athletic Field

Soccer	Baseball
Tennis	Not Used

8. What is the area of the field that is **NOT** being used?

9. **Make Sense and Persevere** How many square units of the field are being used?

10. **Reasoning** A bookstore has a sale. When customers pay for 2 books, they get another book free. If Pat pays for a box of 16 books, how many books does he get for free? How many books does Pat have? Write division and addition equations to show how the quantities are related.

Buy 2, Get 1 Free!

11. **Higher Order Thinking** Cora makes this design with square and triangular tiles. What is the area of the design? How did you calculate your answer?

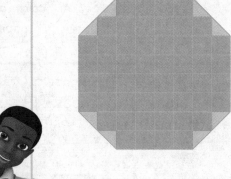

✔ **Assessment**

12. Tyler draws this shape on grid paper. What is area of the shape? Explain how you decided.

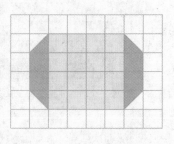

Name _____

☆ Solve & Share

Find the area of the postcard on each grid. What do you notice about the size of the postcard on each grid? What do you notice about the area of the postcard on each grid? Explain.

I can ...
count unit squares to find the area of a shape.

I can also reason about math.

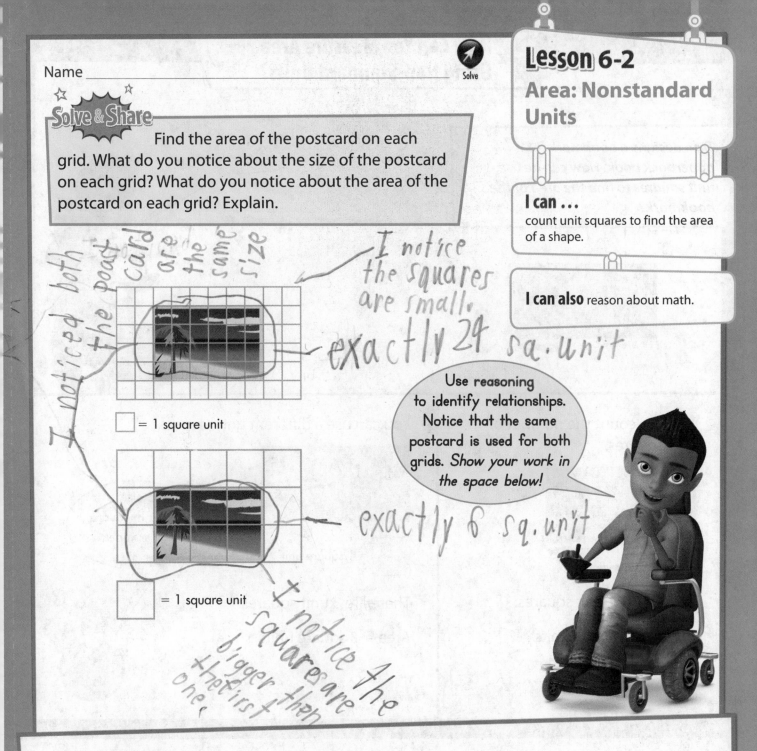

I noticed both the post card are the same size

I noticed the post card

I notice the squares are small.

exactly 24 sq. unit

☐ = 1 square unit

Use reasoning to identify relationships. Notice that the same postcard is used for both grids. *Show your work in the space below!*

exactly 6 sq. unit

☐ = 1 square unit

I notice the squares are bigger then the first one.

Look Back! **Be Precise** Are the measurements of the areas of the postcard shown above the same? Explain.

How Can You Measure Area Using Non-Standard Units?

Essential Question

A

Tran designs a bookmark for a paperback book. How can he use unit squares to find the area of the bookmark?

Unit squares can be different sizes.

B You can count the number of unit squares.

☐ = 1 square unit

There are 32 unit squares.

Area = 32 square units

C You can use a different unit square.

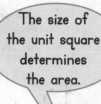

☐ = 1 square unit

There are 8 unit squares.

Area = 8 square units

The size of the unit square determines the area.

Convince Me! Reasoning How are the areas of these two squares alike and how are they different?

They are differrent because one has big sq.unit and the other has small sq.unit.

308 **Topic 6** | Lesson 6-2

☆ Guided Practice ☆

Do You Understand?

1. Which of these shapes has an area of 5 square units? How do you know?

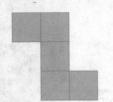 

Do You Know How?

2. Draw unit squares to cover the figures and find the area. Use the unit squares shown.

☐ = 1 square unit   ☐ = 1 square unit

☆ Independent Practice ☆

In **3–5**, draw unit squares to cover the figures and find the area. Use the unit squares shown.

3.

☐ = 1 square unit   ☐ = 1 square unit

4.

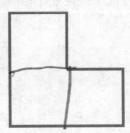 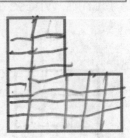

☐ = 1 square unit   ☐ = 1 square unit

5.

 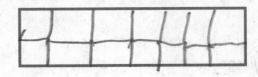

☐ = 1 square unit   ☐ = 1 square unit

Problem Solving

6. Be Precise Ben finds the area of this figure is 14 square units. Draw unit squares to cover this figure.

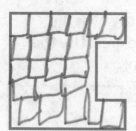

Think about the size of the unit squares you need to use.

---

7. Reasoning Luke eats 6 grapes from the bowl. Then Juan and Luke equally shared the grapes that are left. How many grapes does Juan eat? Show how you used reasoning to solve the problem.

$24 - 6 = 18 \div 2 = 9$

24 grapes

---

8. Construct Arguments Riaz estimates the area of this figure is 45 square units. Martin estimates the area is 48 square units. Whose estimate is closer? Explain.

Martin 48 is the closer because the chart, look at chart.

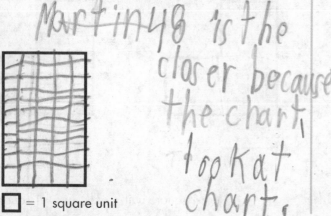

☐ = 1 square unit

9. Higher Order Thinking Theo wants to cover the top of a small table with square tiles. The table is 12 square tiles long and 8 square tiles wide. How many tiles will Theo need to cover the table?

$12 \times 8 = (16 \times 8$

✔ **Assessment**

---

10. Rick found the area of this shape is 21 square units. If he used a larger unit square, would his measurement be greater than 21 square units or less than 21 square units? Explain.

Not same size

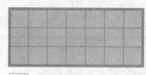

☐ = 1 square unit

Solve & Share

Draw a square to represent 1 unit square. Use your unit square to draw a rectangle that has an area of 8 square units. Compare your shape with a partner's shape. What is the same? What is different?

I can ...
measure the area of a shape using standard units.

I can also be precise in my work.

difference is my square unit is very big and my parthers has smaller square unit,

Be precise. Check your shape to make sure you have used the correct number of unit squares.

different

:1 unit square

Look Back! Reasoning Is the size of your shapes something that is the same or something that is different? Explain.

How Can You Measure Area Using Standard Units of Length?

A

Meg bought this sticker. What is the area of the sticker in square centimeters?

You can measure area in standard units. A square centimeter is a standard unit of area.

B

Here are some standard units of length and area.

DATA	Unit	Square Unit
	inch (in.)	square inch
	foot (ft)	square foot
	centimeter (cm)	square centimeter
	meter (m)	square meter

C Count the unit squares.

☐ = 1 square centimeter

6 unit squares cover the sticker. The sticker is measured in square centimeters.

So, the area of the sticker is 6 square centimeters.

Convince Me! **Be Precise** If square inches rather than square centimeters were used for the problem above, would more unit squares or fewer unit squares be needed to cover the shape? Explain.

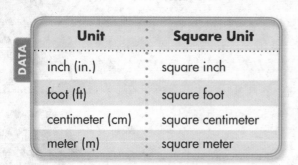

It will take less fewer square because, for example look at the second

Name _____

☆ Guided Practice*

Do You Understand?

1. If Meg's sticker on page 314 measured 2 inches by 3 inches, what would its area be?

6 squar inchs

2. Zoey paints a wall that measures 8 feet by 10 feet. What units should Zoey use for the area of the wall? Explain.

Do You Know How?

In **3** and **4**, each unit square represents a standard unit. Count the shaded unit squares. Then write the area.

3.
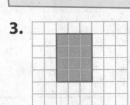
☐ = 1 square ft

4 X 3 = 12

4.
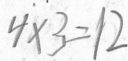
☐ = 1 square m

Independent Practice ☆

In **5–10**, each unit square represents a standard unit. Count the shaded unit squares. Then write the area.

5.
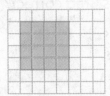
☐ = 1 square in.

4 X 4 = 16

6.
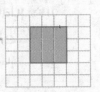
☐ = 1 square ft

7.
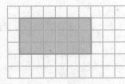
☐ = 1 square in.

3 X 6 = 18

8.
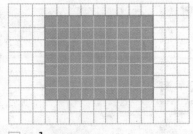
☐ = 1 square m

9.
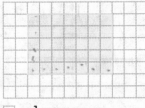
☐ = 1 square cm

5 X 7 = 35

10.
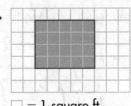
☐ = 1 square ft

Problem Solving

11. Reasoning Mr. Sanchez grows three types of vegetables in his garden. What is the area of the garden that Mr. Sanchez uses to grow lettuce and cucumbers? Explain how to use the units in this problem.

Mr. Sanchez's Garden

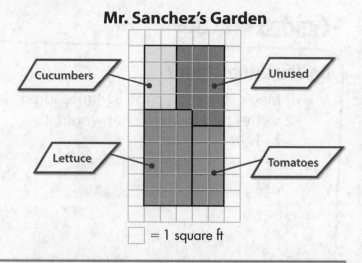

☐ = 1 square ft

---

12. Lisa received 34 text messages on Monday and 43 text messages on Tuesday. She received 98 text messages on Wednesday. How many more text messages did Lisa receive on Wednesday than on Monday and Tuesday combined?

13. Construct Arguments Monica buys a postage stamp. Is the area of the stamp more likely to be 1 square inch or 1 square meter? Explain.

---

14. Algebra Which operation can you use to complete the equation below?

$8 = 56 \boxed{} 7$

15. Higher Order Thinking Brad says a square that has a length of 9 feet has an area of 18 square feet. Is Brad correct? Why or why not?

✔ **Assessment**

16. Each of these unit squares represents 1 square foot. Does each figure have an area of 40 square feet? Choose *Yes* or *No*.

A 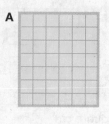 B   C

Shape A	○ Yes	○ No
Shape B	○ Yes	○ No
Shape C	○ Yes	○ No

Help Practice Buddy Tools Games

Another Look!

Count how many unit squares cover this figure.

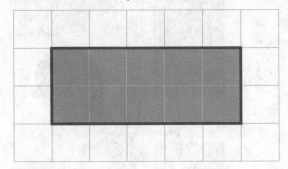

 = 1 square cm

- 10 unit squares cover the figure.
- Each unit square equals 1 square centimeter.

The area of the figure is 10 square centimeters.

You can use standard units of length to help measure area.

In **1–6**, each unit square represents a standard unit. Count the shaded unit squares. Then write the area.

1.

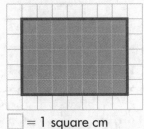

☐ = 1 square cm

2.

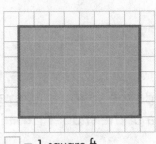

☐ = 1 square ft

3.

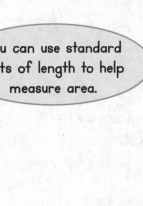

☐ = 1 square m

4.

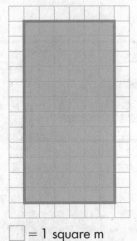

☐ = 1 square m

5.

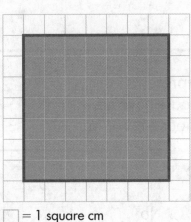

☐ = 1 square cm

6.

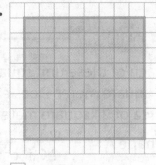

☐ = 1 square in.

In **7** and **8**, use the diagram at the right.

7. **Be Precise** What is the area of Tom's photo? Explain how you know which units to use.

look at the chart. Area= 6x4=24 square unit

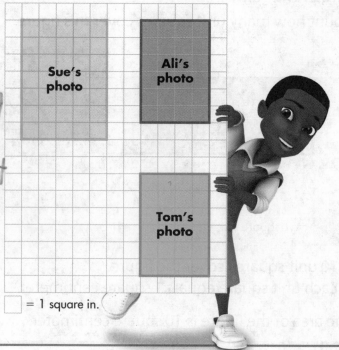

Sue's photo

Ali's photo

Tom's photo

☐ = 1 square in.

8. What is the area in square inches of all the photos? Explain.

---

9. **Construct Arguments** Is the area of a desk more likely to be 8 square feet or 8 square inches? Explain.

becaus it is small

10. Michele has 5 coins worth $0.75 in all. What coins does she have?

---

11. **Higher Order Thinking** Sam made the shape at the right from colored tiles. What is the area of the shape? Explain how you found your answer.

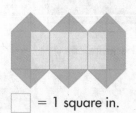

☐ = 1 square in.

12. Each of these unit squares represents 1 square meter. Does each figure have an area of 24 square meters? Choose *Yes* or *No*.

A   B   C

	Yes	No
Shape A	○ Yes	○ No
Shape B	○ Yes	○ No
Shape C	○ Yes	○ No

Name _____

☆ Solve & Share ☆

Jorge is carpeting a square room. One side of the room is 6 meters long. How many square meters of carpet does Jorge need? **Solve this problem any way you choose.**

I can ...
find the area of squares and rectangles by multiplying.

I can also generalize from examples.

You can generalize. What do you know about squares that can help you find the number of square meters of carpet Jorge will need?

6 m

6 m

$6 \times 6 = 36$ square meter

Look Back! **Reasoning** If the sides of the room were 6 feet long, how would the answer to the problem change?

Essential Question **How Can You Find the Area of a Figure?**

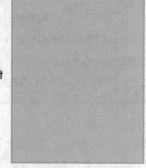

6 ft

8 ft

Mike paints a rectangular wall in his room green. The picture shows the length and width of Mike's wall. A small can of paint covers 40 square feet. Does Mike need more than one small can to paint the wall of his room?

1 can covers 40 square feet

B One Way

Count the unit squares to find area.

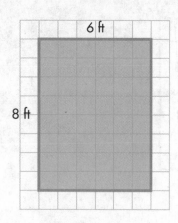

6 ft

8 ft

That's a lot of squares to count!

There are 48 unit squares. The area of Mike's wall is 48 square feet.

C Another Way

Count the number of rows and multiply by the number of squares in each row. There are 8 rows and 6 squares in each row.

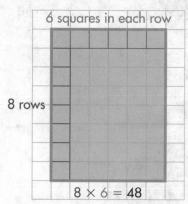

6 squares in each row

8 rows

8 × 6 = 48

The area of Mike's wall is 48 square feet. He will need more than one small can of paint.

Convince Me! **Model with Math** Mike plans to paint a wall in his living room blue. That wall measures 10 feet tall and 8 feet wide. What is the area of the wall Mike plans to paint blue?

Mike's area look like this to help

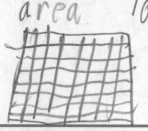

80 square feet

Name _____

Another Example!

The area of another wall in Mike's room is 56 square feet. The wall is 8 feet high. How wide is the wall?

$56 = 8 \times ?$

You can use division. $56 \div 8 = ?$

$56 \div 8 = 7$

The wall is 7 feet wide.

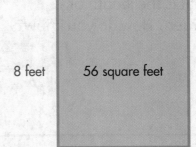

8 feet   56 square feet

? feet

☆ Guided Practice*

Do You Understand?

1. Suji's garden is 4 yards long and 4 yards wide. What is the area of Suji's garden?

2. The area of Michi's garden is 32 square feet. The garden is 8 feet long. How wide is Michi's garden?

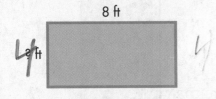

8 ft

4 ft   4

Do You Know How?

In **3** and **4**, find the area of each figure. Use grid paper to help.

3.
   7 in.
3 in. ▭

4.
   9 ft
6 ft ▮   54

☆ Independent Practice ☆

In **5** and **6**, find the area. In **7**, find the missing length. Use grid paper to help.

5.   3 cm
1 cm ▮

6.   4 ft
9 ft ▮   36

7.   7 in.
? in.   35 square in.

---

*For another example, see Set D on page 346.   **Topic 6** | Lesson 6-4   **321**

Problem Solving

8. **Construct Arguments** Jen's garden is 4 feet wide and has an area of 28 square feet. What is the length of Jen's garden? How do you know?

$$28 \div 4 = 7$$

9. **Make Sense and Persevere** Briana has 2 grandmothers. She mailed 2 cards to both of them. In each card she put 6 photographs. How many photographs did Briana mail in all?

10. **Generalize** Kevin thinks he found a shortcut. He says he can find the area of a square by multiplying the length of one side by itself. Is Kevin correct? Why or why not? Yes

11. **Higher Order Thinking** Ryan measures a rectangle that is 9 feet long and 5 feet wide. Teo measures a rectangle that has an area of 36 square feet. Which rectangle has the greater area? Explain how you found the answer.

 Assessment

12. Marla makes maps of Lower Falls Garden. One map is shown at the right.

    Part A

    Complete the boxes in the equation to show the area of the map at the right.

    $\square \times \square = \square$ square feet

    Part B

    Another map has an area of 27 square feet. If the length is 9 feet, how wide is the other map? How do you know?

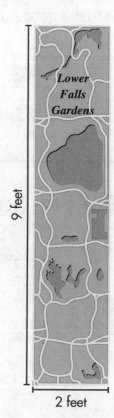

Lower Falls Gardens

9 feet

2 feet

Name _____

Solve & Share

The new reading room floor is a rectangle that is 8 feet wide by 9 feet long. Mrs. Wallace has a rectangular rug that is 8 feet wide by 5 feet long. What area of the reading room floor will not be covered by the rug? *Solve this problem any way you choose.*

I can ...
use properties when multiplying to find the area of squares and rectangles.

I can also model with math to solve problems.

You can draw rectangles on the grid to model with math. *Show your work in the space below!*

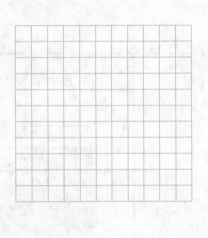

Look Back! **Make Sense and Persevere** Does your strategy change if the rug is in the corner of the room or in the center? Explain why or why not.

Essential Question

How Can the Area of Rectangles Represent the Distributive Property?

A

Gina wants to separate this rectangle into two smaller rectangles. Will the area of the large rectangle equal the sum of the areas of the two small rectangles?

Area = 7 × 8

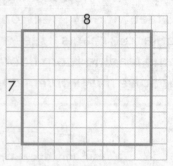

You can use the Distributive Property to break apart facts to find the product.

B Separate the 8-unit side into two parts.

$7 \times 8 = 7 \times (5 + 3)$

C $7 \times 8 = 7 \times (5 + 3) = (7 \times 5) + (7 \times 3)$

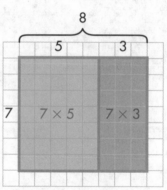

So, the area of the large rectangle is equal to the sum of the areas of the two small rectangles.

Convince Me! **Generalize** Find another way to separate this rectangle into two smaller parts. Write an equation you can use to find the areas of the two smaller rectangles. Is the area of the large rectangle still the same? What can you generalize?

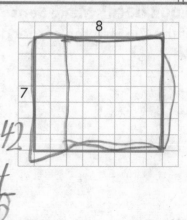

$6 \times 7 = 42$

$2 \times 7 = 14$

56

Name_____

☆ Guided Practice ☆

Do You Understand?

1. Describe a way to separate a 6 × 6 rectangle into two smaller rectangles.

2. What multiplication facts describe the areas of the two smaller rectangles you identified in Exercise 1?

Do You Know How?

Complete the equation that represents the picture.

3.

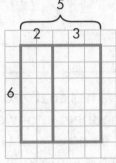

$6 \times \boxed{} = 6 \times (2 + \boxed{})$
$= (\boxed{} \times 2) + (6 \times \boxed{})$

☆ Independent Practice ☆

In **4** and **5**, complete the equation that represents the picture.

4.

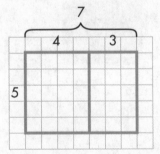

$5 \times \boxed{7} = 5 \times (4 + \boxed{3})$
$= (\boxed{5} \times 4) + (5 \times \boxed{3})$

5.

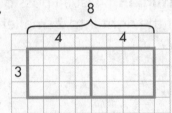

$3 \times \boxed{8} = \boxed{3} \times (4 + \boxed{4})$
$= (\boxed{3} \times 4) + (\boxed{3} \times \boxed{4})$

6. Write the equation that represents the picture.

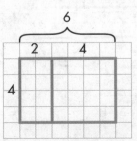

$4 \times 2 \times 4$

You can use the Distributive Property to help find areas of rectangles.

Problem Solving

7. Model with Math Claudia sold 3 shells last week for $5 each and 2 more shells this week for $5 each. Show two ways to determine how much money Claudia made in the two weeks.

$$3 \times 5 = 15 \quad 2 \times 5 = 10$$
$$+ 10$$
$$\overline{25}$$

8. Math and Science Amit wants to replace the roof of his dog house with a new wind-resistant material. The roof has two rectangular sides that are 6 feet by 4 feet. What is the total area of the roof?

$$2 + 4 \times 6 = 36$$

9. Use Structure Chiya has an 8 × 6 sheet of tiles. Can she separate the sheet into two smaller sheets that are 8 × 4 and 8 × 2? Do the two smaller sheets have the same total area as her original sheet? Explain.

Yes It is a double,

10. Higher Order Thinking List all possible ways to divide the rectangle at the right into 2 smaller rectangles.

11. Which equation represents the total area of the green shapes?

Ⓐ $4 \times 8 = 4 \times (6 + 2) = (4 \times 6) + (4 \times 2)$

Ⓑ $4 \times 7 = 4 \times (3 + 4) = (4 \times 3) + (4 \times 4)$

Ⓒ $4 \times 7 = 4 \times (4 + 3) = (4 \times 4) + (4 \times 3)$

Ⓓ $4 \times 7 = 4 \times (5 + 2) = (4 \times 5) + (4 \times 2)$

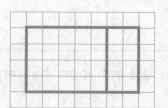

Help Practice Buddy Tools Games

Another Look!

You can use the Distributive Property to break apart multiplication facts to find the product.

> You can separate a rectangle into two smaller rectangles with the same total area.

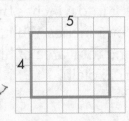

You can write the multiplication fact that represents the area of the large rectangle.

$$4 \times 5 = 20$$

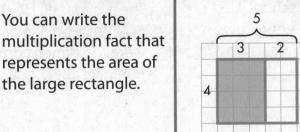

You can write the multiplication facts that represent the area of each of the smaller rectangles.

$$4 \times 5 = 4 \times (3 + 2)$$
$$4 \times 5 = (4 \times 3) + (4 \times 2)$$
$$4 \times 5 = 12 + 8 = 20$$

In **1–4**, complete the equation that represents the picture.

1.

$3 \times \square = \square \times (3 + \square)$

$3 \times \square = (3 \times \square) + (\square \times 2)$

$3 \times \square = \square + \square = 15$

> The areas of the large rectangles are equal to the sum of the areas of the smaller rectangles.

2.

$\square \times 7 = \square \times (\square + 4)$

$\square \times 7 = (\square \times 3) + (4 \times \square)$

$\square \times 7 = \square + \square = 28$

3.

$3 \times \square = \square \times (2 + \square)$

$3 \times \square = (3 \times \square) + (\square \times 4)$

$3 \times \square = \square + \square = 18$

4.

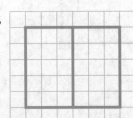

$\square \times 6 = \square \times (\square + 3)$

$\square \times 6 = (\square \times 3) + (5 \times \square)$

$\square \times 6 = \square + \square = 30$

5. Tina divided the rectangle at the right into two smaller parts. Show another way to divide the rectangle into two smaller parts. Write the equation you could use to find the area of the two smaller rectangles.

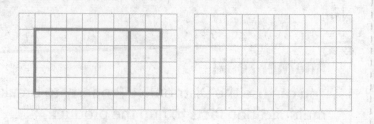

6. Critique Reasoning Lee wants to place 48 photographs on a wall at school. He puts the photographs into 8 equal rows. How many photographs are in each row?

7. Higher Order Thinking George had 1 sheet of paper. He cuts it into 6 inches by 5 inches, and 3 inches by 6 inches. What were the dimensions and total area of his original sheet of paper? Explain.

8. Use Structure Darren has a piece of wood that is 7 inches by 8 inches. Explain how he could divide this large rectangle into two smaller rectangles.

Break apart a problem into smaller problems!

 Assessment

9. Which equation represents the total area of the green shapes?

Ⓐ $3 \times 10 = 3 \times (3 + 6) = (3 \times 3) + (3 \times 6)$

Ⓑ $3 \times 9 = 3 \times (4 + 5) = (3 \times 4) + (3 \times 5)$

Ⓒ $3 \times 9 = 3 \times (3 + 6) = (3 \times 3) + (3 \times 6)$

Ⓓ $3 \times 9 = 3 \times (2 + 7) = (3 \times 2) + (3 \times 7)$

Solve & Share

Mrs. Marcum's desk is shaped like the picture below. The length of each side is shown in feet. Find the area of Mrs. Marcum's desk. **Solve this problem any way you choose.**

I can ...
use properties to find the area of irregular shapes by breaking the shape into smaller parts.

I can also look for patterns to solve problems.

You can look for relationships. Think about how you can break the problem into simpler parts. *Show your work in the space below!*

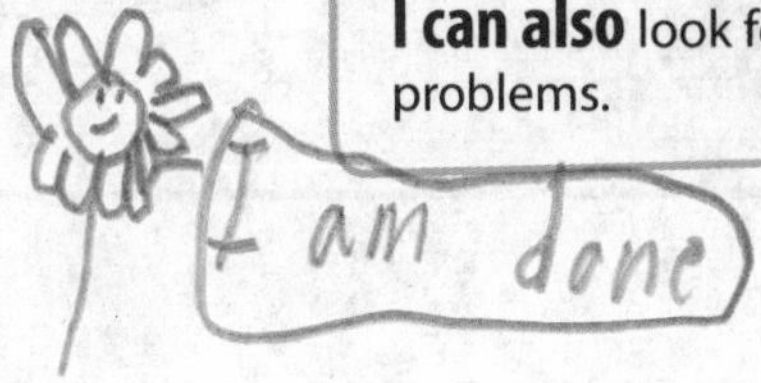

I am done

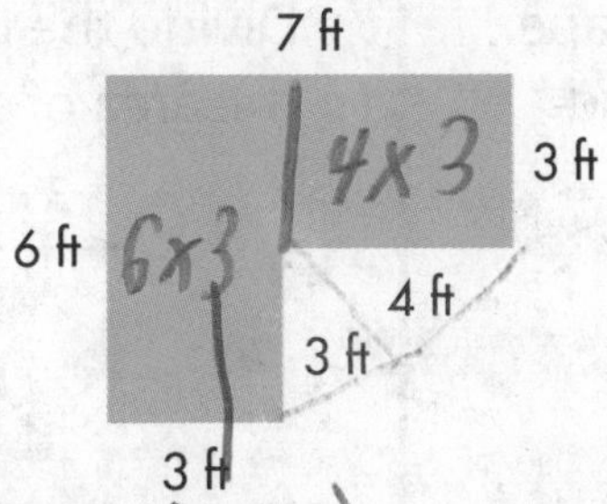

7 ft

4×3 3 ft

6 ft 6×3

4 ft

3 ft

3 ft

$(6 \times 3) + (4 \times 3) = 18 + 12 = 30$ sq. ft

Look Back! **Make Sense and Persevere** How can you check your answer? Is there more than one way to solve this problem? Explain.

How Can You Find the Area of an Irregular Shape?

A

Mr. Fox is covering a miniature golf course putting green with artificial grass. Each artificial grass square is 1 square foot. What is the area of the putting green that Mr. Fox needs to cover?

Look for relationships. Think about smaller shapes that are part of the larger shape.

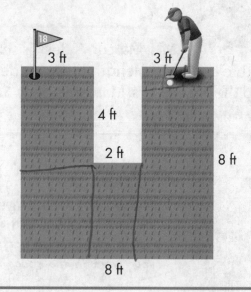

3 ft   3 ft
4 ft
2 ft
8 ft
8 ft

B One Way

You can draw the figure on grid paper. Then count the unit squares to find the area.

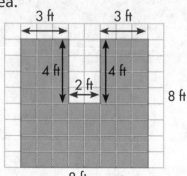

3 ft   3 ft
4 ft   2 ft   4 ft
8 ft
8 ft

The area of the putting green is 56 square feet.

C Another Way

Divide the putting green into rectangles. Find the area of each rectangle. Then add the areas.

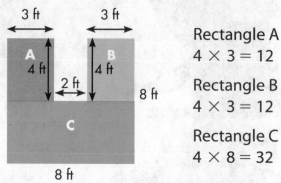

3 ft   3 ft
A   4 ft   2 ft   B   4 ft
C   8 ft
8 ft

Rectangle A
$4 \times 3 = 12$

Rectangle B
$4 \times 3 = 12$

Rectangle C
$4 \times 8 = 32$

$12 + 12 + 32 = 56$. The area of the putting green is 56 square feet.

Convince Me! **Use Structure** Find another way to divide the putting green into smaller rectangles. Explain how you can find the area of the putting green using your smaller rectangles.

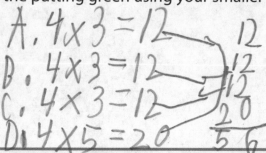

A. $4 \times 3 = 12$ 12
B. $4 \times 3 = 12$ 12
C. $4 \times 3 = 12$ 12
D. $4 \times 5 = 20$ 20
                            56 square feet

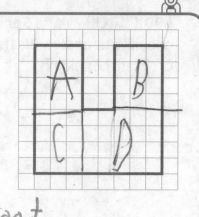

A   B
C   D

Name _____

☆ Guided Practice ☆

Do You Understand?

1. Explain why you can find the area of the putting green on page 332 using different rectangles.

2. **Generalize** Explain what operation you use to find the total area of the smaller rectangles.

Do You Know How?

In **3**, and **4**, find the area of each figure. Use grid paper to help.

3.
2 in.
5 in.
2 in.
5 in.

16 sq. in.

4.
4 cm
← 3 cm
9 cm
6 cm

12
+36
48 sq. cm.

☆ Independent Practice ☆

In **5–8**, find the area of each figure. Use grid paper to help.

5.
1 cm
3 cm
2 cm
4 cm

11 sq. cm

6.
1 cm
1 cm
3 cm
5 cm

7.
1 in.
1 in.
4 in.
2 in.
1 in.
1 in.

8.
5 cm
4 cm
4 cm
1 cm

Problem Solving

9. Reasoning Mr. Kendel is making a model house. The footprint for the house is shown at the right. What is the total area? Explain your reasoning.

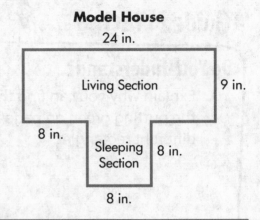

Model House

24 in.

Living Section — 9 in.

8 in.

Sleeping Section — 8 in.

8 in.

---

10. 🄰🄽 **Vocabulary** Fill in the blanks. Mandy finds the _____ of this shape by dividing it into rectangles. Phil gets the same answer by counting _____ .

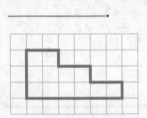

11. Algebra Use a question mark to represent the unknown quantity in the phrase "six times a number is 24." Solve the equation.

---

12. Higher Order Thinking Mrs. Delancy used 3-inch square tiles to make the design at the right. What is the area of the design she made? Explain how you found it.

3 in.

---

13. Jared drew the figure to the right. Draw lines to show how you can divide the shape to find the area. What is the area of the figure?

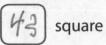

43 square inches

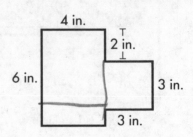

4 in.

2 in.

6 in.

3 in.

3 in.

Help   Practice Buddy   Tools   Games

Homework & Practice 6-6

Apply Properties: Area of Irregular Shapes

Another Look!

How can you find the area of the irregular shape below?

You can count unit squares, or divide the shape into rectangles.

Place the shape on grid paper. Then you can count unit squares.

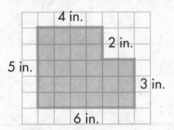

The area of the irregular shape is 26 square inches.

You can divide the shape into rectangles. Find the area of each rectangle. Then add the areas.

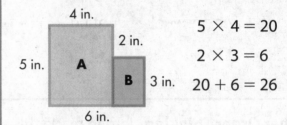

$5 \times 4 = 20$

$2 \times 3 = 6$

$20 + 6 = 26$

The area of the irregular shape is 26 square inches.

In **1–4**, find the area of each irregular shape. Use grid paper to help.

1.

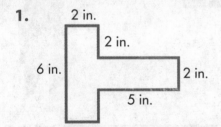

2.

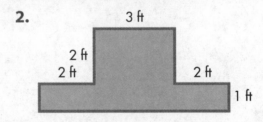

3.

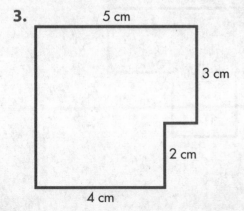

4.

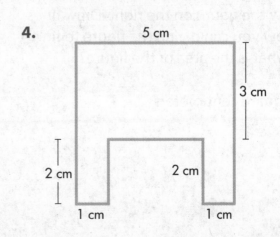

5. Reasoning Tony made this diagram of his vegetable garden. What is the total area? Explain your reasoning.

Vegetable Garden

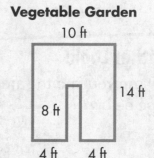

10 ft

14 ft

8 ft

4 ft   4 ft

6. Math and Science Mr. Thomson wants to protect his garage by installing a flood barrier. He connects 2 barriers side by side. Each barrier is 9 feet long by 2 feet high. What is the combined area of the barriers?

7. Number Sense Hadori made this solid figure by paper folding. What is the name of the figure she made? How many faces, edges, and vertices does it have?

8. Higher Order Thinking Jordan made this design from three pieces of square-shaped cloth. What is the total area of the design Jordan made? Explain how you found your answer.

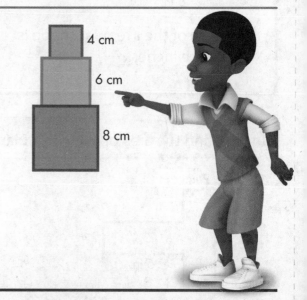

4 cm

6 cm

8 cm

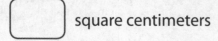
Assessment

9. Daniel drew the figure on the right. Draw lines to show how you can divide the figure to find the area. What is the area of the figure?

[   ] square centimeters

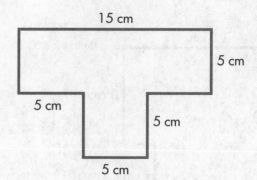

15 cm

5 cm

5 cm

5 cm

5 cm

Name _____

☆ ☆
Solve & Share

Mr. Anderson is tiling his kitchen. He will not need tiles for the areas covered by the kitchen island or the counter. How many square meters of tiles does Mr. Anderson need?

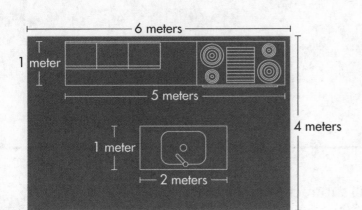

Lesson 6-7
Look for and Use Structure

I can ...
use the relationships between quantities to break a problem into simpler parts.

I can also solve area problems.

Thinking Habits

Be a good thinker!
These questions can help you.

- What patterns can I see and describe?

- How can I use the patterns to solve the problem?

- Can I see expressions and objects in different ways?

Look Back! **Use Structure** Is the tiled area greater than or less than the total area of the kitchen?

How Can You Use Structure to Solve Problems?

A

Janet is painting a door. She needs to paint the entire door except for the window.

What is the area of the part of the door that needs paint?

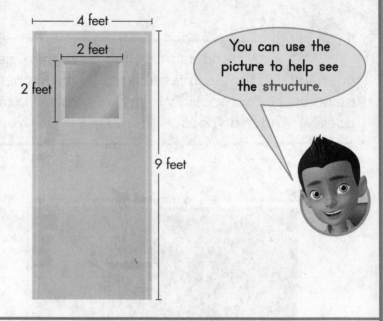

You can use the picture to help see the structure.

What do I need to do to solve this problem?

I need to find the area of the door without the window.

B **How can I make use of structure to solve this problem?**

I can

- break the problem into simpler parts.

- find equivalent expressions.

C

Here's my thinking...

I will subtract the area of the window from the total area.

<u>Find the area of the whole door.</u>
4 feet × 9 feet = 36 square feet

<u>Find the area of the window.</u>
2 feet × 2 feet = 4 square feet

<u>Subtract to find the area that needs paint.</u>
36 − 4 = 32 square feet

The area of the part of the door that needs paint is 32 square feet.

Convince Me! **Use Structure** Janet thinks of a different way to solve the problem. She says, "I can divide the area I need to paint into 4 smaller rectangles. Then I will find the areas of these 4 smaller rectangles." Does Janet's strategy make sense? Explain.

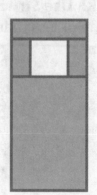

Name _____

☆ Guided Practice *

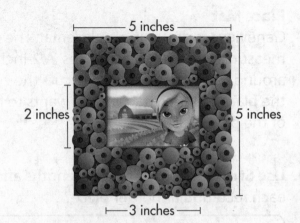

Use Structure

Lil glued beads on the border of the frame. What is the area of the part she decorated with beads?

5 inches

2 inches   5 inches

3 inches

1. How can you think about the total area of the frame?

2. Use what you know to solve the problem.

A picture can help you see equivalent expressions. Think about the structure.

Independent Practice ☆

Use Structure

A keypad has 10 rubber buttons. Each button is 1 centimeter by 2 centimeters. The rest is made out of plastic. Is the area of the plastic greater than the area of the rubber buttons?

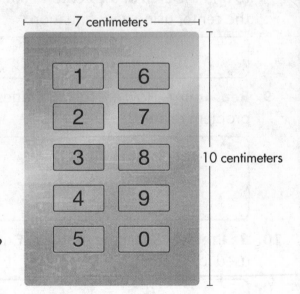

7 centimeters

1	6
2	7
3	8
4	9
5	0

10 centimeters

3. How can you break the problem into simpler parts? What is the hidden question?

4. How can you find the area of all the rubber buttons?

5. Use what you know to solve the problem.

Problem Solving

Place Mat

Genevieve is designing a placemat. The center measures 8 inches by 10 inches. A 2-inch border goes around the center. Genevieve cuts the corners to make the placemat an octagon. She wants to find the area of the placemat.

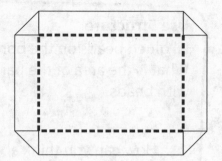

6. **Use Structure** What are the lengths and widths of each rectangular border piece?

7. **Use Appropriate Tools** How can Genevieve find the exact area of the 4 corner pieces using grid paper?

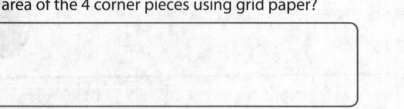

☐ = 1 square in.

8. **Model with Math** What equation can Genevieve use to find the area of the center? Find the area of the center using your equation.

Use structure to simplify a problem.

9. **Reasoning** How are the quantities in this problem related?

10. **Be Precise** Solve the problem. Explain what unit you used for your answer.

Help Practice Tools Games
Buddy

Another Look!

How can you find the area of the shaded part of the figure at the right?

Tell how you can use structure to solve the problem.

- I can break the problem into simpler parts.

- I can find equivalent expressions.

8 cm

5 cm

2 cm

3 cm

Use structure to think of a complex shape as simpler shapes.

Solve the problem.

The shaded area equals the total area minus the non-shaded area.

Find the area of the large rectangle. $5 \times 8 = 40$ square in.

Find the area of the small rectangle. $2 \times 3 = 6$ square in.

Subtract to find the area of the shaded part. $40 - 6 = 34$ square in.

The area of the shaded part is 34 square inches.

Use Structure

A tablet computer has a 1-inch border of plastic around the screen. What is the area of the plastic border?

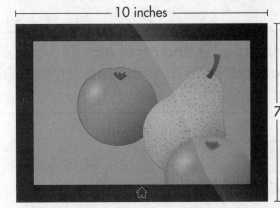

10 inches

7 inches

1. Tell how you can use structure to solve the problem.

2. Find two different ways to express the area of the screen.

3. Use these equivalent expressions to solve the problem.

Playground

Mr. Velasquez built a playground. It has one section with a slide and another section with a swing set. A pathway connects the two areas. The slide is 2 meters high. The areas and the pathway are covered in asphalt. Mr. Velasquez wants to know how much of the playground is covered in asphalt.

Section	Length (meters)	Width (meters)	Area
Swing set	8	3	
Slide	8	2	
Pathway	5	1	

4. **Reasoning** Fill in the table above to show the area of each section. Use the grid to draw a possible diagram of the playground.

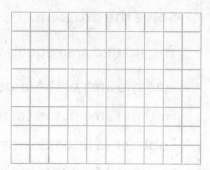

5. **Construct Arguments** Find the total area covered in asphalt. Explain your reasoning using math.

6. **Make Sense and Persevere** Did you use addition or subtraction to solve this problem? Could you have used the other operation instead? Explain.

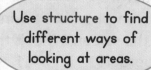

Use structure to find different ways of looking at areas.

7. **Use Structure** Find the area on the grid that is not covered in asphalt. Use this to check your work.

Shade a path from **START** to **FINISH**. Follow the quotients that are odd numbers. You can only move up, down, right, or left.

I can ...
divide within 100.

Start				
15 ÷ 5	45 ÷ 5	40 ÷ 8	36 ÷ 4	6 ÷ 3
28 ÷ 7	12 ÷ 2	90 ÷ 9	63 ÷ 9	0 ÷ 8
48 ÷ 8	50 ÷ 5	81 ÷ 9	9 ÷ 3	56 ÷ 7
20 ÷ 5	48 ÷ 6	42 ÷ 6	10 ÷ 5	6 ÷ 1
30 ÷ 3	16 ÷ 8	35 ÷ 7	45 ÷ 9	56 ÷ 8
				Finish

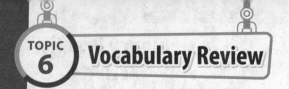

Vocabulary Review

TOPIC 6

Glossary

Word List

- area
- column
- Distributive Property
- estimate
- multiplication
- product
- row
- square unit
- unit square

Understand Vocabulary

Choose the best term from the Word List. Write it on the blank.

1. A(n) _____ has sides that are each 1 unit long.

2. _____ is the number of unit squares that cover a region or shape.

3. You can use the _____ to break apart facts and find the _____.

4. A unit square has an area of 1 _____.

5. When you _____, you give an approximate answer.

Write *always, sometimes,* or *never.*

6. *Area* is _____ measured in square meters.

7. *Multiplication* _____ involves joining equal groups.

8. The *area* of a shape can _____ be represented as the sum of the *areas* of smaller rectangles.

Use Vocabulary in Writing

9. What is the area of this rectangle? Explain how you solved the problem. Use at least 3 terms from the Word List in your answer.

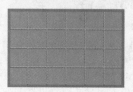

Set A | pages 301–306

A unit square has sides that are 1 unit long.

Count the unit squares that cover the shape. The exact count is the area of the shape.

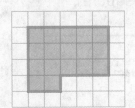

☐ = 1 unit square

17 unit squares cover the shape. The area of the shape is 17 square units.

Sometimes you need to estimate to find the area. First count the full squares. Then estimate partially filled squares.

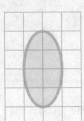

About 6 unit squares cover this shape.

Remember area is the number of unit squares needed to cover a region with no gaps or overlaps.

In **1** and **2**, count to find the area. Tell if the area is exact or an estimate.

1.

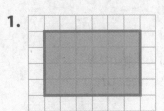

2.

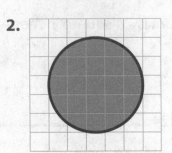

Set B | pages 307–312

Unit squares can be different sizes. The size of a unit square determines the area.

16 unit squares

4 unit squares

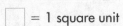 = 1 square unit

☐ = 1 square unit

Area = 16 square units

Area = 4 square units

The measurements are different because different sizes of unit squares were used.

Remember that you can use unit squares to measure area.

Draw unit squares to cover the figures and find the area. Use the unit squares shown.

1.

2.

☐ = 1 square unit

 = 1 square unit

The unit squares below represent square inches.

What is the area of the figure below?

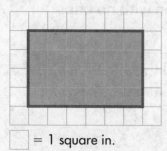

☐ = 1 square in.

24 unit squares cover the figure.
The area of the figure is measured in square inches.

So, the area of the figure is 24 square inches.

Remember that you can measure using standard or metric units of length for unit squares.

In **1** and **2**, each unit square represents a standard unit. Count the unit squares. Then write the area.

1.

☐ = 1 square ft

2.

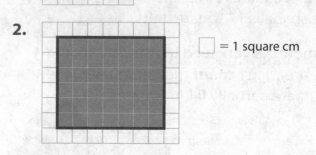

☐ = 1 square cm

You can find area by counting the number of rows and multiplying by the number of squares in each row.

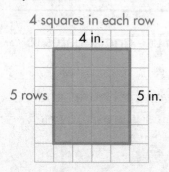

There are 5 rows.
There are 4 squares in each row.

$5 \times 4 = 20$

The area of the figure is 20 square inches.

Remember that you can multiply the number of rows by the number of squares in each row to find the area.

In **1–3**, find the area of each figure. Use grid paper to help.

1.

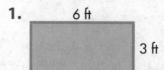

6 ft
3 ft

2.

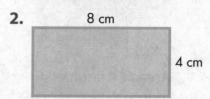

8 cm
4 cm

3.

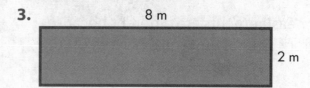

8 m
2 m

Name _____

Set E pages 325–330

You can use the Distributive Property to break apart facts to find the product.

Separate the 5 unit side into two parts.

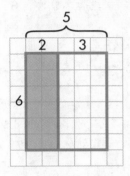

Area of the large rectangle: $6 \times 5 = 30$

Areas of the small rectangles:

$6 \times 2 = 12$

$6 \times 3 = 18$

Add the two areas: $12 + 18 = 30$

You can write an equation to show that the area of the large rectangle is equal to the sum of the areas of the two small rectangles.

$6 \times 5 = 6 \times (2 + 3) = (6 \times 2) + (6 \times 3)$

When you divide a rectangle into two smaller rectangles, the total area does not change!

Remember that you can separate a rectangle into two smaller rectangles with the same total area.

In **1–3**, write the equations that represent the total area of the red shapes. Find the area.

1.

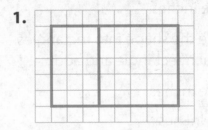

2.

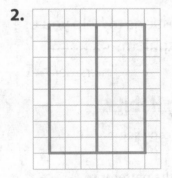

3.

Find the area of this irregular shape.

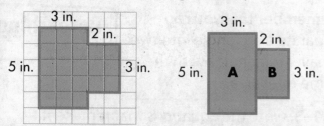

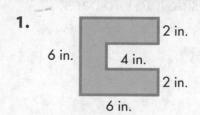

You can place the shape on grid paper and count the unit squares. The area of the shape is 21 square inches.

You can also divide the shape into rectangles. Find the area of each rectangle and add.

$5 \times 3 = 15$ square inches

$3 \times 2 = 6$ square inches

$15 + 6 = 21$ square inches

Remember that you can add smaller areas to find a total area.

In **1** and **2**, find the area of each shape.

1.

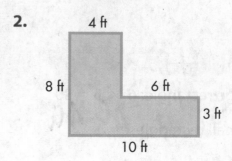

2.

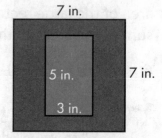

Think about these questions to help you use **structure** in solving problems.

Thinking Habits

- What patterns can I see and describe?

- How can I use the patterns to solve the problem?

- Can I see expressions and objects in different ways?

Remember to look for simpler ways of representing an area.

Debra made this design from 1-inch square tiles. What is the area of the blue tiles?

1. How can you express the area of the blue tiles?

2. Solve the problem. Explain how you solved.

Name _____

Banner Design

Jessie is designing a banner that has red, blue, and white sections.
The **Banner Details** list shows the rules for each color.
The **Jessie's Banner** diagram shows the different sections of the banner.

Banner Details

- Red sections must have a total area greater than 40 square inches.
- Blue sections must have a total area greater than 30 square inches.
- The white section must have an area less than 40 square inches.

Use the **Jessie's Banner** diagram to answer Question 1.

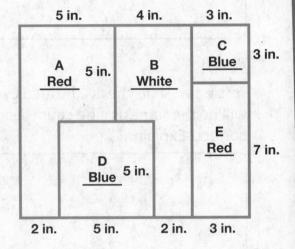

1. To check if his banner fits the rules, Jessie started this table. Complete the table. Use multiplication and addition as needed.

Section	Color	Show How to Find the Area	Area
A	Red		
B	White		
C	Blue		9 square inches
D	Blue		
E	Red	7×3	

Use the table above and the **Banner Details** list to answer Question 2.

2. Is Jessie's banner within the totals in the **Banner Details** list? Explain.

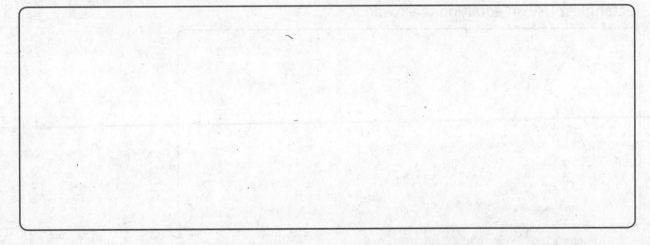

3. Jessie makes a square patch to go on top of the banner.

Part A

Draw unit squares to cover the patch. How many unit squares cover the patch?

Jessie's Patch

= 1 square cm

Part B

Jessie says if he checks the area by multiplying, the area will be the same as if he counts each unit square. Is he correct? Explain.

4. Jessie uses two colors to make the patch. The colors have different areas.

Part A

Explain how to separate the square into two smaller rectangles with different areas. Use multiplication to find the areas of each of the smaller rectangles.

Part B

Is the area of the square equal to the total area of the two smaller rectangles? Use an equation to explain.

Represent and Interpret Data

Essential Question: How can data be represented, interpreted, and analyzed?

Digital Resources

Solve · Learn · Glossary · Practice Buddy · Tools · Assessment · Help · Games

The weather and temperature can change a lot during different seasons.

The seasons can have a huge impact on how we lead our daily lives.

I better prepare for the upcoming season! Here's a project on seasons and data.

Math and Science Project: Seasons

Do Research Use the Internet or other sources to find information about patterns of temperature in the different seasons where you live. Include information about the average monthly temperatures and the record low and high temperatures.

Journal: Write a Report Include what you found. Also in your report:

- For one week, record the daily high and low temperatures in the area where you live. Make a graph displaying this information.

- Find the difference between the highest and lowest daily temperatures from your graph.

Name _____

Review What You Know

A-Z Vocabulary

Choose the best term from the box.
Write it on the blank.

> - multiplication
> - number line
> - equal groups
> - multiples

1. _____ have the same number of items.

2. 0, 2, 4, 6, and 8 are _____ of 2.

3. _____ is used to find a total when joining equal groups.

Multiplication

In **4** and **5**, complete the equation.

4. $5 \times 3 = $ _____

5. $3 \times$ _____ $= 21$

6. Make a bar diagram to represent 4×6.

Multiplication on the Number Line

7. Ed bought 2 bags of grapefruit. There are 6 grapefruit in each bag. How many grapefruit did he buy? Draw jumps on the number line to find the answer.

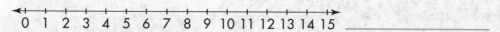

8. Show the multiplication fact 3×4 on the number line. Write the product.

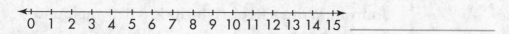

Finding Area

9. Count to find the area of the rectangle.

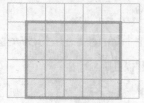

☐ = 1 square inch

_____

356 **Topic 7** | Review What You Know

My Word Cards

Use the examples for each word on the front of the card to help complete the definitions on the back.

scaled picture graph

Plants Sold at the Garden Shop

| April | 🌱 🌱 🌱 🌱 🌱 |
| May | 🌱 🌱 🌱 🌱 🌱 🌱 |

Each 🌱 = 5 plants.

key

Plants Sold at the Garden Shop

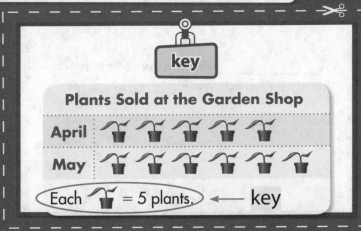

| April | 🌱 🌱 🌱 🌱 🌱 |
| May | 🌱 🌱 🌱 🌱 🌱 🌱 |

Each 🌱 = 5 plants. ← key

scaled bar graph

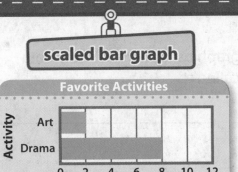

Favorite Activities

scale

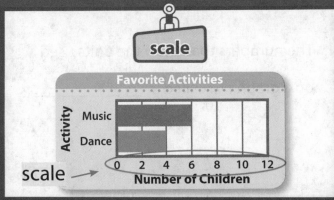

Favorite Activities

scale →

frequency table

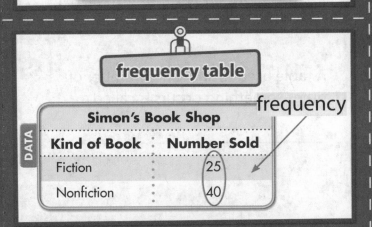

frequency

Simon's Book Shop

Kind of Book	Number Sold
Fiction	25
Nonfiction	40

data

Rico's Paper Chains

Number of Paper Chains	Length
3	6 in.
2	7 in.

data →

survey

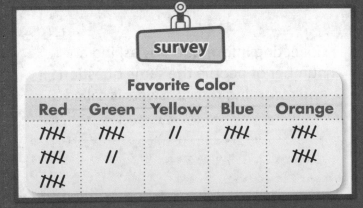

Favorite Color

Red	Green	Yellow	Blue	Orange
⊥⊥⊥⊥	⊥⊥⊥⊥	//	⊥⊥⊥⊥	⊥⊥⊥⊥
⊥⊥⊥⊥	//			⊥⊥⊥⊥
⊥⊥⊥⊥				

My Word Cards

A _____ explains what each symbol represents in a picture graph.

A graph using pictures or symbols to show data is called a

_____.

The numbers that show the units used on a graph are called a _____.

A graph using bars to show data is called a

_____.

Pieces of information are called

_____.

A table used to show the number of times something occurs is called a

_____.

Collecting information by asking a number of people the same question and recording their answers is called a

_____.

Name _____

Solve & Share

Students in Jorge's class took a survey of their favorite cereals and made this graph to show the results. Name at least three facts about the information in the graph.

I can ...
use picture graphs and bar graphs to answer questions about data sets.

I can also look for patterns to solve problems.

You can use structure. How can you find the number of votes for each type of cereal?

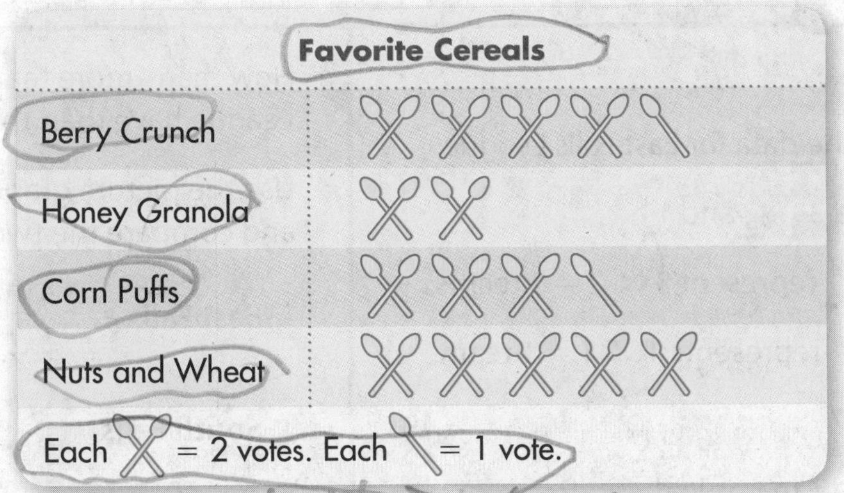

Favorite Cereals

Berry Crunch	X X X X X
Honey Granola	X X
Corn Puffs	X X X X
Nuts and Wheat	X X X X X X

Each X = 2 votes. Each \ = 1 vote.

• table — at the everywhere
• key at the bottom
• Nut and wheat has the most votes

Look Back! **Be Precise** What do the two different symbols on the graph stand for?

Essential Question: How Can You Read Picture Graphs?

A

How many teams are in the East Falls League?

Information you collect is called data. A scaled picture graph uses pictures or symbols to show data.

The scale is the number each picture or symbol represents.

Number of Hockey Teams in Each League

League	Teams
East Falls	✕ ✕ ✕ ╱
North Falls	✕ ✕ ╱
South Falls	✕ ✕
West Falls	✕ ✕ ✕ ✕ ╱

Each ✕ = 2 teams.
Each ╱ = 1 team.

The key explains the scale used in the graph.

B Use the key.

Look at the data for East Falls League.

There are 3 ✕ and 1 ╱ .

The 3 ✕ represent 3 × 2 = 6 teams.

The 1 ╱ represents 1 × 1 = 1 team.

6 + 1 = 7

There are 7 teams in the East Falls League.

C How many more teams does the East Falls League have than the South Falls League?

Use the picture graph to write equations and compare the two rows.

East Falls   ✕ ✕ ✕ ╱
3 × 2 + 1 = 7

South Falls   ✕ ✕
2 × 2 = 4
Subtract: 7 − 4 = 3

The East Falls League has 3 more teams than the South Falls League.

Convince Me! Be Precise Tell something about each league you can find out from the picture graph. It is, East Falls has 7 teams, North Falls has 4 teams, and West Falls has 5 teams, South Falls has 11 teams.

Name _____

Another Example

A scaled bar graph uses bars to represent and compare information. This bar graph shows the number of goals scored by different players on a hockey team. The scale shows the units used.

On this bar graph, each grid line represents two units. Every other grid line is labeled: 0, 4, 8, and so on. For example, the line halfway between 4 and 8 represents 6 goals.

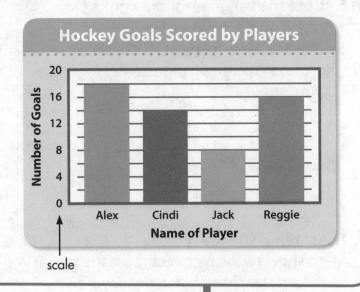

Hockey Goals Scored by Players

Number of Goals / Name of Player

scale

☆ Guided Practice ☆

Do You Understand?

In **1** and **2**, use the bar graph above.

1. How many goals in all did Alex and Reggie score?

   18 goals

Do You Know How?

2. Explain how to find how many more goals Alex scored than Cindi.

Independent Practice ☆

In **3–5**, use the picture graph.

3. Which area has lights on for the most hours each week?

4. Which area has lights on for exactly 50 hours each week?

5. In one week, how many more hours are lights on in the exercise room than in the swimming pool?

Hours of Light Usage at Sports Center
Number of Hours Lights Are on Each Week

Exercise Room	
Locker Room	
Swimming Pool	
Tennis Court	

Each 💡 = 10 hours. Each ▮ = 5 hours.

Problem Solving

In **6–8**, use the bar graph at the right.

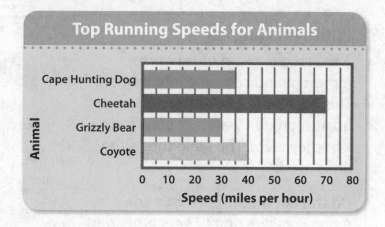

Top Running Speeds for Animals

6. **Be Precise** How many units does each grid line on the graph represent? How do you know?

7. **Reasoning** Use the symbols >, <, or = to show two ways to compare the top speeds of the cheetah and the coyote.

8. **Higher Order Thinking** The top running speeds of which two animals, when added together, equal the top running speed of a cheetah?

cheeth

✓ Assessment

In **9** and **10**, use the picture graph.

9. For which days can you use the equation 9×7 to find how many points were scored? Choose all that apply.

- ☐ October 3
- ☐ October 10
- ☐ October 17
- ☐ October 24
- ☐ None of the days

10. On which days did the football team score fewer than 50 points? Choose all that apply.

- ☑ October 3
- ☐ October 10
- ☑ October 17
- ☑ October 24
- ☐ None of the days

Football Team Scores

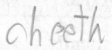

October 3	🏈🏈🏈🏈🏈🏈🏈🏈🏈
October 10	🏈🏈🏈🏈🏈🏈🏈🏈🏈🏈
October 17	🏈🏈🏈🏈🏈
October 24	🏈🏈🏈🏈🏈🏈

Each 🏈 = 7 points.

Basic facts can help you read a picture graph!

Help Practice Tools Games
Buddy

Another Look!

You can use a picture graph or a bar graph to represent and interpret data.

Picture graphs use pictures or parts of pictures to represent data.

Gold Medals Won at 2010 Vancouver Winter Olympics	
Sweden	●●●●●
France	●●
Switzerland	●●●●●●
Russia	●●●

Each ● = 1 gold medal.

Picture graphs have keys to explain the scale being used and what each picture represents.

Bar graphs use bars to represent data.

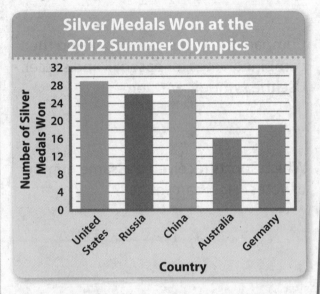

Silver Medals Won at the 2012 Summer Olympics

Bar graphs have scales that show the units used.

Each line in this bar graph represents 2 medals.

In **1–4**, use the picture graph at the right.

1. How many houses were built in City B?

2. How many houses were built in City B and City F?

3. How many more houses were built in City D than in City E in 1 year?

4. Put the cities in order from fewest houses built to most.

Number of Houses Built in 1 Year	
City A	🏠🏠🏠🏠🏠
City B	🏠🏠🏠🏠
City C	🏠🏠🏠
City D	🏠🏠🏠🏠🏠🏠🏠
City E	🏠🏠🏠🏠
City F	🏠🏠🏠🏠🏠🏠

Each 🏠 = 10 houses. Each 🏠 = 5 houses.

5. Higher Order Thinking How many more people chose football or soccer than baseball or basketball?

Favorite Sport

6. Compare the votes for football and the combined votes for baseball and soccer. Use the symbol >, <, or =.

7. Which sports received the same number of votes? How can you tell?

8. Generalize By just looking at the bars, how can you tell which sport got the most votes? The fewest votes? Which sports were they?

✔ **Assessment**

In **9** and **10**, use the picture graph at the right.

9. Which students read more books than Phil? Choose all that apply.

☐ Anders   ☐ Miguel

☐ Jamal   ☐ Tamika

☐ Nancy

10. Which students read fewer than 12 books? Choose all that apply.

☐ Anders   ☐ Miguel

☐ Jamal   ☐ Tamika

☐ Nancy

Books Read

Nancy	📖📖📖📖📖📖📖▯
Tamika	📖📖📖📖📖📖📖📖
Jamal	📖📖📖📖
Phil	📖📖📖📖📖
Anders	📖📖
Miguel	📖▯

Each 📖 = 4 books.   Each ▯ = 2 books.

Name _____

Solve & Share

Mary is helping her teacher count school playground equipment. She records the data in a frequency table. Use the data in the table to complete the picture graph. Write two statements about your completed graph.

I can ...
make a picture graph to record information and answer questions about a data set.

I can also make sense of problems.

DATA

School Playground Equipment		
Equipment	**Tally**	**Number**
Basketballs	𝍷𝍷𝍷𝍷 𝍷𝍷𝍷𝍷	10
Jump Ropes	𝍷𝍷𝍷𝍷 𝍷𝍷𝍷𝍷	10
Bats	𝍷𝍷𝍷𝍷	5
Soccer Balls	𝍷𝍷𝍷𝍷 𝍷𝍷𝍷𝍷 𝍷𝍷𝍷𝍷	15

Favorite Playground Equipment

Basketballs	O O O O O
Jump Ropes	O O O O O
Bats	O O d
Soccer Balls	O O D O O O O d

Each ⚫ = 2 items.   Each ⚫ = 1 item.

You can make sense of problems. How can the tally marks and the key help you represent the data in the picture graph?

Look Back! **Be Precise** How did you know the number of symbols to draw for jump ropes?

A

Sam recorded the number of each kind of bicycle a store sold during one month. He made a frequency table. Use the table to make a picture graph.

You can also collect data with a survey by asking people questions.

Kinds of Bicycles Sold		
Kind of Bicycle	**Tally**	**Number**
Road	ЖЖ ЖЖ	10
Track	ЖЖ ЖЖ ЖЖ ЖЖ	20
Training	ЖЖ ЖЖ ЖЖ	15
Racing	ЖЖ ЖЖ	10

B Write a title for the picture graph.

The title is "Kinds of Bicycles Sold."

Choose a symbol for the key. Decide what each whole symbol and half-symbol will represent.

Each ▲ means 10 bicycles.

Each ◢ means 5 bicycles.

A half-symbol is used to represent 5 bicycles because 5 is half of 10.

C Set up the graph and list the kinds of bicycles. Decide how many symbols you need for each number of bicycles sold. Draw the symbols.

Kinds of Bicycles Sold	
Road	▲
Track	▲ ▲
Training	▲ ◢
Racing	▲

Each ▲ = 10 bicycles.
Each ◢ = 5 bicycles.

Convince Me! **Model with Math** Suppose 25 mountain bicycles were also sold. Draw symbols to show a row in the picture graph for mountain bicycles. Explain how you decided.

Name _____

Guided Practice

You Understand?

...l 2, use the picture graph
...66.

... Explain the symbols that
... the number of training

...sed in the key were
...ycles, how many symbols
...used for the number of road
...old? For the number of track
... sold?

Do You Know How?

3. Use the table to complete the picture graph.

DATA	Favorite School Lunch		
	Lunch	**Tally**	**Number**
	Taco	//	2
	Pizza	TℋL ///	8
	Salad	///	3

Favorite School Lunch

Taco	
Pizza	
Salad	

Each ⬛ = 2 votes.
Each ⸦ = 1 vote.

...dent Practice

...use the data in the chart.

...plete the picture graph.

...bs	
...wks	
...ns	
...drunners	

...h ● = ___ goals. Each ◖ = ___ goals.

...ch two teams scored more goals, the
...s and the Lions or the Hawks and
...Roadrunners?

DATA	Goals Each Team Has Scored		
	Team Name	**Tally**	**Number**
	Cubs	TℋL TℋL	10
	Hawks	TℋL TℋL TℋL TℋL	20
	Lions	TℋL TℋL TℋL TℋL TℋL TℋL	30
	Roadrunners	TℋL TℋL TℋL	15

6. Explain how you decided the number of each symbol to draw to show the goals for the Roadrunners.

Problem Solving

In **7-9**, use the frequency table at the right.

7. Model with Math Make a picture graph to show the data in the table.

Favorite Vegeta	
Kind	**Tal**
Corn	
Green Beans	
Tomatoes	

8. Ask six students in your class which of the three vegetables is their favorite. Record the answers in your picture graph.

9. Make Sense and Pers the difference between and the sum of the even table?

10. Higher Order Thinking Suppose you are going to make a picture graph to show the data in the Simon's Book Shop table. Choose a symbol to stand for 5 books sold. Draw the row for fiction books sold. Justify your drawing.

Simon's Book	
Kind of Book	**Nu**
Fiction	
Nonfiction	
Poetry	
Dictionary	1

✔ **Assessment**

11. The Garden Shop sold 30 plants in May, 35 plants in June, and 25 plants in April. Complete the picture graph for this data. Choose the symbols you will use.

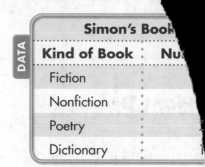

Plants Sold at Garden Shop
April
May
June

Each ___ = 10 plants.   Each ___ =

☆ C

Do Yo

In **1** and
on page 3

1. **Reasoning**
were used for
bicycles sold.

2. If the scale u
▲ = 2 bicy
would be
bicycles s
bicycles

☆
Indepe

In **4–6**,

4. Com

Cu

Ha

Lion

Ro

Eac

5. Whi
Cub
the

*For another

bles	
ily	Number
////	4
//	2
⫽⫽⫽	5

severe What is
the odd number
numbers in the

Shop	
mber Sold	
	25
	40
	20
	5

5 plants.

Name _____

Another Look!

The frequency table shows items that were ordered for lunch. Follow the steps below to learn how to make a picture graph.

Data in a table can be shown in a picture graph.

Items Ordered

Food	Tally	Number
Pasta	卌 l	6
Salad	llll	4
Casserole	卌 卌	10
Fish	卌 llll	9

Items Ordered

Pasta	🍴🍴🍴
Salad	🍴🍴
Casserole	🍴🍴🍴🍴🍴
Fish	🍴🍴🍴🍴🍴

Each 🍴 = 2 meals.
Each 🥄 = 1 meal.

Step 1
Write a title that explains what the picture graph shows.

Step 2
Choose a symbol and a scale.

Step 3
Draw in the graph the number of symbols that are needed for each item.

---

1. Complete the frequency table to show how Ms. Hashimoto's class voted for their favorite type of movie.

Favorite Type of Movie

Type	Tally	Number
Action	卌 lll	
Comedy	lll	
Drama	卌 l	
Animated	卌 卌	

Which two types of movies had more votes, comedy and animated or action and drama?

2. Use the table in Exercise 1 to complete the picture graph.

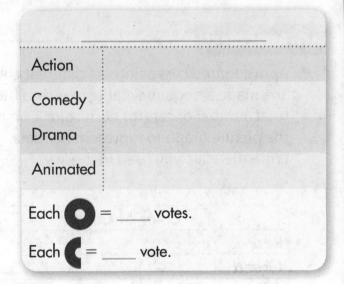

_____

Action	
Comedy	
Drama	
Animated	

Each ⬤ = _____ votes.

Each ◖ = _____ vote.

How did you choose the number that each symbol represents?

3. Math and Science There are 61 days in March and April. Mrs. Dorsey recorded 18 sunny days in March and 12 sunny days in April. How many days were not sunny?

4. 🅰🅩 **Vocabulary** A _____ can also be used to represent and compare the same data set using bars instead of pictures or symbols.

In **5–7**, use the picture graph at the right.

5. Critique Reasoning Pamela made this picture graph showing 14 students' favorite drinks. She drew 3 glasses to represent the 6 students who chose chocolate milk. Is her picture graph correct? Explain.

Favorite Drink

Chocolate milk	🥛 🥛 🥛
Orange juice	🥛 🥛 🥛 🥛

Each 🥛 = 2 students.

6. Higher Order Thinking How would Pamela's picture graph change if 12 students chose grape juice as their favorite?

7. Make Sense and Persevere How would the scale have to change if her picture graph showed the favorite drinks of 70 students?

✔ **Assessment**

8. April counted cars painted 4 different colors. She made a frequency table to record the total number of cars for each color. Complete the picture graph to represent her data. Write the scale you used in the key.

Color of Cars	
Red	
Green	
Silver	
Black	

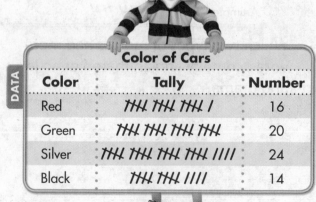

Color of Cars

Color	Tally	Number
Red	𝍬𝍬𝍬 𝍬	16
Green	𝍬𝍬𝍬𝍬	20
Silver	𝍬𝍬𝍬𝍬 𝍬𝍬	24
Black	𝍬𝍬 𝍬𝍬	14

Name _____

Solve & Share

Use the data in the table below to complete the bar graph. What conclusions can you make by analyzing the bar graph?

Daily Reading Log	
Student's Name	**Number of Pages Read**
Yoma	13
Don	10
Bonita	10
Adam	6

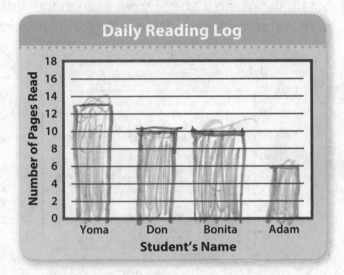

Daily Reading Log

I can ...
make a bar graph to record information and answer questions about a data set.

I can also make sense of problems.

You can use reasoning. You can use the data in the table to help draw the bars on the graph.

Look Back! **Use Appropriate Tools** How can tools such as a ruler help you create a bar graph?

Essential Question **How Do You Make a Bar Graph?**

A

Greg made a table to show the amount of money he saved each month from tutoring. Use the data in the table to make a bar graph.

DATA

Amount Greg Saved Each Month

Month	Amount Saved
January	$25
February	$50
March	$65
April	$40

A bar graph can make it easy to compare data.

B Write a title. Use the same title as in the table.

The title of this bar graph is **Amount Greg Saved Each Month.**

Choose the scale. Decide how many units each grid line will represent.

Each grid line will represent $10.

C Set up the graph with the scale, each month listed in the table, and labels. Draw a bar for each month.

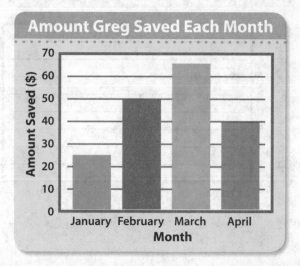

Amount Greg Saved Each Month

Convince Me! **Be Precise** Write new amounts for how much Greg saved in 4 other months. Consider the scale.

In May, Greg saved ___$5___.

In June, Greg saved ___$30___.

In July, Greg saved ___$20___.

In August, Greg saved ___$60___.

Draw bars on the graph to show your new data.

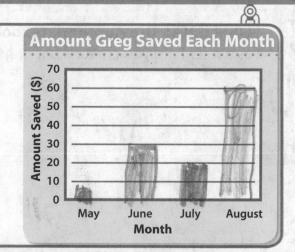

Amount Greg Saved Each Month

---

372 **Topic 7** | Lesson 7-3

Practice Buddy   Tools   Assessment

☆ Guided Practice*

Do You Understand?

In **1–3**, use the bar graph on page 372.

1. **Reasoning** Explain why the bar for January ends between 20 and 30.

   Because 25 is between 20 and 30

2. Suppose Greg saved $35 in May. Between which grid lines would the bar for May end? *40 and 30*

3. How can you tell how much more Greg saved in February than in April?

   February has 50 and April has 40

Do You Know How?

4. Use the table to complete the bar graph.

DATA

Number of People Signed Up for Classes

Class	Tally	Number of People
Chess	Ж I	6
Guitar	Ж Ж	10
Painting	Ж II	7
Writing	Ж IIII	9

Number of People Signed Up for Classes

☆ Independent Practice ☆

In **5**, use the table at the right.

5. Complete the bar graph to show the data.

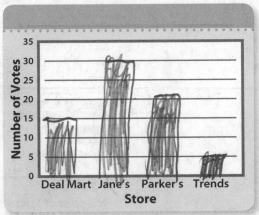

DATA

Favorite Store for Clothes

Store	Tally	Number of Votes
Deal Mart	Ж Ж Ж	15
Jane's	Ж Ж Ж Ж Ж Ж	30
Parker's	Ж Ж Ж Ж	20
Trends	Ж	5

*For another example, see Set B on page 392.

Problem Solving

In **6–8**, use the table at the right.

6. Model with Math Make a bar graph to show the data.

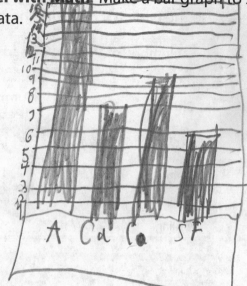

Favorite Kind of Movie

Kind of Movie	Adventure	Cartoon	Comedy	Science Fiction
Number of Votes	16	7	10	6

7. Construct Arguments Which two kinds of movies received about the same number of votes? Explain how to use your bar graph to find the answer.

8. Make Sense and Persevere Each movie ticket costs $8. Jo buys tickets for the number of people who voted for science fiction. How much change does she get from $50?

9. Higher Order Thinking Suppose you are going to make a bar graph to show the data in the table at the right. What scale would you choose? Explain.

Speed of Birds

Kind of Bird	Flying Speed (miles per hour)
Frigate Bird	95
Peregrine Falcon	180
Spin-Tailed Swift	105

Assessment

10. Which information is needed to complete the graph?

Ⓐ How many friends wore pink shoes

Ⓑ The color of shoes with the longest bar

Ⓒ The color of shoes worn by exactly 8 friends

Ⓓ The color of shoes worn by exactly 7 friends

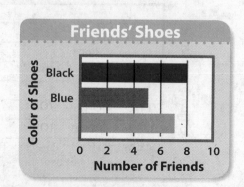

Friends' Shoes

Another Look!

The table below shows the number of birds that visited a bird feeder.

Bird Feeder Visits

Day	Number of Birds
Monday	12
Tuesday	8
Wednesday	14
Thursday	10
Friday	5

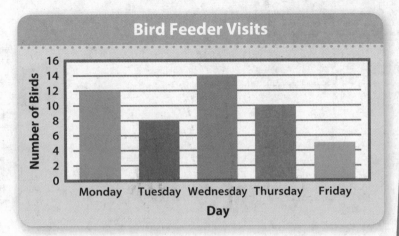

Follow the steps below to learn how to make the bar graph at the right.

Step 1

Write each of the days and label the bottom of the graph "Day."

Step 2

Choose a scale. Number the scale. Label the scale "Number of Birds."

Step 3

Draw a bar for each day. Check that the bar lengths match the number in the table.

Step 4

Give the graph a title.

For **1–3**, use the table at the right.

1. Complete the bar graph to show the data. Remember to add a title.

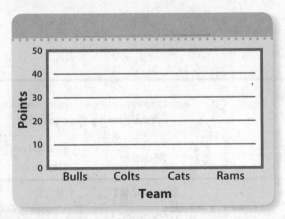

Field Day Results

Team	Points
Bulls	45
Colts	30
Cats	25
Rams	40

2. Explain how to use your bar graph to find the team with the most points.

3. Which team has the shortest bar in your bar graph? Why?

In **4–6**, use the table at the right.

4. **Model with Math** Make a bar graph to show the data.

Favorite States to Visit

State	Number of Votes
New York	25
Florida	35
California	30
Hawaii	20

5. **Construct Arguments** Explain how to use your bar graph to find the state with the least number of votes. Which state is it?

6. **Algebra** The total number of votes for two states can be represented by the equation $35 + ? = 65$. Which state's number of votes makes this statement true?

7. **Math and Science** Dawn made a paper airplane and measured the distance it flew in feet for 30 tosses. The longest distance she measured was 45 feet. The shortest distance was 28 feet. How many more feet is the longest distance than the shortest distance?

8. **Higher Order Thinking** Kim makes a bar graph to record votes for the choice of a class pet. Each grid line represents 4 votes. Fish got 10 votes. The bar for hamster is 3 grid lines higher than the bar for fish. How many votes did hamster get?

✓ **Assessment**

9. **Math and Science** The table at the right shows the average monthly snowfall where Mr. Walker lives. Which would be the best number to use for a scale on a bar graph of the data?

Ⓐ 1   Ⓒ 5

Ⓑ 2   Ⓓ 10

Average Snowfall

Month	Snowfall (Inches)
November	2
December	8
January	12
February	10
March	2

Name _____

★☆ Solve & Share ☆★

The students in Ms. Seymour's class voted for their favorite kind of sandwich. How many more students voted for peanut butter than cheese? How many fewer students voted for tuna than peanut butter?

I can ...
use graphs and other tools to solve word problems.

I can also make sense of problems.

Think about what you are trying to find out to make sense of this problem.

Peanut Cheese
$11 - 7 = 4$ more
$11 - 3 = 8$ more
Peanut Tuna

Ms. Seymour's Class: Sandwiches Chosen

Sandwich

Cheese
Peanut Butter
Tuna
Turkey

0 2 4 6 8 10 12
Number of Students

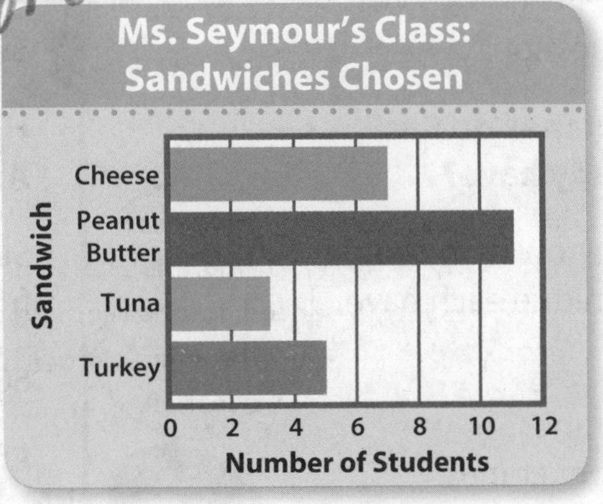

Look Back! **Be Precise** What is the scale for this graph? How do you know the number of votes a bar represents when it is between two lines on this graph?

How Can You Solve Problems Using Graphs?

A

Angela wants Karli and Monique to have a total of 60 paper cranes. The bar graph shows how many paper cranes her friends already have. How many more paper cranes does Angela need to make for Karli and Monique have 60 paper cranes in all?

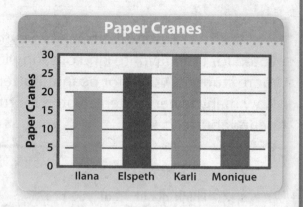

Paper Cranes

This problem has a hidden question!

B Solve the hidden question.

How many paper cranes do Karli and Monique already have?

Use the scale to find how many paper cranes Karli and Monique each have. Then add.

Karli has 30 paper cranes.
Monique has 10 paper cranes.

$30 + 10 = 40$

Together they have 40 paper cranes.

Remember you still need to answer the main question.

C Solve the main question.

How many paper cranes does Angela need to make?

Subtract the number of cranes the friends already have from the total.

$60 - 40 = 20$

Angela needs to make 20 paper cranes.

Convince Me! **Critique Reasoning** Angela says, "I want Ilana and Elspeth to also have 60 cranes in all. I can subtract two times to find how many more cranes I need to make for them." Is Angela correct? Explain.

No, because you need to find how many Ilana and Elspeth.

☆ Guided Practice ☆

Do You Understand?

1. Look at the graph on page 378. Explain whether you would add, subtract, multiply, or divide to find how many more paper cranes Karli already has than Monique.

2. How does a bar graph help you compare data?

Do You Know How?

In **3**, use the bar graph.

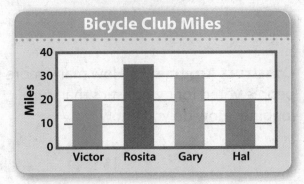

Bicycle Club Miles

3. How many more miles did Hal and Victor ride than Rosita?

☆ Independent Practice ☆

In **4–6**, use the picture graph at the right.

4. How many more red T-shirts were sold at Ultimate T than at Jazzy's?

   5 more

5. How many fewer green T-shirts were sold at Jazzy's than at Ultimate T?

6. How many more blue and red T-shirts were sold at Jazzy's than green T-shirts were sold at Ultimate T?

   15 more

T-Shirt Sales		
	Jazzy's	**Ultimate T**
Blue	👕👕🧍	👕
Red	👕👕	👕👕🧍
Green	🧍	👕👕👕

Each 👕 = 10 T-shirts. Each 🧍 = 5 T-shirts.

Problem Solving ☆

In **7–9**, use the bar graph at the right.

7. **Number Sense** How many people voted for their favorite type of exercise? How can you find the answer?

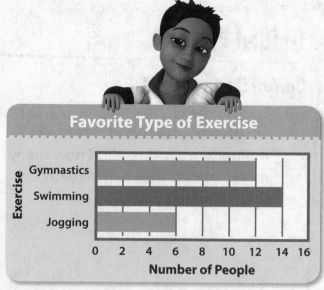

Favorite Type of Exercise

8. **Construct Arguments** How many more people voted for gymnastics than for jogging? How do you know?

6 more look at chart.

9. How many fewer people voted for swimming than for gymnastics and jogging?

---

10. **Make Sense and Persevere** Leslie delivers papers on weekdays and Saturdays. She delivers 6 papers each weekday and 16 papers on Saturday. How many papers does Leslie deliver during the entire week?

28

11. **Higher Order Thinking** What kinds of comparisons can you make when you look at a bar graph or a picture graph?

 Assessment

12. Daryl made a bar graph to record the number of books read by each member of a reading club.

How many fewer books did Alice read than Sandra and Daryl? Explain.

Books Read by Reading Club Members

Another Look!

Students were asked to name their favorite type of dog. The picture graph shows the results of the survey.

Students' Favorite Dogs	
Dog	**Number Counted**
Beagle	🐕 🐕 🐕
Collie	🐕 🐕 🐕 🐕 🐕
Shepherd	🐕 🐕 🐕
Poodle	🐕
Dalmatian	🐕 🐕

Each 🐕 = 2 votes. Each 🐕 = 1 vote.

You can use graphs to compare data and draw conclusions.

Some conclusions you can draw from the picture graph include:

- Shepherd was chosen by exactly 5 students.
- 2 fewer students chose dalmatian than chose beagle.
- 2 more students chose collie than chose beagle or poodle.

In **1–4**, use the bar graph at the right.

1. How many more votes did punch get than water?

2. How many fewer votes did milk get than juice and water?

3. How many more votes did juice get than punch and water?

4. What is the difference between the number of votes for juice and the number of votes for water and milk combined?

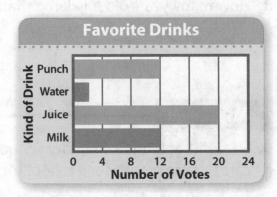

In **5** and **6**, use the picture graph at the right.

5. **Generalize** Which type of shoe was sold least at Just Shoes? How do you know?

6. **Construct Arguments** How many more pairs of boots than pumps were sold at Just Shoes? How did you find your answer?

Girls' Shoes Sold at Just Shoes

Sneakers	
Sandals	
Pumps	
Boots	

Each 👟 = 4 pairs.　　Each 👟 = 2 pairs.

In **7** and **8**, use the bar graph at the right.

7. **Higher Order Thinking** Jared, Alicia, Lydia, and Tray are cousins. Jared is 8 years older than Alicia. Lydia is 4 years younger than Tray. Tray is 18 years younger than Jared. Alicia is 22. Complete the graph to show their ages.

8. How many years older is Jared than Lydia?

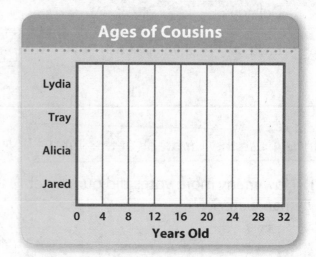

Ages of Cousins

Lydia

Tray

Alicia

Jared

0　4　8　12　16　20　24　28　32
Years Old

✓ **Assessment**

9. Students at King Elementary School washed cars to raise money for a school trip.

How many more cars did the 4th graders and the 6th graders wash than the 5th graders? Explain.

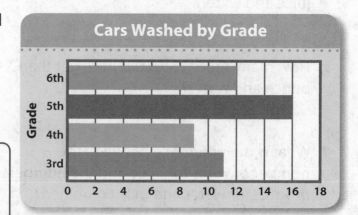

Cars Washed by Grade

6th

5th

Grade 4th

3rd

0　2　4　6　8　10　12　14　16　18

Name _____

Solve

Solve & Share

Action books and mystery books cost $5 each. Biography books cost $10 each. A librarian has $100 to spend on new books. She collected some information about the kinds of books that students checked out to read last month.

How should the librarian spend the money? Use math words and symbols to explain your thinking.

I can ...
be precise when solving math problems.

I can also use data in graphs.

Books Read Last Month

Thinking Habits

Be a good thinker!
These questions can help you.

- Am I using numbers, units, and symbols appropriately?

- Am I using the correct definitions?

- Am I calculating accurately?

- Is my answer clear?

Look Back! **Be Precise** How did you use words and symbols to explain your answer?

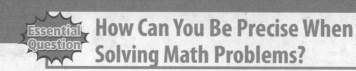

How Can You Be Precise When Solving Math Problems?

A

Bella has a bakery. She will use the bakery items at the right to make a gift basket worth $40. Bella wants the basket to have more than one of each bakery item. Show one way to make a gift basket.

Bakery Items Available

Wheat Loaves ($4 each)

Cinnamon Buns ($2 each)

Muffins ($1 each)

Each 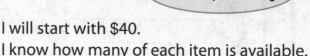 = 2 items

What do I need to do to make a gift basket?

I need to be precise. I will decide how many of each item to put in a basket so the total is exactly $40.

B **How can I be precise in solving this problem?**

I can

- correctly use the information given.

- calculate accurately.

- decide if my answer is clear and appropriate.

- use the correct units.

C

Here's my thinking...

I will start with $40.
I know how many of each item is available.

3 wheat loaves × $4 = $12
$40 − $12 = $28

9 cinnamon buns × $2 = $18
$28 − $18 = $10

10 muffins × $1 = $10
$10 − $10 = $0

All calculations are correct. My gift basket has 3 wheat loaves, 9 cinnamon buns, and 10 muffins. The total is exactly $40.

Convince Me! **Be Precise** Is there another way to make a gift basket that totals exactly $40? Explain.

Practice Buddy   Tools   Assessment

☆Guided Practice*

Be Precise

Use the graph on page 384. Suppose Bella wanted to make a gift basket worth $25 instead. The gift basket must also have more wheat loaves than muffins. Show one way Bella can make the gift basket.

To be precise, you need to check that the words, numbers, symbols, and units you use are correct and that your calculations are accurate.

1. What given information will you use to solve?

2. Show and explain one way Bella can make the gift basket.

Independent Practice ☆

Be Precise

Derek is making a tile pattern that will be 30 inches long. The graph shows how many of each length of tile Derek has. He wants to use more than one of each length of tile in his pattern. Show one way to make the pattern.

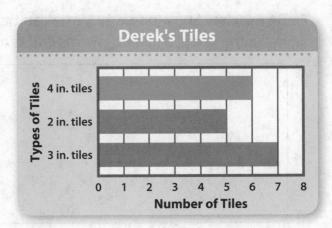

Derek's Tiles

3. What given information will you use to solve?

4. Show and explain one way Derek can make the pattern.

Problem Solving

Picture Planning

Marta has $50 to spend on sketches.
She wants to display them in an array
of 3 rows, with 4 sketches in each row.
Marta wants to include each type of
sketch at least two times in her array.

Sketch Types and Pricing

Landscape ($2 each)	☐ ☐ ☐ ☐ ☐ ☐ ⊏
Animal ($4 each)	☐ ☐ ☐ ☐
Portrait ($10 each)	☐ ☐ ☐ ☐ ☐ ⊏

Each ☐ = 2 sketches in stock.
Each ⊏ = 1 sketch in stock.

5. **Reasoning** How many sketches does
Marta want?

6. **Make Sense and Persevere** What is a good plan for
solving the problem?

7. **Be Precise** Show one way Marta can buy sketches to
make the array. Use math words and symbols to explain.

> Be precise when
> analyzing the symbols, words,
> and numbers displayed in a
> picture graph.

8. **Use Structure** Suppose Marta wants to make an array of
4 rows, with 3 sketches in each row. Would your answer
still work? Explain.

Another Look!

Wynton made a picture graph to record the music he would like to download. He has $35 to spend on music. He wants to buy at least 1 of each type of item. He wants to buy more singles than albums. What is one way Wynton can spend $35 on music?

When you are precise, you use math symbols and language correctly.

Tell how you can be precise when solving this problem.

- I can correctly use the information given.

- I can make sure my calculations are accurate.

Solve. Use math words and symbols to explain your thinking.

5 singles × $2 = $10   35 − 10 = $25 left

3 albums × $6 = $18   25 − 18 = $7 left

1 collection × $7 = $7   7 − 7 = $0 left

Wynton has spent exactly $35.
He has bought more singles than albums.

Music to Download	
Singles ($2)	♩ ♩ ♩ ♩
Albums ($6)	♩ ♩ ♩
Collections ($7)	♩ ♩

Each ♩ = 3 items.

Be Precise

Casie made a picture graph to record the points that third-grade students scored on a test. Mrs. Wilson's group scored 40 points in all. There are 11 students in Mrs. Wilson's group. What is one way Mrs. Wilson's group may have scored 40 points?

1. Tell how you can be precise when solving this problem.

2. Solve. Use math words and symbols to explain your thinking.

Test Scores	
Point Types	**Number of Students**
2 points	😀 😀 😀 😀
4 points	😀 😀 😀
6 points	😀 😀 😀

Each 😀 = 3 students.

Pizza Party!
Ms. Chavez is planning a class party. There are 28 students at the party. She wants to get at least 1 of each type of pizza and have enough pizza so each student gets 2 slices. Delivery takes 20 minutes. Ms. Chavez has $55 to spend.

Ready To Go Pizza Delivery

Pizza Type	Number of Pizzas Available
Cheese ($6 each)	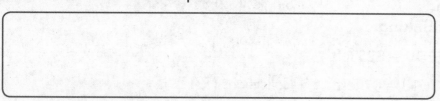
Pepperoni ($8 each)	
Supreme ($10 each)	

Each 🍕 = 8 slices.

3. **Reasoning** How many slices of cheese pizza are available? How do you know?

4. **Make Sense and Persevere** How many slices of pizza does Ms. Chavez need? Explain.

5. **Model with Math** Show how to find the number of pizzas Ms. Chavez should order.

Be precise. Make sure your answer is clear and appropriate.

6. **Be Precise** Show one way Ms. Chavez can order enough pizzas. Use math words and symbols to explain your thinking.

7. **Make Sense and Persevere** Which information did you not need to help you solve the problem?

Name _____

Fluency Practice Activity

Find a partner. Get paper and a pencil. Each partner chooses a different color: light blue or dark blue.

Partner 1 and Partner 2 each point to a black number at the same time. Both partners multiply those numbers.

If the answer is on your color, you get a tally mark. Work until one partner has seven tally marks.

I can ...
multiply within 100.

Partner 1

| 5 |
| 8 |
| 4 |
| 3 |
| 10 |

48	90	35	20
50	72	27	9
60	30	12	15
45	18	27	25
36	28	21	56
40	56	70	24

Partner 2

| 7 |
| 3 |
| 9 |
| 5 |
| 6 |

Tally Marks for Partner 1

Tally Marks for Partner 2

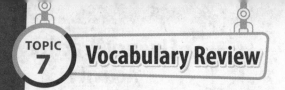

Vocabulary Review

A-Z
Glossary

Understand Vocabulary

Rainy Days

| April | |
| May | |

Each 🌂 = 2 days

Graph A

Word List

- data
- frequency table
- graph
- key
- scale
- scaled bar graph
- scaled picture graph
- survey

Complete each sentence with *scaled picture graph*, *scaled bar graph*, *key*, or *scale*.

1. The _____ in Graph A shows that each umbrella represents 2 days.

2. Graph A is a _____ .

3. The _____ in Graph B increases by 5.

4. Graph B is a _____ .

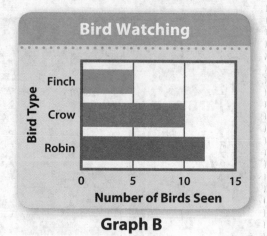

Bird Watching

Graph B

Bird Type: Finch, Crow, Robin
Number of Birds Seen: 0, 5, 10, 15

Write T for *True* or F for *False*.

_____ 5. A survey is the only way to collect data.

_____ 6. A scaled bar graph has a key.

_____ 7. Data from a frequency table can be used to make a scaled bar graph.

Use Vocabulary in Writing

8. Suppose you found out the number and type of pets your classmates have. Explain how you can display that information. Use at least 3 terms from the Word List in your answer.

Name _____

Set A pages 359–364

Picture graphs use pictures or parts of pictures to represent data.

The scale is the number each picture represents. The key explains the scale that is used.

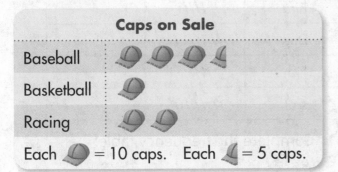

Caps on Sale

Baseball	
Basketball	
Racing	

Each 🧢 = 10 caps.   Each 🧢 = 5 caps.

Bar graphs use bars to represent data. You can use a scale to find how much a bar represents.

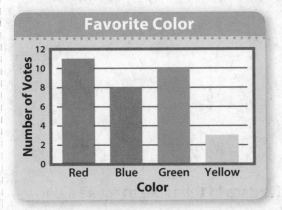

Favorite Color

Number of Votes / Color — Red, Blue, Green, Yellow

Each line in this bar graph represents 2 votes.

Remember to use a key or scale. The number of pictures in picture graphs and the lengths of bars in bar graphs help to compare data.

Reteaching

In **1–3**, use the picture graph on the left.

1. How many more baseball caps are on sale than racing caps?

2. How many more baseball caps are on sale than basketball and racing caps?

3. How many fewer basketball caps are on sale than baseball caps?

In **4–7**, use the bar graph on the left.

4. Which color got the most votes? How many votes did that color get?

5. How many fewer votes were for yellow than for green?

6. How many more votes were for red than for blue?

7. What is the difference between the votes for red and the votes for blue and yellow combined?

This frequency table shows data about the number of coins Mark has.

Mark's Coins

Coin	Tally	Number of Coins
Penny	//// ///	8
Nickel	//// ////	10
Dime	//// /	6

You can use the data to make a picture graph. Picture graphs include a title, symbol, and a key to show the scale.

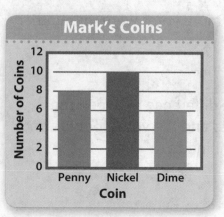

Mark's Coins

Coin	Number of Coins
Penny	⬤ ⬤ ⬤ ⬤
Nickel	⬤ ⬤ ⬤ ⬤ ⬤
Dime	⬤ ⬤ ⬤

Each ⬤ = 2 coins.

In this picture graph, each symbol equals 2 coins.

You can also use the data to make a bar graph.

1. Label the bottom and side of the graph.

2. Choose a scale.

3. Draw a bar for each type of coin.

4. Include a title.

Remember a frequency table includes tally marks or numbers. A picture graph uses pictures to show data.

In **1** and **2**, use the frequency table below.

Dan's class voted for their favorite pet. The results are shown in this frequency table.

Favorite Pet

Pet	Tally	Number
Bird	////	
Dog	//// //// ////	
Fish	//// /	
Cat	//// ///	

1. Complete the frequency table.

2. Use the data in the frequency table to make a picture graph.

3. Use the data in the table to make a bar graph.

Name _____

Set C pages 377–382

You can use data from bar graphs or picture graphs to draw conclusions.

In a picture graph Erica recorded the number of magazines she read. How many more magazines did she read in April and May than in June?

Magazines Read

April	
May	
June	

Each [NIGHT GOLF] = 2 magazines.

You can solve 2-step data problems.

There are 6 symbols for April and May. There are 3 symbols for June.

$6 - 3 = 3$. There are 3 more symbols for April and May.

Each symbol represents 2 magazines. $3 \times 2 = 6$. Erica read 6 more magazines in April and May than in June.

Remember you can use tables and graphs to make comparisons. Sometimes you need to find and answer hidden questions.

In **1–6**, use the picture graph below.

Trees in Park

Maple	
Oak	
Beech	
Elm	

Each 🌳 = 6 trees.

1. How many more maple trees than elm trees are there?

2. How many fewer beech trees are there than maple trees?

3. How many trees are **NOT** maple trees?

4. How many more maple and beech trees are there than oak trees?

5. How many fewer oak trees are there than beech and elm trees?

6. If the city wants to have 24 elm trees, how many more elm trees does it need to plant? Explain how to solve.

Think about these questions to help you **attend to precision**.

Thinking Habits

- Am I using numbers, units, and symbols appropriately?

- Am I using the correct definitions?

- Am I calculating accurately?

- Is my answer clear?

Use the bar graph below to solve **1** and **2**.

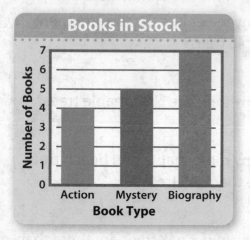

Remember to use words, numbers, and symbols to show your reasoning.

In **1** and **2**, use the bar graph at the left to solve.

Jackie has $50 to spend on books. She has made a bar graph to show the number of each type of book the store has in stock. Jackie wants to buy at least 2 of each type of book. Show one way Jackie can spend $50 on books.

Action books cost $5.

Biographies cost $10.

Mysteries cost $5.

1. What given information will you use to solve the problem?

2. Show one way Jackie can spend $50 on books. Use math words and symbols to explain your thinking.

Glossary

A.M. The time between midnight and noon.

acute angle An angle that is open less than a right angle.

addends Numbers added together to give a sum.
Example: $2 + 7 = 9$

Addend   Addend

angle A figure that is formed where two sides meet.

angle measure The degrees of an angle.

area The number of unit squares needed to cover a region.

array A way of displaying objects in equal rows and columns.

Associative (Grouping) Property of Addition The grouping of addends can be changed and the sum will be the same.

Associative (Grouping) Property of Multiplication The grouping of factors can be changed and the product will be the same.

benchmark fraction A commonly used fraction such as $\frac{1}{4}$, $\frac{1}{3}$, $\frac{1}{2}$, $\frac{2}{3}$, and $\frac{3}{4}$.

capacity (liquid volume) The amount a container can hold measured in liquid units.

centimeter (cm) A metric unit of length.

column An arrangement of objects or numbers, one above another.

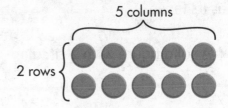

5 columns

2 rows

Commutative (Order) Property of Addition Numbers can be added in any order and the sum will be the same.

Commutative (Order) Property of Multiplication Numbers can be multiplied in any order and the product will be the same.

compare To decide if one number is greater than or less than another number.

compatible numbers Numbers that are easy to add, subtract, multiply, or divide mentally.

compensation Choosing numbers close to the numbers in a problem to make computation easier and then adjusting the answer for the numbers chosen.

compose To combine different parts.

conjecture A statement that is believed to be true, but it has not been proven.

cone A solid figure with a circle as its base and a curved surface that meets at a point.

cube A solid figure with 6 same-size squares as its faces.

cylinder A solid figure with 2 circular bases.

data Pieces of information.

decompose Breaking a number into parts.
Example: $\frac{2}{5}$ can be broken into $\frac{1}{5} + \frac{1}{5}$.

degrees (°) A unit of measure for angles.

denominator The number below the fraction bar in a fraction, which shows the total number of equal parts.

difference The answer when subtracting one number from another.

digits The symbols 0, 1, 2, 3, 4, 5, 6, 7, 8, and 9 used to write numbers.

Distributive Property A multiplication fact can be broken apart into the sum of two other multiplication facts.
Example: $5 \times 4 = (2 \times 4) + (3 \times 4)$

dividend The number to be divided.
Example: $63 \div 9 = 7$

↑
Dividend

division An operation that tells how many equal groups there are or how many are in each group.

divisor The number by which another number is divided.
Example: $63 \div 9 = 7$

$\uparrow$
Divisor

dollar sign A symbol ($) used to indicate money.

edge A line segment where 2 faces meet in a solid figure.

eighth One of 8 equal parts of a whole.

elapsed time The total amount of time that passes from the starting time to the ending time.

equal (equality) When the two sides of an equation have the same value.

equal groups Groups that have the same number of items.

equation A number sentence that uses an equal sign (=) to show that the value on its left side is the same as the value on its right side.

equilateral triangle A triangle with all sides the same length.

equivalent fractions Fractions that name the same part of a whole or the same location on a number line.

estimate To give an approximate number or answer.

even number A whole number that can be divided by 2 with none left over.

expanded form A number written as the sum of the values of its digits.
Example: $476 = 400 + 70 + 6$

face A flat surface of a solid that cannot roll.

fact family A group of related facts using the same numbers.

factors Numbers that are multiplied together to give a product.
Example: $7 \times 3 = 21$

$\uparrow \quad \uparrow$
Factor　Factor

foot (ft) A customary unit of length. 1 foot equals 12 inches.

fourth One of 4 equal parts of a whole.

fraction A symbol, such as $\frac{1}{2}$, used to name a part of a whole, a part of a set, or a location on a number line.

frequency table A table used to show the number of times something occurs.

gram (g) A metric unit of mass, the amount of matter in an object.

half (halves) One of 2 equal parts of a whole.

half hour A unit of time equal to 30 minutes.

hexagon A polygon with 6 sides.

hour A unit of time equal to 60 minutes.

Identity (Zero) Property of Addition The sum of any number and zero is that same number.

Identity (One) Property of Multiplication The product of any number and 1 is that number.

inch (in.) A customary unit of length.

intersecting lines Lines that cross at one point.

inverse operations Two operations that undo each other.

key The explanation for what each symbol represents in a pictograph.

kilogram (kg) A metric unit of mass, the amount of matter in an object. One kilogram equals 1,000 grams.

kilometer (km) A metric unit of length. One kilometer equals 1,000 meters.

L

line A straight path of points that is endless in both directions.

line plot A way to organize data on a number line.

line segment A part of a line that has 2 endpoints.

liter (L) A metric unit of capacity. One liter equals 1,000 milliliters.

M

mass A measure of the amount of matter in an object.

meter (m) A metric unit of length. One meter equals 100 centimeters.

mile (mi) A customary unit of length. One mile equals 5,280 feet.

milliliter (mL) A metric unit of capacity.

millimeter (mm) A metric unit of length. 1,000 millimeters = 1 meter.

minute A unit of time equal to 60 seconds.

mixed number A number with a whole number part and a fraction part. *Example:* $2\frac{3}{4}$

multiple The product of a given whole number and any non-zero whole number. *Example:* 4, 8, 12, and 16 are multiples of 4.

multiplication An operation that gives the total number when you join equal groups.

N

nearest fourth inch A measurement that ends with a $\frac{1}{4}$, $\frac{2}{4}$, $\frac{3}{4}$, or full inch.

nearest half inch A measurement that ends with a $\frac{1}{2}$ or full inch.

not equal When two sides of a number sentence do not have the same value.

number line A line that shows numbers in order using a scale. *Example:*

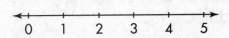

numerator The number above the fraction bar in a fraction, which shows how many equal parts are described.

O

obtuse angle An angle that is open more than a right angle.

octagon A polygon with 8 sides.

odd number A whole number that cannot be divided by 2 with none left over.

open number line A number line which only displays the numbers being computed.

order To arrange numbers from least to greatest or from greatest to least.

ounce (oz) A customary unit of weight.

P

P.M. The time between noon and midnight.

parallel lines Lines that never cross each other.

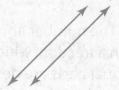

parallel sides Sides of a polygon that go in the exact same direction; if the sides cross when they are made longer, they are not parallel.

parallelogram A quadrilateral with 2 pairs of parallel sides.

pentagon A polygon with 5 sides.

perimeter The distance around a figure.

perpendicular lines Two intersecting lines that form right angles.

pint (pt) A customary unit of capacity. One pint equals 2 cups.

place value The value given to the place a digit has in a number.
Example: In 946, the place value of the digit 9 is *hundreds*.

point An exact position often marked by a dot.

polygon A closed figure made up of straight line segments.

pound (lb) A customary unit of weight. One pound equals 16 ounces.

product The answer to a multiplication problem.

Q

quadrilateral A polygon with 4 sides.

quart (qt) A customary unit of capacity. One quart equals 2 pints.

quarter hour A unit of time equal to 15 minutes.

quotient The answer to a division problem.

R

ray A part of a line that has one endpoint and continues endlessly in one direction.

rectangle A parallelogram with 4 right angles.

rectangular prism A solid figure with 6 rectangular faces.

regroup (regrouping) To name a whole number in a different way.
Example: 28 = 1 ten 18 ones

remainder The number that is left over after dividing.
Example: $31 \div 7 = 4$ R3

Remainder

rhombus A parallelogram with all sides the same length.

right angle An angle that forms a square corner.

round To replace a number with a number that tells about how much or how many to the nearest ten, hundred, thousand, and so on.
Example: 42 rounded to the nearest 10 is 40.

row An arrangement of objects or numbers, one to the side of another.

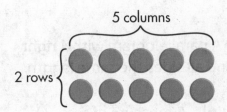

5 columns

2 rows

S

scale The numbers that show the units used on a graph.

scaled bar graph a graph that uses bars to show data.

scaled picture graph a graph that uses pictures to show data.

second A unit of time. 60 seconds equal 1 minute.

side A line segment forming part of a polygon.

sixth One of 6 equal parts of a whole.

solid figure A figure that has length, width, and height.

sphere A solid figure in the shape of a ball.

square A parallelogram with 4 right angles and all sides the same length.

square unit A measure of area.

standard form A way to write a number showing only its digits.
Example: 845

straight angle An angle that forms a straight line.

sum The answer to an addition problem.

survey To collect information by asking a number of people the same question and recording their answers.

T

tally mark A mark used to record data on a tally chart.
Example: = 5

third One of 3 equal parts of a whole.

time interval An amount of time.

trapezoid A quadrilateral with only one pair of parallel sides.

triangle A polygon with 3 sides.

triangular prism A solid figure with two triangular faces.

unit angle An angle with a measurement of 1 degree.

unit fraction A fraction representing one part of a whole that has been divided into equal parts; it always has a numerator of 1.

unit square a square with sides 1 unit long, used to measure area.

unknown A symbol that stands for a number in an equation.

vertex of a polygon The point where two sides of a polygon meet.

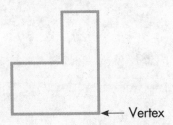

← Vertex

week A unit of time equal to 7 days.

weight A measure of how heavy an object is.

word form A number written in words. *Example:* 325 = three hundred twenty-five

yard (yd) A customary unit of length. One yard equals 3 feet or 36 inches.

Zero Property of Multiplication The product of any number and zero is zero.

Photographs

Photo locators denoted as follows: Top (T), Center (C), Bottom (B), Left (L), Right (R), Background (Bkgd)